THE ROYAL ROAD TO CARD MAGIC

JEAN HUGARD
AND
FREDERICK BRAUÉ

DOVER PUBLICATIONS, INC.
Mineola, New York

Bibliographical Note

This Dover edition, first published in 1999, reproduces exactly the text of the same title as published in 1951 by The World Publishing Company, Cleveland and New York.

Library of Congress Cataloging-in-Publication Data

Hugard, Jean, 1872–1959.
    The royal road to card magic / Jean Hugard and Frederick Braué.
        p.   cm.
    Originally published: Cleveland: World Pub., 1951.
    Includes index.
    ISBN 0-486-40843-4 (pbk.)
    1. Card tricks. I. Braué, Frederick, 1906– . II. Title.
GV1549.H756   1999
793.8′5—dc21   99-17024
                                                          CIP

Manufactured in the United States of America
Dover Publications, Inc., 31 East 2nd Street, Mineola, N.Y. 11501

For
Millie and Annette

CONTENTS

PART TWO

PART THREE

INTRODUCTION
by PAUL FLEMING

MODERN magic is a most entrancing pursuit, whether followed as a vocation or a hobby. One need only attend a national convention of the Society of American Magicians or the International Brotherhood of Magicians to learn that conjuring is an art to which its devotees, both amateur and professional, apply themselves with rare enthusiasm. In return for their expenditure of time and effort, they reap the apparently ample reward of being able to entertain their friends, their business associates, or the general public by catching coins in the air, causing chosen cards to rise solemnly from the pack, reading the minds of spectators, and engaging in other harmless bits of deception. It should be added that the satisfaction experienced by the magician in baffling his audience seems to be matched by that of the spectators; for in conjuring that is frankly nothing more than entertainment,

> "Doubtless the pleasure is as great
> Of being cheated as to cheat,"

as a seventeenth century poet once said.

There are many branches of magic, but none likely to be more rewarding to the amateur—for whom primarily the present book was written—than magic with cards. Card tricks may, in general, be performed wherever and whenever the card conjurer, an audience, and a pack of cards come together. Card tricks are, in many instances, utterly dumbfounding to the uninitiated; and they give the impression of demanding great skill on the part of the magician. "Nearly every modern conjurer of any pretensions of skill commences with a card trick," wrote Edwin T. Sachs some seventy years ago, in one of the great classics of magical literature. "There is something about a good card trick well executed that always takes with an intelligent audience," he continued. "When a performer does not commence with cards, it is generally because he does not possess skill enough to do anything effective with them, although he will generally make a virtue of necessity (at which conjurers are particularly apt), and give some totally different reason."[1] This emphasis upon the skill needed in performing card tricks was far more warranted in Sachs' time than it is in 1947, though it is only fair to say that practically all the card sleights he explained are still used, in one form or another, by the most expert card magicians of the present day. It is equally true, however, that many new and easy methods have been devised which enable one to perform a considerable number of excellent card tricks with surprisingly little practice.

In support of this statement, we cite Chapter I of the present work, in which the learner is taught to "false shuffle" a pack of cards. This is an exceedingly simple sleight, which can be mastered readily by anyone who is able to do a *genuine* overhand shuffle. Yet the false shuffle, as here employed, is a most worthy substitute for "the pass," a very difficult sleight which was once considered the most basic of card principles, but which, in the present treatise does not make its appearance until the student is half way through the book and has been taught dozens of extremely effective tricks. The pedagogical method adopted by the authors—that of first explaining the "mechanics" of a sleight, and then showing its practical application in several striking feats— is an admirable one in teaching conjuring. Not only is the student led, step by step, from the easy to the more difficult and from the simple to the more complicated sleight, but throughout the process he gets encouragement and enjoyment in the actual performance, from the very outset, of really first-rate magic. Indeed, the amateur who masters no more than the first chapter of *The Royal Road to Card Magic* will have at his command a half-dozen very good card tricks!

But it is a safe bet that no one who begins the book will be able to stop with the first chapter. The rapid progress he is sure to make and the prospect of adding increasingly effective tricks to his repertory will carry him along from chapter to chapter, from

[1] Edwin T. Sachs, *Sleight-of-Hand*, Berkeley Heights, N. J., Fleming Book Company, 4th (American) Ed., 1946, p. 177.

wonder to wonder, until he finds himself—unless he has far less than average zeal and talent for this sort of thing—an expert card conjurer, well equipped to give drawingroom, club, and perhaps even stage performances. This book, though it assumes no previous knowledge of the subject on the part of the reader, provides information that will enable him to present not only "parlor magic" but many of the truly great card tricks—tricks which helped to build the reputations of such masters of magic as Robert-Houdin, Alexander Herrmann, David Devant, and one of the greatest card artists of all time, the late Nate Leipzig.

The Royal Road to Card Magic was written by two authorities who are particularly well equipped for the task. The senior author, Jean Hugard, has given a long lifetime to the study and presentation of magic. In both his native Australia and his adopted America, he was widely known as an outstanding professional magician until his recent retirement from active stage work. Some fifteen years ago, he was invited to write a textbook on magic—and has been writing ever since! In this time he has turned out more than a dozen monographs that have been accorded the highest praise by specialists in each of the several branches of conjuring which were thus dealt with. But proof of his scholarship, industry, and genius for clear exposition is most evident in the larger books that he has written, edited, or translated: *Encyclopedia of Card Tricks*, which deals with non-sleight-of-hand feats; *Greater Magic*, a thousand-page tome on general magic; *Modern Magic Manual*, an exceptionally fine *general treatise* on conjuring; *Magic without Apparatus*, a translation of an unrivalled work on pure sleight-of-hand, Gaultier's *La Prestidigitation sans Appareils; The Fine Art of Magic*, a book of original magic, now in process of manufacture; and finally the present volume. Mr. Hugard is also editor and publisher of *Hugard's Magic Monthly*, a lively little journal which has won the enthusiastic support of several thousands of magician-subscribers.

Somewhat less than a decade ago, Mr. Hugard struck up a correspondence with Frederick Braué, a native Californian who had been a close student of magic since early boyhood and had developed into a successful, part-time professional. Mr. Braué is a generation or so younger than Mr. Hugard, in terms of physical years, but they are amazingly alike in their love of conjuring, the breadth and depth of their knowledge of the subject, and their conviction that a feat of magic, to be worthy of the name, must have charm as well as mystery, must not only bewilder but delight the spectator. The like-mindedness of these two wizards doubtless accounts, in large measure, for the success of their collaborations, which date from the production, in 1940, of their *Expert Card Technique*, the foremost treatise on *advanced* card magic, which the reader may wish to tackle when he has mastered the instructions given in the present book. The next Hugard-Braué product was their *Miracle Methods Series*, which contains thus far four small volumes, each dealing with a specialized branch of card conjuring. Then came *The Invisible Pass*, in which they gave the world of magic a vastly improved method for performing this important card sleight. We understand that these tireless collaborators, having completed *The Royal Road to Card Magic*, are already busy on yet another work on conjuring, the nature of which we are not at liberty to reveal at this time.

What we have said about our authors is by way of assuring the reader that he is in safe hands. Jean Hugard and Frederick Braué are sound theorists and practical experts, who have learned through long experience the best tricks to present and the best ways to present them. The explanations they give are full, clear, and accurate, and will enable the reader, with a moderate amount of practice, to become a competent performer. We can recall, without too great effort, our own initiation into the mysteries of card conjuring, a good many years ago. Remembering vividly the months of drudgery that preceded the actual performance of any tricks, we cannot help envying a little the beginner of today who sets forth on *The Royal Road to Card Magic*—certainly a shorter and smoother road than was plodded by magicians of the past, and one quite as likely to take the traveler to his destination.

PREFACE

MANY years ago David Devant, the great English conjurer, was approached by an acquaintance new to sleight-of-hand with cards. "Mr. Devant," said this young man, "I know three hundred tricks with cards. How many do you know?" Devant glanced at the youth quizzically. "I should say," the magician responded drily, "that I know about eight."

Devant was making a point with which all professional magicians are familiar. To perform card tricks entertainingly you must not only know how the tricks are done, but *how to do them.* There is a vast difference between the two, and if proof were needed, one need only watch the same feat performed by a novice and by an expert card conjurer. The novice knows the mechanics of so many tricks that he cannot do any one feat really well; the professional performs a smaller number of tricks which he knows how to present in such a way as to create the greatest possible impression upon those who watch.

We cannot emphasize too strongly that knowing the secret of a trick is not the same as knowing how to perform that trick; and that knowing the secret of hundreds of tricks is of little value unless each can be performed smoothly and entertainingly. It is far better to know only a few tricks which can be performed with grace, skill and effect.

In writing this book, we have attempted to teach you card tricks which may be performed anywhere, at any time, under any circumstances, for any company, and using any pack of cards. You will not need "trick" packs of cards, nor special cards, nor expensive accessories. This is most important, for it means that no matter where you may be, you need only borrow a deck of cards when called upon to entertain; the ability to amuse and interest will be literally at your finger tips.

To ensure that you *will* be a good card magician, we have introduced you to the mysteries of card magic progressively.

Each chapter describes a new sleight or principle and a selection of tricks follows in which that particular sleight, and those already learned, are the only ones used. We do not suggest that all the tricks in each section should be mastered before you pass on to the next sleight. You should, however, select at least two of them and learn them so well that you can perform them smoothly and entertainingly before going any farther. These tricks have been chosen with the greatest care and every one of them is effective if properly done. If you find that, in your hands, a certain trick falls flat, you can rest assured that the fault is yours, and that further study is required.

Clearly, to travel the royal road to card magic, you must begin with the fundamental principles and learn these well, as you would in learning any other art. Fortunately, the study of card conjuring is a delightful task and one that is no less than fascinating. For this reason, we have found that the student is inclined to race ahead to explore the distant pastures which he is sure (and rightly!) are lushly green. We cannot blame you if you, too, wish to rush through this book, but we would rather have you emulate the tortoise than the hare. By making haste slowly, by really learning what is given you in one chapter before proceeding to the next, you will, in the end, be a far better card magician.

By adhering to our plan of study, you will not only learn practical sleights and subtleties, but you will simultaneously add to your repertoire of good card tricks which will surprise and please all those who see them. Best of all, you can begin performing tricks of sleight-of-hand as soon as you have mastered the first chapter, and thus at once learn through practical experience before audiences how tricks must be presented to achieve the greatest effect from them. Then, too, we have inserted in each chapter feats which are self-working—effects which require no skill on the part of the performer. These will give you an opportunity for concentrating your whole attention on acting your part in such a way as to bring out the trick's greatest possible effect.

We reiterate that there is a vast difference between *doing* and *performing* card tricks. Since your primary purpose in performing sleight-of-hand with cards is to entertain those who watch, it is not enough that you should achieve technical perfection alone. You must also make your tricks amusing and interesting by weaving about a trick's basal plot a pleasant discourse which will divert the spectators. We have tried to show you how this is done by outlining talk—or "patter"—for most of the tricks. Naturally, your patter should be in keeping with your own personality, gay and amusing if you have an ebullient personality, more factual if you are a more serious person. For this reason you should use the patter we have suggested only as an illustration of how the bare bones of a trick may be clothed in talk and action to make the *presentation* a striking one.

True art, we have been told, holds the mirror to nature. This is especially true of conjuring with cards. Complete naturalness of action, speech and manner is the essence of the art. There is a school of card conjuring in which the artist, by the mere rapidity of his actions, attempts to impress his audience with the great skill he possesses. We urge you to eschew this type of card work and instead strive at all times for a natural, relaxed, graceful handling of the cards.

There are a number of general rules governing good card magic which you should always keep in mind:

1. Never tell beforehand what you purpose to do. Forewarned, the audience conceivably may discover the method. Wait until the climax, when all the necessary secret preparations have been made, before announcing what you will do.

2. Do not repeat a trick, unless you can duplicate the effect by another means.

3. *Never* reveal the secret of a trick. Many good card tricks are so simple that to reveal the method is to lower yourself in the estimation of the audience, which has given you great credit for a skill which you then confess you do not possess!

4. Use misdirection to help you conceal the vital sleight or subtlety employed in a trick. Misdirection is simply the diversion of the audience's attention during the moments when a sleight or subtlety is made use of. Let us say, for instance, that you must make use of the sleight known as The Pass in the course of a trick. You can divert attention from your hands by addressing

a remark to someone, at the same time glancing at him; all eyes will turn to the person you have addressed as he makes his response. You can divert attention by requesting someone to hand you a nearby object, which has the same effect of turning everyone's gaze, for an instant, towards the object; and in that instant you perform your secret sleight. You can divert attention by having someone show to others a card which he holds; as everyone glances at it, you perform the necessary sleight.

5. Know what your patter will be for a given trick. Not only will your patter help in entertaining your audience, but it aids in concealing the *modus operandi* of the feat. Since a certain amount of a person's powers of concentration must be devoted to assimilating that which you say, he cannot analyze quite so clearly that which you do.

Finally, we should mention that we have not included the more recondite and difficult card sleights, such as the second and bottom deals, which in any event are performed well by only a few top-flight card experts. Later, when you have learned all that we have given in this book, you may, if you like, progress to these sleights, which you will find in *Expert Card Technique*, and other books. For the time being we urge you to confine your knowledge of card magic to this book, learning how to do, and how to perform, the fine tricks which we give.

And now we have talked to you long enough; you are impatient to savor the good things to come. To you we say *"Bon Voyage!"* as we stand aside to let you start your journey up the royal road to card magic.

JEAN HUGARD
FREDERICK BRAUÉ

November 1, 1947

PART ONE

I

THE OVERHAND SHUFFLE, I

I T IS our intention to show you the royal road to card magic, and the first stage of our journey is to instruct you in the use of the overhand shuffle and to explain the many purposes which it serves.

Anyone who plays cards has learned to execute the overhand shuffle. It is a simple operation, yet it is the first step—and a very important one—on the road to the mastery of card magic. It is essential that you master this first step before continuing on your journey, and for this reason we urge you to learn the various shuffles and perform the many fine tricks which they make possible before you pass on to the other sections.

Each succeeding chapter in this book, except the last, leads to the one which follows and supplements the one which preceded. By resisting the impulse to learn everything at once but by practicing each step as you go, you will, with a speed that will amaze you, soon have traveled the entire road; when finally in that way you have reached its end, you will be a far more competent card conjurer than will the more impatient reader.

With this final word of caution, we now start you on your pleasant journey.

POSITION OF THE PACK IN THE HANDS

It is essential that the cards be handled neatly and precisely, and the first requisite towards acquiring this neatness of execution is the position of the pack in the hands.

1. Hold your left hand half closed, palm upwards, and place the pack in it, face downwards, so that the third phalanx of the index finger is bent against the outer left corner. The middle and

3

ring fingers, slightly bent, rest against the face of the bottom card; the little finger curls inwards so that its side rests against the inner end, and the thumb rests on the top card, its tip near the middle of the outer end.

The pack should slope downwards toward the left at an angle of about forty-five degrees, its lower side resting along the palm of the hand. In this position the pack can be gripped, as in a forceps, between the index and the little fingers by pressing them against the opposite ends (Fig. 1).

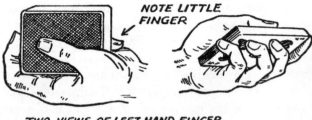

TWO VIEWS OF LEFT HAND FINGER POSITIONS FOR OVERHAND SHUFFLE

Fig. 1

This position of the pack gives one perfect control of the cards and should be strictly adhered to. The grip should be firm but light; in fact, the lightest touch possible, consistent with security, must be cultivated from the outset.

Execution of the Overhand Shuffle

1. Holding the pack as described above, seize the lower half with the right hand between the top phalanx of the thumb, at the middle of the inner end, and the top phalanges of the middle and ring fingers at the middle of the outer end. Bend the index finger lightly on the upper side of the deck, letting the little finger remain free.

2. Lift this lower packet upwards to clear the other portion of the pack, then bring it downwards over the other cards until its lower side touches the left palm. Press the left thumb against the top card of this packet and simultaneously lift the right hand so that the card, or cards, pulled off by the left thumb fall on top of the packet retained in the left hand.

3. Repeat this action until all the cards held by the right hand have been shuffled off onto those held by the left hand. Pat the upper side of the deck with the outstretched fingers of the right hand to square the cards. Since the overhand shuffle is generally repeated, this action is absolutely essential to a clean execution.

In making this shuffle *do not look at your hands and the cards.* Practice this from the outset and so form the habit, which is an essential factor in the maneuvers which follow and are done under cover of the action of this shuffle.

The speed at which the shuffle is executed should be about the same as that used by any card player, neither too fast nor too slow, and the tempo should be an even one throughout.

USING THE OVERHAND SHUFFLE

Controlling the Top Card

1. Holding the deck as explained, lift it with the right hand, and with the left thumb draw off the top card only in the first movement of the shuffle. Without the slightest pause or hesitation shuffle the other cards onto this one until the shuffle has been completed. The top card is now at the bottom of the pack.

2. Again lift the entire pack and repeat the shuffle you have just made down to the last card, which we know was the card originally at the top. Drop this card on top of all the others in the last movement of the shuffle. After a few trials you will find that this last card will cling to the thumb and fingers without any conscious effort on your part.

In this sleight, as well as in the others to follow, the action must become automatic so that you can look at, talk with, and give your whole attention to your audience. Only in this way can you convince the onlookers that the shuffle is genuine, and you should never forget that it is at this very starting point that illusion begins or is destroyed. If you stare fixedly at your hands while shuffling, suspicion will inevitably be aroused, and if a spectator suspects that you have "done something" the illusion of your magic is gone.

In practicing this shuffle and those that follow, it is a good plan to turn the top card face upwards so that at the finish you can see at a glance if you have made it correctly.

CONTROLLING THE BOTTOM CARD

1. Lift the lower half of the pack to begin the shuffle, and in so doing press lightly on the bottom card with the tips of the left middle and ring fingers, holding it back and thus adding it to the bottom of the packet remaining in the left hand.

2. Shuffle off the cards remaining in the right hand, and repeat the action if desired. Nothing could be simpler than this control, and the sleight is valuable because of its ease and naturalness.

RETAINING THE TOP AND BOTTOM CARDS IN POSITION

1. Grip the entire pack with the right hand to start the shuffle, at the same time pressing lightly on the top card with the left thumb and on the bottom card (Fig. 2), with the left middle and

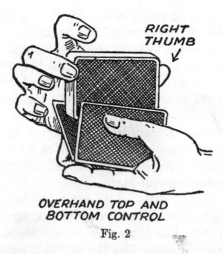

RIGHT THUMB

OVERHAND TOP AND BOTTOM CONTROL

Fig. 2

ring fingers holding them back so that all the cards except these two are lifted clear, the top card falling upon the bottom card. Continue the shuffle, without pause, until completed.

2. Pat the upper side of the deck square and repeat the moves exactly as before by lifting out all but the top and bottom cards, then shuffle off to the last card of those held in the right hand,

the card originally at the top, and drop it back again on the top.

Be careful not to pull the cards away sharply in the first movement of the shuffle, making the top and bottom cards come together with a "click." Use a light touch. Note that by placing two known cards at the bottom and a third at the top, all three cards can be controlled by this valuable artifice. Practice the sleight in this way until you can do it with ease and certainty.

Top Card to Next to Bottom and Back to the Top

1. Lift the pack for the shuffle, retaining the top and bottom cards in the left hand as in the preceding sleight. Shuffle the cards in the right hand onto the two cards in the left hand without hesitation. The card originally on the top is now next to the bottom card.

2. Again lift the pack, retaining the top and bottom cards in the left hand. Shuffle off the cards in the right hand upon the two in the left, allowing the bottom card to fall last, thus returning the top card to its original position.

Later you will find that this sleight is useful for showing that a chosen card which you are controlling is neither at the top nor at the bottom of the pack.

The Run

In magical parlance, this term means the pulling off of cards one by one from the right hand packet with the aid of the left thumb in the course of the shuffle. To make the run, press the left thumb lightly on the back of the top card of the right hand packet while holding this latter packet just tightly enough to allow one card only to escape. It is very important that the single cards be drawn off at the same tempo as the rest of the shuffle, so that there will be no hesitation at the start of the shuffle or its end.

A few minutes' practice with cards that are in good condition will prove how easy the sleight is, yet it is one of the most useful in the card man's arsenal.

THE INJOG

This term is applied to the subterfuge of causing a card to project about one quarter of an inch from the inner end of the deck. It is one of the oldest stratagems in magic, having been in use for three and a half centuries. It was first mentioned in Scott's *Discouverie of Witchcraft,* published in 1584.

The action of jogging a card is a simple one. In the course of the shuffle, when a card is to be jogged, move the right hand slightly towards the body, draw off one card with the left thumb, then move the hand back to its former position and continue the shuffle in the usual way. The card thus jogged should rest on the little finger tip, which enables you to know, by sense of touch alone, that the card is in the proper position (Fig. 3).

LITTLE FINGER UNDER JOG. FOREFINGER AT CORNER OF OTHER END.
Fig. 3

It is advisable at the start to make the card protrude about half an inch and, in shuffling off the remaining cards from the right hand, to make them lie irregularly so that the protruding card is covered and concealed. With practice the jogging of the card can be reduced to approximately a quarter of an inch. Here again it is most important that there shall be no alteration in the tempo. The card must be jogged and the shuffle continued without the least hesitation.

THE UNDERCUT

This sleight is used to bring the cards directly under a jogged card to the top of the pack, in the following manner:

A card having been jogged and the shuffle completed, bring the right hand upwards from a position a little below the left hand, so that the point of the thumb will strike against the face of the jogged card, lifting it and the cards above it slightly; then move the right hand outwards with the lower packet, the thumbnail scraping against the face of the jogged card while the middle and ring fingers close on the outer end of the packet. Lift the packet clear and throw it on the top of the deck. This action brings the jogged card to the bottom and the card directly below it to the top of the pack.

To undercut to a jogged card is a very simple action if the right thumb strikes *upward*, not inward (Fig. 4).

RIGHT THUMB BENDS
JOG BEFORE PUSHING
THE CARD INTO PACK.

Fig. 4

OVERHAND SHUFFLE CONTROL

A large proportion of card tricks consist of having a card selected, noted, and returned to the middle of the deck, which is then shuffled. The chosen card is revealed by the magician in some startling way. To do this the chosen card must be controlled, and one of the easiest, best, and most natural methods is by using the overhand shuffle. Here are the moves:

1. Let us suppose that a card has been freely chosen by a spectator. While he notes what it is, you begin an overhand shuffle and, when you have shuffled about half the cards into your left hand, move that hand toward the spectator, tacitly inviting him to replace his card. He puts it on the top of those in your left hand and you immediately resume your shuffle by *running* three cards flush on top of the chosen card, jogging the next card, and shuffling off the remainder freely.

2. Undercut below the jogged card, as explained in the preceding section, and throw the packet on top. The chosen card will then be the fourth card from the top of the pack and you can deal with it as you please.

For example, possibly in the course of the shuffle the chosen card may have arrived at the top or bottom of the pack; therefore you take off three cards from the top and spread them face outwards, asking the spectator if his card is among them. *Never* say, "You see your card is not there." You are not supposed to know whether it is or not. Throw the three cards casually on the table. Then show several cards at the bottom. Finally gather up the three cards by placing the pack on them and picking up all together.

You have the chosen card on the top, yet the onlookers will be convinced, if you have done your part simply and naturally, that the chosen card is lost in the pack and beyond your control. Thus you have succeeded in the most important part of the trick, for whenever a chosen card is controlled in some abnormal fashion your purpose is defeated. The real illusion of card magic begins with the conviction on the part of the spectator that his card is lost among the others. Without that conviction the trick has already failed.

RETAINING TOP STOCK

The overhand shuffle control is extremely useful in tricks where it is necessary to retain a card or cards at the top of the pack while giving the impression that you are shuffling the cards.

To do this, undercut the lower half with the right hand, and, in the first movement of the shuffle, injog the first card drawn off by the left thumb. Upon it shuffle the rest of the cards held in the right hand. Undercut below the injogged card and throw this packet on top. Although you have seemingly mixed the cards, you have retained the desired cards at the top.

OVERHAND FALSE SHUFFLE

Many fine card feats depend on the fact that the pack has been arranged in a certain order familiar to the magician. To retain that order while apparently mixing the cards thoroughly, proceed as follows:

1. Begin an overhand shuffle by undercutting half the deck.

2. Run five cards onto the original upper half of the deck. That is to say, pull off five cards singly with the left thumb,

then throw the remaining packet on top making it protrude about half an inch beyond the outer end of the cards in the left hand (Fig. 5).

3. Press the tip of the left index finger against the face of this protruding packet and seize the cards below it by the ends, between the right thumb and middle finger. Lift them, again run five cards, and throw the remainder on top.

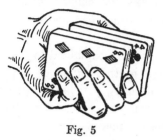

Fig. 5

The whole pack will be in its original order.

The action consists simply of reversing the order of five cards in the middle of the deck and then, by reversing these same five cards again, bringing them back to their original order, the rest of the cards not having been disturbed. Done smoothly and rather rapidly, not looking at your hands and while addressing the spectators, the shuffle is completely deceptive.

OVERHAND SHUFFLE PRACTICE ROUTINE

The best method of practicing the various overhand shuffles is to go through them in sequence as follows:

1. Turn the top card face upward.
2. Shuffle it to the bottom and back to the top again.
3. Shuffle it to the bottom. Shuffle again, retaining it there, then shuffle it back to the top.
4. Reverse the card now at the bottom. Shuffle, retaining the top and bottom cards in position.
5. Shuffle the top card to the next to bottom and back to the top.

The two reversed cards should be at the top and bottom. Check your work.

6. Control the top reversed card only by means of the overhand shuffle control, which will give you facility in the run, the injog, and the undercut.

Again check your work. The original top card should now be the fourth from the top of the pack. If that is the case and you have made the shuffles smoothly, you have made excellent progress toward acquiring this most useful of all card sleights. Practice until you can make the shuffles without looking at your hands, and at the same time keep up an easy flow of conversation.

With the simple principles explained in the preceding sections, which can be learned in the course of a pleasant half-hour's toying with a pack of cards, you have a golden key which will unlock the door to many of the most entertaining card tricks it is possible to perform. Since the best way to learn to do magic is to do magic, in the next section several tricks are explained in which the principles you have already learned are put to use

TRICKS WITH THE OVERHAND SHUFFLE

Having acquired facility with the overhand shuffle and the various maneuvers accomplished by its use, the royal road to card magic with all its surprising twists and turns opens before you a vista of exciting adventures, of which you are the protagonist.

A good card trick—and by that we mean a card trick which entertains, surprises, amuses, and puzzles an audience—has certain attributes:

1. It has a simple plot. It must not be confusing to those who watch.

2. The *modus operandi* is simple.

3. It is interesting.

4. It has a surprising denouement.

The following tricks afford excellent practice in applying the different principles you have learned and will start your repertoire with some of the finest feats of card magic, the first of which is:

It is always a good rule to begin a series of card feats with a short, startling effect, one that will arouse the interest of the onlookers immediately and stimulate their interest in the marvels to follow. In this effect one half of the pack is placed face to face with the other half, yet, on the word of command, the cards right themselves so that all of them face the same way.

Whenever possible you should use a borrowed deck, and we shall suppose that one has been handed to you with the request: "Show us some card tricks."

1. Take the pack and place it face down on your left hand. With your left thumb spread the cards by pushing them over

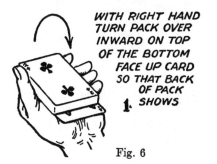

WITH RIGHT HAND
TURN PACK OVER
INWARD ON TOP
OF THE BOTTOM
FACE UP CARD
SO THAT BACK
OF PACK
1. SHOWS

Fig. 6

to the right hand under pretense of examining the backs. "These seem to be ordinary cards," you say. "Let's see the faces." Close the deck into the left hand and square the cards, holding them in dealing position.

2. Take hold of the outer end of the deck between the right thumb on top and the fingers on the bottom, lift it and turn it over inwards—that is to say, towards your body—and lay it in your left hand, face upwards. Spread the cards as before, showing the faces and remarking, "Just ordinary cards, aren't they?" Close the pack into the left hand again and square it, but this time, in doing so, let the lowermost card slip off the tip of the right thumb and push the rest of the cards forward about an inch (Fig. 6).

3. Grasp the outer end of the deck as before and turn it over inward onto the left hand and onto the face-up card. Square the pack and hold it in your left hand so that it slopes down-

ward a little; thus no one can see the reversed card now on the bottom.

4. Cut off about half the cards by grasping them at the ends between the right thumb and middle finger. Turn the right hand over with a little flourish to show the face card of this packet

TAKE HALF OF PACK
IN RIGHT HAND AND
SHOW FACE WHILE
TURNING LEFT HAND
OVER TO EXPOSE BACK
OF WHAT WAS BOTTOM CARD

Fig. 7

and look at that card yourself, saying, "I turn one half of the cards face upward, so." As you say this, quietly turn your left hand over, bringing it back upwards, thus bringing the reversed card uppermost (Fig. 7).

HALF IS PLACED FACE UP ON BACK OF
LEFT HAND

LOWER HALF IS NOW PLACED ON TOP
OF FACE UP HALF APPARENTLY PUTTING
TWO HALVES FACE TO FACE

Fig. 8

5. Still keeping your eyes fixed on the face card of the packet in your right hand, continue: "I'll put this packet face upwards on the back of my left hand." Do so (Fig. 8). The packet in the left hand, which the spectators think is face downward, is really face upward with a single reversed card on top.

6. Draw out the packet from your left hand, grasping it at the sides near the ends, as you say, "These face-down cards I'll place on the face-up packet," and you do so, being careful to slope the packet so that no glimpse can be had of its bottom card. Take the pack off the back of your left hand and replace it in that hand, which you turn palm upwards, between the tips of the thumb on one side and the fingers on the other. With the right hand turn the pack over sideways three times, each time taking it between the left thumb and fingers as you say, "You see half the pack faces one way, the other half the reverse way." The third turn will bring the single reversed card to the bottom.

7. "I want to test these cards to see if I shall be able to do anything with them. I shall therefore order all the face-up cards to turn face downward. Let me show you what I mean. I take one of the face-up cards, so." Draw out the bottom card by the end toward your body, deliberately turn it face downwards on the top of the pack. "*Allez oop!*" you exclaim, and, with a flourish, you spread the whole pack on the table. All the cards are face downwards. "Excellent! You have trained your cards well. I am sure we shall have a great success with them."

The most important thing for the beginner at card magic to bear in mind is this: A conjuring trick is just what the performer makes of it. It may be composed of the simplest elements, yet, given a plausible plot and dressed with appropriate patter, it can be transformed into an imposing illusion. In other words, it is not so much what you do as what you make the onlookers think you do.

The preceding trick affords an example of this fact. Merely to take the cards and go through the motions of apparently reversing them would be a tame affair, a mere curiosity. Asserting that the cards are intelligent, that they can be trained to act by themselves puts a different complexion on the matter. The onlookers are amused by your fairy tale; they take a greater interest in the performance and sometimes actually persuade themselves that there might be something in it after all.

It has been said that "the proper way to do tricks is to do

tricks." That is true, provided it is borne in mind that the tricks must not only be *done* but must also be *presented* or *acted* properly. Good presentation can only be acquired by actual performance before an audience, even if it is composed only of your home circle. Confidence in yourself is the main thing. If you know that you can do the trick without any possible hitch, then you can devote your whole attention to "putting across" the fairy tales which you are telling. To help you in gaining this confidence, we shall from time to time explain tricks which practically work themselves—self-workers, as they are called.

The art of interspersing these self-workers with tricks that call for skill is an important principle of card magic. The most eminent magicians use self-workers; but they use only the good ones, never those which call for endless dealing of cards or obvious mathematical principles. Some of the good self-workers are gems of subtlety and misdirection. Some of them depend on faults of observation on the part of the spectators; many depend on the inability of most people to understand properly what is being done.

The trick that follows is one of the latter kind and, when you have performed it, you will be astonished at the effect it causes. It is called:

A Poker Player's Picnic

Taking a pack of cards which has been thoroughly shuffled, a spectator cuts it into four piles. Turning the top card of each packet himself, he finds that he has actually cut to the four aces.

Preparation. If you make this your first trick, you must beforehand place the four aces on the top of the pack. If you wish to do it following other tricks, or with a borrowed deck, then you must get the aces to the top secretly. *Never* attempt to do that furtively. Run over the faces of the cards, holding them so that no one else can see them and at the same time saying, "I suppose these are ordinary cards?" Watch for an ace, cut the deck to bring it to the bottom as you look up and say, "Is there a joker in the pack? If so, I don't want that card."

Continue running through the cards; each time you find an

ace separate your hands just enough to be able to push it to the bottom with the left thumb as you glance at the spectators and make some casual remark. If there is a joker, discard it.

If you do the work openly and casually, to the onlookers you are merely toying with the cards and your actions pass without special notice.

Procedure. The steps are as follows:

1. If you are beginning with this trick and you have the aces at the top of the pack, well and good. If, however, you have had to sort them to the bottom as we have just explained, then you turn the pack face downwards and make an ordinary overhand shuffle. When you reach the last half-dozen cards run them— that is to say, pull them off with the left thumb one by one, thus bringing the four aces to the top.

2. Execute the overhand shuffle control, retaining top stock (see page 10), again leaving the aces on the top.

3. Offer to demonstrate how gamblers cheat at cards and comment casually that their skill is greatly overrated. "As a matter of fact," you say, "almost anyone can duplicate their feats with very little practice." Single out one of the spectators. "You look as though you might be a good poker player. Will you help me?"

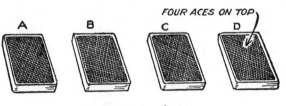

POKER PLAYER'S PICNIC

Fig. 9

4. Place the pack before your assistant and request him to cut it into four packets about equal. He does this, and for the purpose of our explanation we shall call these packets A, B, C, and D, the four aces being the four cards at the top of D (Fig. 9).

5. Instruct him to pick up A, remove three cards from the top of the packet and place them at the bottom, then deal one card from the top onto each of the other three packets.

6. Have him take B and repeat exactly the same process, putting three cards to the bottom and dealing one card on each of the other three packets. Have him do the same with C and D. (Follow this procedure with the cards and you will at once see that the three cards that are placed one by one on D are finally moved to the bottom of that packet, and then three aces are placed on top of each of the other packets quite unwittingly by the spectator himself.)

7. Recapitulate what has been done. "You will recall that you yourself cut the cards and that I did not touch them at any time. I picked you for this demonstration because you have a poker face. Let's see if I judged you correctly—let's look at the cards at which you cut." At your direction, the assistant turns over the top card of each packet and to his astonishment finds each card to be an ace.

Note particularly that at the end of the trick you emphasize that the *assistant cut the cards,* but do not mention that he also moved cards about. You do this deliberately because you want him to forget about this part of the trick. The average person has great difficulty in recalling the details of any fairly complex action. Capitalize on this weakness by stressing a part of what he did and suppressing another part. This expedient is often used in magic. You will be amazed, sometimes, to hear the assistant describe the trick and state that he *shuffled* the cards and then cut to the four aces, which he certainly did not do. This unconscious distortion will enhance your reputation and at the same time bring you considerable secret amusement.

A Pocket Discovery

A card having been freely selected by a spectator, noted and replaced in the deck, the pack is shuffled and then placed in a spectator's pocket. Any number having been chosen, the magician draws cards from the pocket singly and produces the selected card at the number chosen.

1. Begin by handing the pack to a spectator and asking him to shuffle it and while doing so to think of any card. When he has done that, instruct him to take that card out of the pack

and hand the remaining cards to you. Turn away and have him show the card to the rest of the company.

This method of having a card taken by a spectator is a good one, not only because it is obvious that he has a free choice but also because the onlookers will think of it as merely having been "thought of," which enhances the effect immensely. Note, too, that it is wise to have a chosen card shown to the audience. Nothing is more annoying than to find, on reaching the climax of your feat, that the drawer has forgotten which card he chose. That precaution also prevents a spectator from

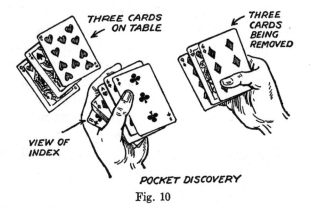

THREE CARDS ON TABLE

THREE CARDS BEING REMOVED

VIEW OF INDEX

POCKET DISCOVERY

Fig. 10

naming a card wrongly in order to embarrass you; this, sad to relate, some people are tempted to do.

2. You now have to control the chosen card for your own purposes, and this you do by using the overhand shuffle control. That is, you shuffle off about half the pack onto your left hand, have the card replaced on this packet, run three cards flush, injog the next card, and shuffle off. Undercut below the injogged card and throw on top. The chosen card now lies fourth from the top of the pack.

3. It is necessary for you to know the chosen card, and to secure this information you must glimpse the index of the fourth card, as follows:

Continue, as explained in the section referred to above, by remarking that the shuffle may have brought the chosen card near the top or bottom. Lift off the top three cards, show them, and drop them face down on the table. Turn the pack face up-wards in your left hand, take off several cards with your right hand, at the same moment pressing the top card of the pack (the chosen card, now resting against the left palm) to the left just enough to expose the index (Fig. 10).

Since this action takes place on the side of the deck away from the audience, it is imperceptible to them. Show the cards in your right hand, replace them on the bottom of the pack, turn the pack face downwards, and drop it on the three cards on the table. You have the chosen card on the top of the pack and you know what card it is, although everyone should be con-vinced that it is unknown to you and buried in the deck.

4. "Let us put the cards to a harder test," you say. "Will you, sir, kindly empty your breast pocket?" As he does this you can generally contrive to cause some amusement over the hetero-geneous articles thus brought to light. Hand the pack to him telling him to put it in his pocket, but you must note carefully which way the cards face as he does so.

"Now that the cards are out of my possession, will you, sir, name any number you please—say between one and twelve, just to save time." Suppose he says, "Eight." "Very well, this is what I propose to try: Seven times I will take a single card from your pocket and at the eighth draw I will order the chosen card to jump into my hand. Ready?"

5. Draw out seven cards in succession from the face of the pack, counting them and laying them face downwards on the table. "Eight, you said. Very well, now for the eighth card." Plunge your hand into the pocket, calling out, *"Allez oop!"* Then, without withdrawing the hand, "A card has leapt into my hand!" Lean forward, let your right ear rest against the pocket. "The card tells me it is a seven. The seven of —" Then take the card out and hold it face downwards. "Will you, sir, be kind enough to complete the name?" "The seven of hearts." Turn the card face upwards and show that you have succeeded.

The feat is made up of the simplest possible elements, but properly presented it never fails to create amusement and wonder-ment.

TELEPATHY PLUS

Having turned the conversation to the subject of mind reading, an easy matter at the present time, ask permission to attempt an experiment of that nature. Explain that you have had some success with objects that can be pictured mentally and pretend to select with great care some person as concentrator and transmitter.

1. Hand him a pack of cards and have him shuffle it thoroughly, then instruct him to deal a row of five spot cards of differing suits and values. If picture cards or cards of the same value turn up, they are to be discarded.

Suppose that the row, when completed, consists of

9H   5S   AD   3S   7C

Everyone must be convinced that these cards have been chosen by chance alone.

2. Take back the pack and invite the spectator to select, mentally, any one of the five cards and to concentrate deeply on its suit and value. In order not to be suspected of detecting the card by the direction of his gaze, turn your head away as he looks at them. When he announces that he has set his mind upon a card, turn the five cards face downwards as they lie, but in the meantime you have memorized their values, taking no notice of the suits, by saying to yourself, "Ninety-five, one thirty-seven." In memorizing figures always divide them into groups in this fashion; never try to remember separate figures.

3. In order to understand the following process of shuffling the cards, we should explain that its object is to place the five cards secretly at positions from the top of the pack corresponding with their values. Thus at the conclusion the ace of diamonds must be the top card, the three of spades the third card, the five of spades the fifth card, and so on.

To do this, assume a poker face, look steadily at the spectator, and pick up the nine of hearts (the card of the highest value of the five), its face towards yourself, letting no one else get a glimpse of it. Look at it gravely, then lay it on the top of the pack in your left hand.

Recalling that the next highest card is the seven of clubs, begin an overhand shuffle by running one card flush on top of the nine of hearts, injog the next card, and shuffle off. Undercut at the injog and throw on top.

4. Repeat your pantomime of studying the spectator's face as if to read his innermost thought, take up the seven of clubs, look at it, and then put it on the top of the pack. The next highest card being the five of spades, again you have to run one card flush, injog the next card, shuffle off, undercut, and throw on top.

5. Repeat the same process with the three of spades; but with the ace of diamonds, after placing it at the top, you must injog the first card, shuffle off, and undercut. When the undercut is thrown on top, the five cards will now be at the numbers from the top denoted by their values, and you are master of the situation. Needless to say, throughout the shuffling you have refrained from staring at your hands and have kept up a running fire of entreaties to your subject to concentrate upon his card.

6. Hand the pack to the spectator, addressing him somewhat after this fashion: "I have obtained from you a distinct impression of a certain card. If I were to name that card and you agreed that it is the one of which you are thinking, others would almost certainly believe that you were merely being complaisant. There would be no certainty that I really have read your thoughts.

"For this reason I have arranged matters so that the proof must be accepted by all—that is, *if* I have succeeded. The pack is in your hands; I cannot tamper with it, and my proof is this: I have placed your card in a certain position which I could only have done by knowing what card it is. Please name the card upon which you have concentrated. The five of spades! I knew it! And, knowing it is a five, I placed that very card fifth from the top. Deal four cards face down, please. Now turn up the fifth card. The five of spades! Thank you, sir; I have never worked with anyone possessing greater powers of concentration."

Take back the pack, gather up the cards just dealt face downwards, and shuffle the pack. In tricks of this nature it is always advisable to carry on at once with another that depends on an entirely different principle.

THOUGHT STEALER

This trick follows naturally after the preceding feat, since it duplicates the effect of the other by an entirely different means. This course should be followed wherever possible when you are requested to repeat a trick.

1. Turn to one of the spectators and say, "There are skeptics in every group, and it may well be that in your secret thoughts you believe that by some hocus pocus the feat you have just witnessed was not genuine mind reading. If I can divine your thought will you agree that there is more to this than meets the eye? You will. Very well, let's see if you are as admirable a concentrator as I think you are."

2. As you say this, idly run through the pack and remove these cards

2C   6S   5H   7S   4D   QD

one at a time in that order, placing the six of spades slightly overlapping the two of clubs, the five of hearts overlapping the six of spades, and so on with the others (Fig. 11).

THOUGHT STEALER

Fig. 11

3. "Now, sir," you continue, "while I turn my back, I shall ask you to think of one of these cards. Will you do that?" Turn away. When the spectator says he is ready, turn around. "Now, sir, you are the only person in this room who knows the name of the card you have mentally selected. That is right, is it not? Good. Then be sure to keep your mind fixed on it."

Gather up the six cards by sliding them together, retaining their order, and place them on the top of the pack. Thus the top card is the two of clubs and the sixth card the queen of diamonds.

4. Continue, "Once again I shall offer proof that I can actually read minds." As you say this, begin an overhand shuffle by lifting the lower half of the deck, run nine cards, injog the next card, and shuffle off. Undercut at the injog and throw on top. Your sequence of six cards now runs from the tenth card to the sixteenth card from the top of the pack.

5. Hand the pack to the spectator, saying, "I shall now offer my proof. I want you to spell the name of your card mentally and for each letter in its name I want you to deal a single card. For example, if you thought of the ace of diamonds, you will spell *a-c-e o-f d-i-a-m-o-n-d-s*. Is that clear? Don't forget the *of*."

When the spectator says that he understands, have him make the deal and then say: "Now I want you to pick up the last card you dealt, hold it face downwards and think intently of the card you chose mentally, which is unknown to the rest of us. You've done that? Now, for the first time, please name your card." The spectator does so. "Thank you. Will you be so good as to look at the card which you hold?"

He does so and finds that he is holding the very card which he selected mentally.

The explanation is a simple one. Each card, after the first, spells with one letter more than the preceding card, thus: two of clubs (10 letters), six of spades (11 letters), five of hearts (12 letters), and so on. Since there are several cards in the deck which will fit into each position, you will be able to pick them out quickly and apparently at random. This subtle principle should be borne in mind, for there are many effective feats which can be performed with it.

PINKIE DOES IT

A spectator having freely selected a card, noted it, and returned it to the deck, the cards are thoroughly shuffled. Holding the deck upright in your left hand, the bottom card facing the spectators, place your index finger on the upper end. The chosen card is named and as you lift your index finger that very card is seen to rise from the deck clinging to it. The card is shown to have risen from the middle of the deck, and the spectator may remove it from that position himself.

1. Hand the deck to a spectator to shuffle, then have him remove one card and hand the pack to you. Have him show the card to others as you turn away.

2. Use the overhand shuffle control to bring the card to the top, then shuffle it to the bottom and back to the top.

3. Stand with your left side to the audience holding the deck upright in your left hand, the bottom card facing the onlookers, between the first phalanx of your thumb on one side, a little below the middle of that side, and the first phalanges of your index and middle fingers on the other side. Rub your right fingers along the upper end of the pack, squaring it, and with the tip of your middle finger push down a small packet, making a step at the back of the deck (Fig. 12).

BACK VIEW SHOWING STEP

Fig. 12

4. Gravely rub your right index finger vigorously on your left sleeve and then apply it against the top of the deck, holding the other three fingers flexed. Lift the finger slowly, and nothing happens. "I wonder what is the matter?" you say. "I expected your card to rise out of the deck. Oh, of course, it must be named first! What was your card?"

5. The card is named. Rub your right index finger on your sleeve again and apply it against the top of the deck, then straighten out your little finger so that its tip presses against the top card (the chosen card, now the rearmost card). With the little finger push the rear card upwards until it touches the

index finger, then raise the right hand, maintaining the pressure of the little finger so that the card appears to cling to the index finger (Fig. 13).

6. When the bottom of the rising card reaches and clears the top of the stepped packet, push its lower end forward against the cards in front of the step, and at the same moment press your left little finger against the bottom of the stepped packet, squaring it with the deck. Flex your little finger and the card will remain protruding from the deck.

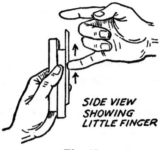

SIDE VIEW
SHOWING
LITTLE FINGER

Fig. 13

7. Tilt the deck forward to show that this is actually the case and invite the spectator to remove his card and the deck and to examine them carefully—and your index finger, too, if he so desires.

The rising of a card from the deck has been a favorite feat with magicians and audiences for many generations. There are many ways of doing the trick with mechanical means, but this impromptu method will be found to create as much astonishment as the most complicated mechanical method *if* you present the feat as if you, yourself, really believe that the card rises spontaneously.

A CARD AND A NUMBER

A chosen card should always be revealed in as striking a manner as possible. This effect affords a double surprise, for you divine a number merely thought of and use this number to find a chosen card.

1. Have a card chosen by a spectator, noted by him, and returned to the pack. Bring it to the top by using the overhand shuffle control.

2. Shuffle the cards by the overhand method, running the chosen card to the bottom and back to the top.

3. Address a second spectator. "Will you please think of a number between five and twenty? You have one? When I turn my back whisper your number to the person who selected a card." Turn your back, turn the top card—the selected card—face upwards and dig your thumbnail into it near the two index corners. This will make a bump on the back of the card which you will feel with your right thumb when dealing the cards. Replace the card face down on the top.

4. Turn around and give the pack to the second spectator. "I want you to deal, silently, cards to the number of which you are thinking. This will impress that number on your mind and help me to get the right impression. I will turn away as you deal." Do so. When he announces that the deal is completed, instruct him to replace the dealt cards on the rest of the pack.

5. This done, face front again and take the pack. "My trick is this," you say. "I shall attempt to read your thoughts and so get the number of which you are thinking." As you speak, shuffle the cards—using the overhand shuffle control, retaining top stock (see page 10), to keep the upper half of the deck unchanged.

6. Continue, "As I deal cards, please think intently of your number." Deal the cards, one by one, counting them aloud, until you feel the bump under your right thumb. Let us say that this is the sixteenth card. Remove it, holding it in your right hand face downwards.

7. Announce that this is the number he thought of, and when he agrees ask him, "Do you know how I knew that is your number?" He will admit that he does not know. Turn to the spectator who chose the card and ask him, "What was the name of the card you selected?" When he names it, slowly turn up the card you hold. It is that very card!

II

THE RIFFLE SHUFFLE

THIS is the shuffle ordinarily used by card players, but in spite of its almost universal use it is rarely done neatly or even smoothly. Nearly always the cards are bent far too much and then pushed together clumsily. The proper way to execute the shuffle should be acquired at the outset, not for appearances' sake alone but because it will enable you later to apply various secret maneuvers to the shuffle with ease and certainty. Here is the proper procedure:

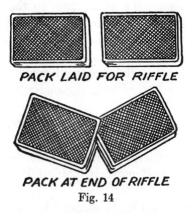

PACK LAID FOR RIFFLE

PACK AT END OF RIFFLE

Fig. 14

1. Place the deck on the table in front of you, its sides parallel with the edge of the table. With your right hand cut off half the cards and place the packet end to end with the other packet (Fig. 14).

2. Put your hands on the packets, your thumbs against the adjacent inner corners, your index fingers resting on the backs near these ends and your middle, ring and little fingers against

28

the outer sides. Your hands thus assume identical positions on their respective packets.

3. Seize the packets between the thumbs and the middle and ring fingers. Raise the inner corners with the thumbs, bending

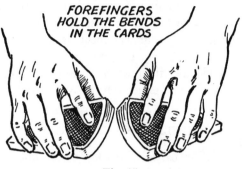

Fig. 15

the cards *very slightly* against the downward pressure of the index fingers (Fig. 15).

4. Begin to release or riffle the ends of the cards of each packet so that they interweave. Regulate this release of the corners so that a card, or several cards, falls from each packet alternately.

5. When this action has been completed and all the ends of the cards are interlaced, seize the outer ends of the packets be-

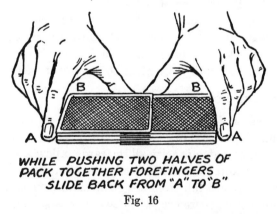

WHILE PUSHING TWO HALVES OF PACK TOGETHER FOREFINGERS SLIDE BACK FROM "A" TO "B"

Fig. 16

tween the thumbs and the index and middle fingers and push the packets inwards, telescoping them until they are almost but not quite flush.

6. To square the deck neatly and gracefully, place the thumbs at the middle of the inner side of the deck, their tips touching one another, and the index fingers against the ends near the outer corners. Now move the thumbs outwards along the side of the deck and the index fingers inwards along the ends, and by their pressure squeeze the cards flush (Fig. 16). When the tips of the thumbs and index fingers meet at their respective inner corners, the deck will be squared perfectly.

The riffle shuffle has its greatest use when the performer is seated at a table. It can effectively be alternated with the overhand shuffle.

RIFFLE SHUFFLE CONTROL

To retain a card or cards on the top or the bottom of the deck by means of this shuffle is a simple matter.

RETAINING A CARD AT THE TOP OF THE DECK

When the cut is made for the riffle shuffle, the card to be retained becomes the top card of the cut packet. Therefore you have merely to see that all the cards of the left-hand packet have fallen before you release the last few cards of the right-hand packet. When the packets are telescoped the required card will again be the top card of the deck.

A packet of six or eight cards can be retained on the top in the same way by holding them back until all the cards of the left-hand packet have fallen. It is not advisable, however, to use the maneuver with more than that number of cards.

RETAINING THE BOTTOM CARD OR CARDS

In this case the cards to be controlled are on the bottom of the left-hand packet. In grasping that packet with the left thumb and fingers, do not seize all the cards; allow a small packet to remain on the table and raise only the corners of those above it. The first cards to fall from the right-hand packet will fall on top of these cards; therefore, when the deck is squared, the card or cards being controlled will again be on the bottom of the deck.

Sometimes it becomes necessary to add one card to the top of the deck. This can easily be done by the riffle shuffle. In lifting the corners of the left-hand packet, press the index finger on the top card of that packet and draw it a little over the left thumb. It is an easy matter then to hold it back until the last card of the right-hand packet has been released.

RIFFLE SHUFFLE IN THE AIR

It is surprising that in this nation of bridge players so many persons who know how to make a neat riffle shuffle at the table do not know how to make the same shuffle away from a table. To be able to riffle shuffle in the air is a particularly useful weapon for the card conjurer who has to perform under varying conditions. This form of the riffle shuffle is not difficult, but it does require some practice to perform it neatly.

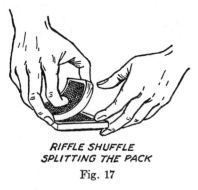

RIFFLE SHUFFLE
SPLITTING THE PACK
Fig. 17

1. Take the pack face downwards in the right hand with the thumb at one end, the middle, ring and little fingers at the other, and the index finger bent so that its nail rests against the middle of the back of the top card. Turn the pack to a vertical position with the thumb at the top and the faces towards the left.

2. Place the left hand, palm upwards, a couple of inches to the left of and a little above the tips of the right fingers. Bend the middle of the pack outwards by pressing outwards, with the right forefinger at the middle and the thumb and fingers inwards at the ends. Allow about half the cards to fall forward onto the left fingers in a horizontal position (Fig. 17).

3. Place the tip of the left thumb momentarily on the back of this packet and move the left forefinger up to take its place.

4. With the tips of the right fingers bend the left-hand packet upwards and place the left thumb on the middle of its upper end. The two packets are thus held facing each other and with exactly the same grip by each hand—thumbs at the top, index fingers at the middle of the backs, and the other three fingers gripping the lower ends (Fig. 18).

5. Turn both hands palm downwards, bend the ends of both packets upwards by pressure against the forefingers, and hold the packets with the inner ends close together in the shape of a shallow V, the point of which is away from the body.

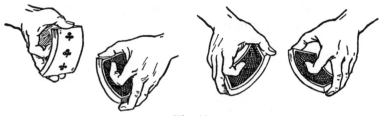

Fig. 18

6. Allow cards to slip from each thumb alternately, interlacing the corners.

7. Press the packets flush by bringing the hands together, and square the pack.

If the positions are taken correctly it will be found that the lower end of each packet will be held firmly between the first phalanx of the index finger at the back and the first phalanges of the other three fingers at the face. The grip must be held firmly until all the cards have been riffled off by the thumbs.

TRICKS WITH THE RIFFLE SHUFFLE

An Instinct for Cards

The purpose of the riffle shuffle is to mix the cards thoroughly, its very essence being that after a genuine shuffle the position of any particular card cannot be known. You may therefore find it hard to believe that a card unknown to you can be placed anywhere in the deck and the cards then genuinely riffle shuffled and cut, yet you can infallibly find that card and reveal it. The secret is so ingenious, and still so simple, that this is one of the few feats which can be repeated without fear of discovery. The only skill required is the ability to riffle shuffle the deck.

Preparation. Place the thirteen cards of one suit, say diamonds, in sequence from ace to king, at the top of the deck. Put the deck in its case and the case in your pocket.

Procedure. Here are the steps in this trick:

1. Take the case from your pocket and remove the cards and shuffle them, retaining the diamond sequence at the top by means of the overhand shuffle control, retaining top stock. Cut off about two-thirds of the deck and complete the cut. The sequence of diamonds will then run from about the twentieth card, the ace, to the thirty-third, the king.

2. Place the pack before a spectator, request him to cut it, remove the card he cuts to, replace the cut, and square the deck perfectly. You may add, "Better cut somewhere near the middle, so that I cannot possibly know the card to which you cut." But even without this admonition most people will cut somewhere near the middle, between the twentieth and thirty-third cards; thus they are sure to remove one of the diamonds. Turn away and move a pace or two from the table so that no one can suspect you might see the card.

3. With your back still turned, instruct the spectator to show the card to everyone; then cut the pack anywhere he likes, replace the card at that point, square the deck, and give it a riffle shuffle.

It is most effective to have the spectator himself make the shuffles and cuts, but if there is no one present who can shuffle cards neatly you may make the shuffles yourself. In such case call particular attention to the genuineness of the shuffles.

4. Next have the spectator cut the pack and complete the cut, riffle shuffle again, and finally cut again and complete the cut. Under these conditions you will find that everyone will be confident that you cannot possibly discover the selected card.

5. Turn around and take the pack, run through it slowly, glancing at the spectator from time to time as though studying his expression. You will find that despite the shuffles and cuts, which seemingly mix the cards indiscriminately, actually the

diamonds have been distributed among the other cards *in sequence*, with each succeeding higher value to the right. This is because the first shuffle distributed them through *half* the deck and the second shuffle throughout the *entire* deck. The cuts, of course, do not have any effect upon the sequence, though they may affect its starting point.

When the chosen card was replaced in the pack, it was not placed at the point from which it was taken; therefore, in order to find it, look for one card of that suit which is *out of sequence*. Let us say that you find that the diamonds run in the following order:

$$4 - 5 - 6 - K - 7 - 8 - 9 - 10 - J - Q - A - 2 - 3$$

The chosen card is the king, the only card out of sequence.

6. Remove the king and place it face downwards on the table. Rub it gently with the tip of your right second finger and have the selected card named. Turn the card face upwards showing that you have the correct card.

This perplexing feat may also be performed with the pack in hand. With the diamond sequence at the center, spread the cards and have one removed, making certain that it is taken from among the diamonds, an easy enough matter. Have it replaced at a point other than that from which it was taken. The rest follows as in the out-of-hand method.

MIRROR OF THE MIND

This is another method of performing the preceding effect, but here the necessary preparation is made more quickly. The method is not so clean-cut, but we give it as an alternative procedure.

Preparation. Place the thirteen cards of one suit, say hearts, in any order on the top of the pack. Note and remember the top card, which we shall assume is the six of hearts. Put the deck in its case and the case in your pocket.

Procedure. The method is as follows:

1. Take the cards out of the case and make the overhand shuffle control, retaining top stock, thus retaining the hearts on the top.

2. Hand the deck to a spectator, turn your back, and move

away a pace or two. Request him to deal any small number of cards, from one to twelve, face downwards on the table, urging him to do this silently so that you cannot count the cards dealt. When he has done this, tell him to look at and remember the next card and replace it on the cards he still holds, then pick up the packet of dealt cards and place it on top of all. The bottom card of this packet is your key card, the six of hearts, the first card dealt, and it is now directly above the chosen card.

3. As in the preceding feat, have the pack riffle shuffled twice, with a completed cut after each shuffle.

4. Take the pack and spread the cards face upwards on the table from *left to right*. Have the spectator grasp your wrist, then pass your hand over the line of cards from end to end, urging him to concentrate upon his card. When you see your key card, the six of hearts, look for the next heart *to its right*; this will be the chosen card. Move your hand away from this card and then abruptly, as though drawn by a strong magnetism, place your forefinger upon it and push it out from the spread.

ULTRA CARD DIVINATION

There is a fascination in the thought that the future can be foretold, and this trick capitalizes on this interest in divination. You write down the name of a card and place the memorandum to one side. A card is selected, and this is the one you prophesied.

1. Borrow a pack of cards and, holding it face upwards, count the cards into your right hand, reversing their order in the count, under pretense of making sure that it is a full deck. Note the thirty-fourth card and remember it, because this card, which will be thirty-fourth from the top of the pack after the count, is the one you will "predict."

2. Take a slip of paper and on it write the name of the thirty-fourth card. After writing the prediction, fold the slip twice and then stand it on the edges with the pencil underneath it (Fig. 19).

3. Cut off about half the pack, but not more than twenty-six cards, and have these shuffled and spread face downwards on the table.

4. Address a spectator, saying, "Kindly push a card out of the spread." When he has done so, have a second and third spectator

also push out a card. Gather the rest of the cards and replace them on the pack.

5. Hand the deck to still another spectator and have him turn the first of the three cards face upwards. Instruct him to deal as many cards below it, face downwards, as may be needed to bring

THE PROPHECY FOLDED

Fig. 19

its value to ten. For example, if the card is a seven, he will deal three cards. If a two, he will deal eight cards. But if the card is a court card it is arbitrarily called a ten, and in this case no cards are dealt because none are needed.

6. Have the same done with the other two cards.

7. Now tell the spectator to add the values of the three cards which were selected and deal that number of cards from the pack and place the next card aside.

8. Point out that the card has been selected in the fairest possible manner. "Before you even touched the cards," you say, "I wrote the name of a card on a slip of paper and thereafter never touched it." Lift the pencil with the slip on it and offer it to the spectator. "Will you read what I wrote?" He reads aloud the name of the card. Slowly turn the card face upwards. It is the card which you predicted!

III

FLOURISHES

FLOURISHES are certain movements with the cards which do not come under the heading of sleights, since they are done openly. In general they are used to show elegance in handling the cards; sometimes, however, they serve a more useful purpose, that of misleading the audience as to the moment when an effect is really brought about. Used in moderation they are a decided asset to the card conjurer, but when carried to extreme lengths they defeat the very object that the magician should always have in mind, namely, that the effects he produces are done by magic and not by skill. A series of brilliant flourishes leaves only the impression of juggling skill on the minds of the onlookers, and the performer's feats are dismissed by them with the remark, "He's clever with his hands." The simple flourishes which follow are legitimate, for some of them are already in fairly general use among card players.

DISPLAYING THE TOP CARD

A. For Intimate Performances. Instead of taking the card off the pack with the right hand to show it to the onlookers, make the following moves:

1. Hold the pack in the left hand in dealing position.

2. Push the top card off about an inch to the right with the left thumb.

3. Bend the top phalanx of the index finger under the card, near the upper right corner, and bend the same phalanx of the middle finger on the back of the card, which is thus gripped between the two fingers (Fig. 20). Insert the tips of the ring and

little fingers under the card and with them grip the rest of the pack.

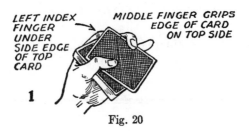

Fig. 20

4. Extend the index finger and middle finger, carrying the card away to the right and turning it face upwards in the action. At the same time press the thumb on the back of the pack (Fig. 21).

This pretty little flourish can be used to good advantage for counting off a small number of cards when it is necessary to name them as they are counted. Each card is taken by the right hand as it is flicked off and turned face upwards by the left hand.

B. For Intimate Performances. When a chosen card has been found, for example after dealing to a certain number or on the

DISPLAYING TOP CARD

Fig. 21

last letter after having spelled its name, the following is a neat method for displaying it:

1. Push the card off with the left thumb and take it by the middle of its right side between the top phalanges of the right middle finger on its back and of the ring finger on its face (Fig. 22).

2. Place the tip of the right thumb on its face and turn the card to a vertical position between the tips of the thumb and middle finger, bringing the face of the card toward you (Fig. 23).

3. Place the tip of the index finger on the face of the card and move the thumb to the back. Release the middle finger and with the thumb cause the card to revolve, bringing its face outwards and toward the spectators (Fig. 24).

This intriguing little flourish provides a momentary pause and thus heightens the climax, which is the revelation of the card. Also, since it brings the face of the card toward you first, you gain a precious moment in the event of a mishap which should

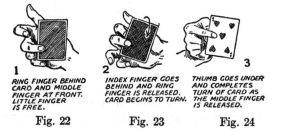

1
RING FINGER BEHIND
CARD AND MIDDLE
FINGER AT FRONT.
LITTLE FINGER
IS FREE.
Fig. 22

2
INDEX FINGER GOES
BEHIND AND RING
FINGER IS RELEASED.
CARD BEGINS TO TURN.
Fig. 23

3
THUMB GOES UNDER
AND COMPLETES
TURN OF CARD AS
THE MIDDLE FINGER
IS RELEASED.
Fig. 24

be a very rare occurrence, but accidents will happen to the most careful of card conjurers.

C. For Platform Performances. On the platform this would be your handling:

1. Push the card off with the left thumb and grasp it at the inner right corner between the right thumb and index finger, holding as little of the card as possible.

2. Move the card slowly to your right, so that it does not obscure your face. Hold it at about shoulder height, turning it vertically face outwards.

The Ruffle

The object of this flourish is to produce a crackling sound with the cards at the moment that some feat of magic is accomplished. The purpose is to mislead the audience into the belief that the feat is actually done at that moment.

A. With Both Hands. Proceed as follows:

1. Hold the pack in the left hand, as for dealing, but with its outer end protruding about an inch over the index finger.

2. Press the left thumb firmly down on the middle of the back of the top card and with the tip of the right middle finger bend the outer ends of all the cards upwards about an inch (Fig. 25).

TWO HAND RUFFLE
Fig. 25

3. Release the ends of the cards by drawing the right hand away sharply. Being freed thus in rapid succession, the cards strike one against the other and produce the sharp crackling sound required.

MIDDLE FINGER RUFFLES EDGE OF PACK DOWNWARD. INDEX FINGER IS BENT UNDER THE PACK.

SINGLE HAND RUFFLE
Fig. 26

Some performers get into the habit of using this flourish almost continuously with neither rhyme nor reason. This is not only inartistic but also irritating to the audience, and it betrays nervousness on the part of the performer. The flourish should be used only for the purpose of misleading the onlookers as to the moment when a certain effect is supposed to take place.

B. With One Hand. In this case the method is somewhat different:

1. Hold the deck in the left hand as for dealing.

2. Bend the index finger under the deck and with the first phalanx of the middle finger bend the cards downwards toward the palm of the hand.

3. Allow the cards to slip off the tip of the middle finger by bending that finger inwards, producing a prolonged crackle (Fig. 26).

A slight wave of the hand will cover the action.

C. With a Single Card. Sometimes it is desirable to produce a similar sound with one card—for example, when one card is

RING AND MIDDLE
FINGER SNAP DOWN
ON FACE OF CARD.

SINGLE CARD RUFFLE

Fig. 27

apparently changed to another. To do this, hold the card in either hand between the index finger and thumb. Rest the other three fingers, one above the other on the index finger. To produce the required sound, press the three fingers inwards and let them escape and strike against the card in rapid succession (Fig. 27).

THE CLICK

A single sharp clicking sound can be produced at any moment desired in the following way:

1. Hold the pack in the left hand as for dealing.

2. Bend the ring finger under the deck and with the tip of the

little finger bend two or three of the bottom cards downwards and inwards against the bent ring finger (Fig. 28).

RING FINGER BENT IN UNDER THE PACK. LITTLE FINGER BENDS CORNER OF CARD DOWN AND ALLOWS IT TO SNAP BACK.

THE CLICK
Fig. 28

3. Press outwards with the ring finger and let the cards escape by moving the little finger away. A sharp click will be heard as the cards strike against the bottom of the deck.

SPREAD AND TURNOVER

A. On a Cloth-Covered Table. This flourish has a very pretty effect as a preliminary to the execution of an opening trick. The cards are spread on the table in a row showing the backs, then they are turned over simultaneously to show the faces.

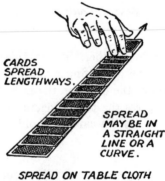

CARDS SPREAD LENGTHWAYS.

SPREAD MAY BE IN A STRAIGHT LINE OR A CURVE.

SPREAD ON TABLE CLOTH
Fig. 29

Two conditions are required for perfect results: first, the table used must have a cloth on it to provide the necessary friction to prevent the cards from sliding; second, the cards themselves must be in good condition.

1. Place the pack on the table toward your right, the sides parallel with the edge of the table nearest you.

2. With a swift movement of the right hand to the left, pressing down slightly on the top card, spread the cards, thus causing a separation of about an inch between each card and the one following it (Fig. 29).

3. Slip the index finger of the right hand under the card at the extreme right and turn it over in the direction in which the cards lie. This action will cause all the other cards to turn over.

When facility has been acquired in spreading the cards in a fairly long line, the knack of spreading them in an arc of a circle will give you little trouble. The effect of the turnover is then much prettier.

The spread may be used for a very attractive flourish, first described by Robert-Houdin in *The Secrets of Conjuring and Magic* (1868). A comparatively recent addition makes the little feat even more effective.

LEFT HAND TAKES CARD
FROM FAR END AND
WITH ITS EDGE
CONTROLS
MOVEMENT.

FIRST ARRANGE A FEW OF THE
CARDS AS SHOWN ABOVE.
SPREAD TURN OVER

Fig. 30

1. After spreading the cards in a long line on the table lengthwise, in such a way that about two-thirds of each card is covered by the one above it, slip the right index finger under the first face-down card.

2. Turn this card to an upright position.

3. Take one card in the left hand, hold it vertically with its sides parallel to the table top, and place the middle of its lower side on the top edge of the upright card (Fig. 30).

4. Draw this card toward the left, pressing it lightly on the top edge of the other cards as they move up into a vertical position. All the cards turn over in succession.

5. On reaching the other end of the line, do not let the cards fall flat. Move the card in the left hand back in the opposite direction and turn the line of cards face downwards as at the start.

If the cards have been spread carefully, the flourish may be repeated several times before letting the cards fall flat in their original position. The effect is intriguing.

B. On a Bare Table. For this flourish proceed as follows:

1. Grasp the pack at the ends between the right thumb and the middle and ring fingers, pressing the tip of the index finger on the middle of the pack.

2. Pull the ends of the deck upwards with the thumb and two fingers, at the same time pressing downwards with the index finger.

3. Place the pack on the table so that only the middle part of the bottom card touches the table surface (Fig. 31).

CARDS SPREAD SIDEWAYS.

SPREAD WITHOUT CLOTH

Fig. 31

4. Move the cards from left to right swiftly, allowing the ends to slip off the tips of the fingers and thumbs, and at the same time maintaining the pressure of the index finger on the back of the top card. The result will be the formation of a perfect and symmetrical ribbon of cards, accompanied by a light riffling sound which is very effective. The length of this ribbon spread will be

governed by the amount of pressure exerted by the index finger.

Note that in this case the cards are spread sideways, not lengthwise as in situation *A*. The method may also be used on a cloth-covered table. It is excellent for use when a card is reversed at or near the bottom of the pack (see page 13). In starting the spread, let half a dozen cards slip off the thumb and fingers before moving the hand, so that these cards will be bunched together and prevent the reversed card from being seen. The onlookers will be convinced that all the cards are face downwards without your commenting on this fact.

GATHERING THE RIBBON-SPREAD PACK

When (as in A above) the cards have been spread, turned face upwards, and face downwards again—or when (as in B) they have been ribbon-spread for the selection of a card—the whole pack can be gathered with a rapid sweep of the right hand. To do this, slip the fingers of the right hand under the lowermost card at the extreme end of the line and slide it under all the others, following the line of the pack. The cards are all brought into the hand, the thumb falling on the last card.

The action can be made as rapidly as you wish with perfect safety.

SPRINGING THE CARDS

This is a favorite flourish with card conjurers, and when well done the effect is brilliant. With the hands held apart the cards are made to leap from one hand to the other. The moves are as follows:

1. Hold the pack in the right hand, by the ends, between the thumb and the middle and ring fingers.

2. Bend the cards by squeezing on the ends, so that the convex side of the pack is toward the inside of the hand. They will then naturally tend to spring from the fingers.

3. Place the left hand about six inches away from the right hand, in position to catch the cards; continuing the pressure on the pack, allow the cards to escape, one by one, and catch them in the left hand (Fig. 32).

The distance between the hands can be increased with practice, and the flourish should be accompanied by a swing of the body toward the left, so that the hands describe an arc of a circle.

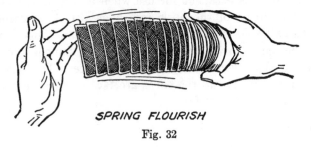

SPRING FLOURISH

Fig. 32

The right hand should follow the last card and be brought against the cards in the left hand with a loud smack.

A FLOURISH COUNT

This is a striking method of counting a small packet of cards.

1. Hold the packet vertically in the left hand between the crotch of the thumb and the outermost joint of the middle finger.

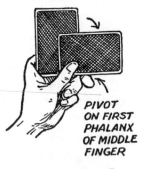

PIVOT ON FIRST PHALANX OF MIDDLE FINGER

FLOURISH COUNT

Fig. 33

2. Push the top card to the right with the tip of the left thumb, pivoting it on the middle finger at the middle phalanx, until it projects at right angles from the packet (Fig. 33).

3. Remove this card and repeat for each remaining card.

THROWING A CARD

It is often necessary to throw a card or cards out to the audience. When this is done with neatness and precision it creates a marked impression of the performer's dexterity. The flourish depends on a little knack by means of which the card is made to revolve rapidly in its own plane. To do this:

1. Hold the card in your right hand, near the outer end, between the forefinger and the middle finger (Fig. 34).

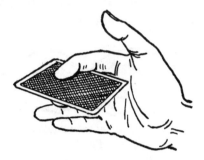

THROWING A CARD
Fig. 34

2. Draw the hand back near the left breast, bending the wrist inwards. Extend the arm rapidly, letting the card go but at the same moment giving it a spinning motion by a sharp backward jerk of the hand. It is this spinning motion in the card's own plane that carries the card to a distance; otherwise the resistance of the air would cause it to fall at your feet.

When throwing cards to an audience, slant them upwards so that, their velocity expended, they flutter down upon the spectators.

By starting the throw at an upward angle of about forty-five degrees and throwing the card only a couple of yards, the card can be made to return to your hand so that you can catch it with the tips of the fingers. This very pretty effect, known as the *boomerang card*, is the basis of several fine tricks with cards.

WATERFALL SHUFFLE

This is a flourish applied to the riffle shuffle. It has come into common use among card players, and its use by the card conjurer is therefore entirely justified.

1. Proceed exactly as described for the riffle shuffle, interlacing the ends of the two packets for about half an inch.

2. Place the thumbs on the back of the packets at the point of junction, and slide the middle, ring, and little fingers under the outer ends of the packets, at the same time moving the hands toward each other and bending the packets (Fig. 35).

OVERLAPPING CARDS
Fig. 35

3. Raise the hands and the pack about breast high, maintaining the pressure of the thumbs and fingers; then, by slightly relaxing the pressure of the hands on the outer ends of the cards and at the same time continuing the downward pressure of the thumbs, allow the cards to fall from the bottom separately onto the fingers of both hands held together (Fig. 36).

THE WATERFALL
AFTER RIFFLE SHUFFLE
Fig. 36

In making the preliminary shuffle the cards should be allowed to fall as nearly as possible in regular rotation, a card from one hand falling on a card from the other. The cards should be interlaced just sufficiently to be held in position by the thumbs, for the higher the arch that is formed the longer and more effective the fall of the separate cards becomes.

THE FAN

This useful method of displaying cards also makes possible a very fine card control and force which we shall mention later.

I

Fig. 37

1. Hold the pack in the right hand at the inner end, between the index and middle fingers at the face and the thumb on the top, all the fingers paralleling the inner end (Fig. 37).

2. Place the left hand at the outer end in the same position, the fingers below and the thumb above and paralleling the end. Spread the cards in an arc with the left thumb as the left fingers

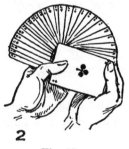

2

Fig. 38

draw the cards to the left, the bottom cards being the last to be fanned. Straighten the right fingers so that the cards will pass over them as they are fanned.

The completed fan appears as in Fig. 38.

ONE-HAND FAN

This surprising flourish is particularly effective, the cards spreading into a wide fan in a flash. It may be performed with either hand.

1. Hold the pack vertically in the right hand, between the middle phalanges of the middle and ring fingers at one end and the thumb at the other. Rest the index and little fingers lightly at the sides (Fig. 39).

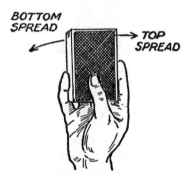

LITTLE FINGER AND
INDEX HOLD THE DECK
LIGHTLY AT THE SIDES

ONE HAND FAN
Fig. 39

2. Hold the pack upright by a pressure of the fingers at the sides and remove the thumb, placing its tip at the middle of the back.

3. Remove the index and little fingers, grasping the pack between the tips of the ring and middle fingers at the face and the thumb at the back.

4. Spread the cards in a fan by an opposite pressure of the thumb and fingers very similar to that used in snapping the fingers. When the cards are completely fanned they are grasped by the index finger only, at the face, with the fan resting along the palm and the length of the thumb at the back.

A reverse action closes the fan, bringing it to its original position.

The knack of making the one-hand fan is not easily acquired, but as with all things practice makes perfect.

THUMB FAN

This graceful flourish should be performed with cards in good condition. It is not only pretty to see, but makes possible a version of the famous *diminishing cards* trick (see page 276).

1. Hold the pack at one end between the left thumb, above, and the index finger, below.

2. Place the right hand over the pack and press the tip of the thumb firmly against the left side near the outer corner.

3. Sweep the thumb in a circle to the right, drawing the top cards with it and spreading those below them in a fan. The thumb exerts a diminishing pressure, as it sweeps to the right, which is quickly learned.

A small fan is formed by placing the tip of the left thumb at the inner right corner in grasping the pack. A larger fan is made by placing the thumb at the inner left corner. To make a rosette, place the thumb at the center of the pack.

RIGHT HAND   KEEP BEND IN CARDS
                              WHILE FANNING

LEFT   RIGHT

1   **2**

HOLD PACK AT ENDS
AND SQUEEZE TO
BEND THE CARDS

Fig. 40   Fig. 41

By securing one of the modern colorful bridge packs, many pleasing patterns can be formed by fanning the cards by this method and by grasping the pack at the four corners—in which case, when the outer corners are grasped, the fan is made in reverse, that is, by moving the thumb from right to left.

PRESSURE FAN

This modern two-handed method of making a fan insures an absolutely symmetrical fan.

1. Hold the pack at the ends between the right thumb and the middle and ring fingers, the first finger curling at the top (Fig. 40).

2. Place the pack in the crotch of the left hand, the tip of the left thumb resting on the inner left corner at the back, the index finger slanting diagonally across the face of the pack.

3. Bend the cards downwards over the left index finger, and spread them in a fan by sweeping the right hand in a circle to the right, allowing the cards to slip from under the finger tips (Fig. 41).

This handsome flourish is useful in offering the cards for a choice.

IV

THE GLIDE

THIS sleight is one of the easiest and most useful to the card magician. In its original form it was used merely to substitute one card for another, but since the turn of the century other and excellent uses of the sleight have been evolved, some of which we shall describe. The basic action of the glide is this:

1. Hold a pack of cards face downwards in the left hand—the thumb at one side, the fingers at the other—its outer side pressing against the middle phalanx of the index finger, near the outer left corner, and the first (innermost) phalanx of the little finger. Rest the tip of the ring finger lightly against the middle of the face card. The third (outermost) phalanges of the index and middle fingers are bent inwards but take no part in the action to follow.

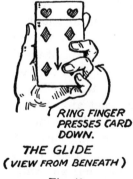

RING FINGER
PRESSES CARD
DOWN.

THE GLIDE
(VIEW FROM BENEATH)

Fig. 42

2. Press backwards with the tip of the ring finger, forcing the face card back about an inch and making it protrude beyond the inner end of the deck (Fig. 42). This shows the sleight as seen

from below; viewed from above, the cards appear to be in normal position, the protruding card being concealed by the back of the hand.

3. Bring the right hand palm upwards over to the deck, press its middle finger tip against the outer end of the second lowermost card, which is now exposed, and draw this card outwards about an inch; then seize and remove it with the aid of the thumb. Finally move the left little finger backwards and with it press the protruding card flush with the deck.

A little practice will show that the sleight is an easy one to do, yet it must be performed smoothly and without looking at the hands.

To illustrate the uses to which the glide can be put, we shall describe first an extraordinarily good trick known as Design for Laughter.

DESIGN FOR LAUGHTER

This is a trick in which the magician appears unknowingly to have made a mistake which insures the failure of his feat. The more certain the spectators are of this, the more they enjoy his predicament and the more astonished and appreciative they are when the trick proves to be successful after all.

1. First shuffle the pack, then have a spectator choose a card freely. Have him show the card to everyone while you turn your head away. This is important, for all must know the card or they will not enjoy the feat. Next have the card replaced and control it to the top of the deck by means of the overhand shuffle control. Finally shuffle the chosen card to the bottom and leave it there.

2. Place the deck on the table before you and announce what you propose to do somewhat after this style: "One of the most difficult feats with cards is that known as the *location by cut*. Let me show you what I mean." Turn to the spectator who chose the card, saying, "Will you assist me, sir? I must make two conditions, however—first, that you will not at any time name your card or give me any indication that I have discovered it; second, that when you cut the cards, as I shall instruct you, you will say to yourself, 'This I cannot fail to do.' That, of course, is an application of the principles of Dr. Coué, the eminent French

psychologist, to feats of skill with cards. It is surprising that, when a person cuts with complete confidence, he will actually cut to a card which he has chosen and which has been shuffled into the pack."

3. Gravely describe a circle around the deck with your extended index finger, then move your finger to make a cross above it. "I now ask you to cut off about one-third of the cards as you say to yourself, 'This I cannot fail to do.' Fine! Place the cut here." Indicate that he is to place the packet to the right of the deck. "Now cut off about half the remaining cards, using the same formula, and place them to the right of the first cut. Thank you."

There are now three packets on the table and the chosen card is at the bottom of the left-hand packet.

4. Square the packets carefully and continue, "There can be no doubt that you have cut at your card. However, I cannot know *which* of the cards is your card, so I must again ask you not to give me any indication by word or gesture as to which it may be."

Pick up the right-hand packet face downwards in your left hand in position for the glide. Turn it so that the face card can be seen by everyone, glance at it, and say, "This is not your card." Turn the packet face downwards, draw out the face card and place it face downwards at your right on the table. Drop the remainder of the packet on the right-hand packet of the two on the table.

5. Pick up this combined packet in the same manner, lift it to show the face card, look at it yourself, and say, "Nor is this your card." Draw it off and lay it face downwards beside the first tabled card.

6. Place the combined packet on the one remaining on the table, pick up all the cards, holding them ready for the glide, lift the pack, and show the face card. It is the chosen card, but you keep a poker face and say as you execute the glide and remove the next card, "Apparently you lack confidence in yourself, for that is not your card either."

In spite of your previous instructions, someone may try to interrupt you at this point, for everyone sees that it *is* the chosen card. If so, take no notice and at once draw out the next card above the glided card and use it as a pointer. Touch each of the three tabled cards in turn counting, "One, two, three cards and none of them yours." Replace this pointer card on the face of the deck and lift the deck so that all can see it. This subtle move not only conceals the chosen card but finally convinces the onlookers that the chosen card has been placed on the table.

7. Turn to another spectator and ask him to name a number, say between five and ten. "The chosen card will infallibly be at that number," you say. Suppose seven is named. Still holding the deck face downwards, draw out the face card and deal it face upwards on the table, counting "One." Execute the glide and draw out the card above it, deal it on the table, and count "Two." Continue to draw out and deal indifferent cards to the count of "Six." Then draw out the glided card and hold it face downwards, counting "Seven."

"Here is your card," you say confidently. "Will you now for the first time name your card?"

8. The spectator names the card you hold. Here is where your ability to act convincingly will be of prime importance. Pretend to be taken aback upon hearing the card named. Repeat its name and glance covertly at the card on the table which the spectators believe to be the chosen card.

Usually at this point someone, with no little glee, will tell you that the chosen card is on the table and that you have made a mistake. Occasionally, because of courtesy, no one will fall into the trap. In either case, after a moment you brighten and say, "That's right. Here's the card!" Turn over the card you hold and show that it is the required card.

It is at this point that the trick is most enjoyable. You will find invariably that someone will reach for the tabled card, which should be, but is not, the chosen card. The laughter and puzzlement which this action provokes will repay you a hundredfold for the slight effort you have made in mastering the trick.

The Observation Test

The glide, as we have shown, is a useful sleight with which many effects can be had. Here is another use to which it can be put—one that enables you to vanish one card and make another appear in its place.

1. Shuffle the pack, have a card drawn and noted, and when it is replaced control it to the face of the pack by means of the overhand shuffle control.

2. Turn the pack with the face toward yourself, so that no one can see the cards, and run through them, removing the four two-spots and placing them at the face of the pack in black, red, black, red order. "This is a test of your powers of observation," you explain. "I shall use the four two-spots to make the test."

3. Remove the *five* cards at the face of the pack without showing how many you take. Turn them face downwards and hold them in the left hand in readiness for the glide. The top card is the chosen card, and under it are the four two-spots.

4. "I shall ask you to remember the sequence of the colors," you continue. Remove the bottom card with the right hand and deal it face upwards on the table, calling its color, "Red."

5. Deal the card now at the bottom face upwards on the first card in the same way. "Black."

6. Glide back the card now at the bottom. Remove the two cards above it as one by grasping them at the outer end between the right thumb, above, and the fingers, below. As they are drawn from the left hand, press against their sides with the left index finger and thumb, thus keeping the two cards in perfect alignment. Deal these two cards face upwards as one upon the first two cards, saying "Black." The cards should be dealt neatly one on top of the other.

7. Take the last card, saying, "And this naturally must be red." Show it, drop it face upwards on the other cards. You have shown four cards and all are two-spots. Pick them up, square them with the face toward yourself, and mix the cards without revealing how many you hold. Be sure that the chosen card is third from the top when you finish. "A good mixing," you say, turning them face downwards. Take them in your left hand in readiness for the glide.

8. "I'll do that again." Repeat the actions from step No. 4 through step No. 6 and you will hold one card face downwards in your left hand. This is the chosen card.

9. Place it face downwards to your right. Pick up the other cards, place them on the pack, and hold the pack in your hands. "This is where I test your powers of observation," you explain. "You see, I made you think that you should observe the *color* of the cards as I dealt the two-spots. That was a trick, for now I want you to tell me the *suit* of the last card." As you say this, idly cut the pack, thus burying the other cards.

10. The spectators may succeed or fail in naming the proper two-spot, but, no matter what their answer, you say, "I'm sorry, but you were observing the colors so closely that you failed to notice the values of the cards." Have the chosen card named, turn the card on the table face upwards, and show that it is not a two-spot, as expected, but the chosen card.

V

THE GLIMPSE

IN MAGIC the term glimpse is applied to the act of sighting and taking note of any particular card secretly. There are many ways of doing this; some of the methods have graduated into the conjuring class from the gaming table and require considerable skill to execute properly. The best of these will be considered later. In the meantime let us take up first the one that is most easily acquired.

BOTTOM-CARD GLIMPSE I

We shall suppose that you have handed the deck to a spectator to be shuffled. When he has done that, hold out your right hand to take back the deck, purposely holding it rather high so that he will have to raise his hand to give you the deck. Take the pack with your thumb underneath it on the face card, your fingers on the back. At that moment it is natural for you to glance at the cards, and by tilting them ever so little with the thumb you can glimpse the index of the bottom card at the inner left corner (Fig. 43). Immediately look at the spectator and address him with some such short remark as this, "You are satisfied that you have mixed the cards thoroughly?"

Do not tilt the pack so far that the whole of the face card is visible to you. Slope it just enough to see the index only. Also do not turn your gaze toward the pack as you tilt it; you should be looking at the pack only as you take it. Get the glimpse and then look at the spectator. Make the action a natural one, and no one will have the least suspicion that you have seen the bottom card.

Immediately after making the glimpse, execute an overhand

shuffle, controlling the sighted card by keeping it at the bottom or sending it to the top of the pack.

Sometimes the spectator will play into your hands. Many laymen make the shuffle roughly, and often you can glimpse the

SLIGHTLY
TILTED

GLIMPSING BOTTOM CARD.
THE TILT OF DECK SHOWN HERE
IS EXAGGERATED FOR CLARITY

Fig. 43

bottom card either as the shuffle is made or as the cards are being squared after the shuffle. Always make a point of watching for this. If you do not sight the card, then resort to the method explained above.

Bottom-Card Glimpse II

This is a bold method but a good one.

Offer the pack for shuffling and when it is returned hold it face downwards at the ends between the right thumb and fingers. Say: "Kindly notice—nothing up my sleeves," and draw back the

LEFT HAND TURNS OVER AND POINTS
GIVING GLIMPSE OF BOTTOM CARD

Fig. 44

right sleeve with the left hand. As the right arm is extended, tilt the pack enough to enable you to glimpse the index of the bottom card.

Bottom-Card Glimpse III

Offer the pack for shuffling and when it is returned hold it in the left hand as for dealing, face downwards. Thumb off about a dozen cards from the top and take these in a fan in the right hand, letting it be clear that you do not see the faces.

Hold the hands well away from your body as you say, "You will certify that these cards are well mixed?" Run your left index finger over the faces of the fanned cards, from right to left, with the back of the hand toward yourself (Fig. 44). Note the bottom card of the pack, which faces you, and instantly avert your gaze. Your eyes must not dwell on the card but flick it in passing.

Replace the fanned cards on the deck in the left hand.

Top-Card Glimpse I

Take the pack in the left hand, as for dealing, but with the index finger curled up over the outer end and the thumb lying flat against the left-side edge.

Gesture to someone, saying, "Will you help me?" As you make this gesture, turn the back of the hand uppermost, bringing the

DRAWING EXAGGERATED FOR CLARITY.

THE GLIMPSE OF TOP CARD

Fig. 45

deck face upwards. Push the top card to the right with the left fingertips; this will expose the inner index (Fig. 45). Return the hand to its original position.

Riffle shuffle the pack, retaining the top card in position but making sure that the original bottom card is lost near the bottom of the pack in the event that someone may have noticed it and may be following it.

FAN PEEK

This is a method of ascertaining which card a spectator chooses from among a number of cards.

Hold the cards vertically and thumb them from the left into the right hand, inviting someone to touch any card and remember it. Place the left thumb against the lower edge of the card he touches, at the index corner, and drop the hands somewhat, never glancing at the cards.

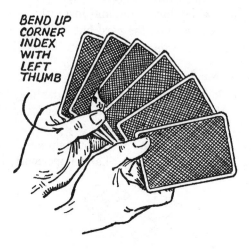

THE FAN PEEK

Fig. 46

Raise the fan again, saying that you wish him to be sure to remember his card, and instantly raise the index corner with the thumb, glimpsing the index (Fig. 46), and remove the thumb. Close the pack and hand it for shuffling.

Wherever possible a chosen card should be glimpsed by one or another of the methods given above as soon as possible after its replacement in the pack. In the event that the card is accidentally lost, or if a spectator insists on being allowed to shuffle the cards himself, knowledge of what the card is still leaves you master of the situation.

For other methods of glimpsing, refer to the palm glimpse (page 88) and the double-lift glimpse (page 143).

To illustrate the usefulness of the glimpse there is no better trick depending on it than the one next described.

TRICKS WITH THE GLIMPSE

Gray's Spelling Trick

A spectator replaces a selected card in the pack, which is honestly squared and shuffled. The name of the card is then spelled mentally by the spectator, who applies one letter to each card dealt by the magician. On reaching the last letter the spectator calls "Stop!" He names his card. The last card dealt is turned face upwards and proves to be the very card he selected.

1. Hand the deck to a spectator and have him shuffle the cards thoroughly. Take the pack back, glimpsing the bottom card, and then shuffle overhand retaining the card on the bottom. Suppose this card is the five of spades.

2. Spread the pack and have a card freely chosen, noted by the drawer, and shown to several persons near by. This is a precaution it is wise to take, because it gets others interested and prevents any subsequent misnaming of the card, either by carelessness or by design.

3. Holding the deck by its sides at the tips of your thumb and your middle and ring fingers, draw out the lower half with your right thumb and middle finger, making what is termed an under-cut. Let the packet in your left hand fall onto the palm, and hold out that hand for the replacement of the chosen card on top. Immediately drop the right-hand packet on it and square the deck openly.

Be careful to hold the right-hand packet face downwards, and do not glance at it. Some performers take the glimpse of the bottom card at this time. A very bad practice, widely open to detection.

4. The position now is that the chosen card is in the middle of the deck, with the glimpsed card, the five of spades, immediately above it. Shuffle overhand in this manner: Lift the whole pack and freely shuffle off about one-third of the cards, let about another

third of the cards fall in a block, and then shuffle the remaining cards freely. Thus the two cards, the glimpsed card and the chosen card, must remain together in the middle. It is true that a casual shuffle is not likely to separate them, but it is best to be certain.

5. Square the cards and say, "Some people imagine that a magician can steal a card out of the pack without anyone seeing him do it. Let me show you that your card is still buried among the other cards." Turn half left, hold the deck in your left hand, the bottom card facing the spectators, and push the cards off one by one, with the left thumb taking them with the right hand. Do this at a fairly rapid pace, but not too fast. As you begin, say, "You might think I detect your card by your expression when you see it; therefore I shall not attempt to watch you." This is your excuse for looking at the cards as you run them off.

6. Watch for the index of the five of spades. The moment you see it, note the card you have just taken in your right hand, which will be the chosen card. Let us suppose that this card is the ten of hearts. Begin at once to spell ten of hearts mentally, saying to yourself *t* for the ten of hearts you have already taken in your right hand, *e* as you take the five of spades (the glimpsed card) *n* for the next card, *o* and *f* for the next two, and so on until you arrive at the letter *s*.

7. At this point separate your hands rather widely, look at the spectator, and ask him, "Have you seen your card?" He replies, "Yes." Bring your hands together, at the same time gripping the packet in the left hand between the thumb and index finger and extending the other fingers so that you can slide the right-hand packet under the left-hand packet smoothly. Do this quietly, without looking at your hands, while saying to the spectator, "Very well. No use going any farther."

8. You now have everything set for the climax, so you tell the spectators what you are going to do. "I shall deal cards from the top and as I do so I want you, sir, to spell the name of your card mentally, one letter for each card. Suppose your card is the queen of hearts; as I deal the first card you will say to yourself *q*, for the next card *u*, the third card *e*, and so on; and don't forget the *o-f*. Is that clear? Very well. When you come to the last letter

just call 'Stop!' and the card in my hand at that moment will be the very card of which you are thinking. Impossible, you say? Well, let's try it."

Deal the cards deliberately and keep a check on the spelling yourself, for you know the card.

9. When the spectator calls "Stop!" keep the card in your hand face downwards and say, "Now, sir, you have thought of a card—" (ignore the fact that he actually took it from the pack and replaced it) "—and you have spelled its name mentally. Would you be surprised to find that the cards have arranged themselves automatically so that this card at which you called 'Stop' is your card? You would. Then name your card."

"The ten of hearts."

Turn the card face upwards slowly and reveal that very card.

The above feat can be made even more effective in the following way:

1. Follow the same procedure up to the point at which you have spelled out the name of the chosen card and have arrived at the last letter, in step No. 6. At once note the next card, which let us say is the king of hearts. Continue running cards and mentally spell this card, taking one card for each letter until you reach the *s*; then separate your hands and ask the spectator if he has seen his card. As before, in putting the two packets together you place the right-hand packet underneath that in your left hand.

2. Turn the deck face downwards and you are set to spell out, first, the king of hearts. Explain to the spectator the peculiar property of playing cards by which, under certain conditions, they place themselves in position to be spelled out and appear on the final letter. "For example," you say, "suppose I name a card, any card—let us say the king of hearts—and spell it out dealing a card for each letter. We shall find the king of hearts in that position.

"You don't believe me. Very well, let's try."

Spell *k-i-n-g o-f h-e-a-r-t-s*, dealing one card for each letter, and turn up the king of hearts on the final *s*. "You see, the result is infallible if you concentrate on the card you want to appear.

You take the deck, think intently of your card, then spell it mentally, dealing a card for each letter, as I did."

3. The spectator follows your instructions and stops the deal on his last letter. You ask him, "Have you spelled the name of the card of which you are thinking?"

"Yes."

"Would you be surprised if the next card is your card? You would? Very well. Name your card." He does so. "Now turn the card yourself!" He does so and you have a climax that will astonish the onlookers and one that you yourself will enjoy.

ROUND AND ROUND

This fine self-working trick makes use of the fan peek.

1. Take any ten cards from the pack and have them shuffled. Turn your back and instruct the spectator to look at and remember the top card, after doing which he is to think of any small number and silently transfer that number of cards one by one from top to bottom.

2. Turn around, take the cards, and point out that you cannot know which card he has chosen; at the same time study the faces of the cards. Thumb them off, face upwards, into the right hand one by one, reversing their order. Scrutinize the cards closely and glance at the spectator occasionally as though plumbing his thoughts.

Shake your head and, still holding the cards with their faces toward yourself, take the five bottom cards in the right hand. Glance at them, then at those in the left hand, holding them well apart. Again shake your head disconsolately, saying, "I'm having trouble with you!" Bring the hands together and place the right-hand cards above the others, at the top of the packet.

By this means you have, first, reversed the order of the ten cards, and, second, placed the first five cards below the second five.

3. Return the cards to the spectator, turn your back, and instruct him to transfer silently as many cards from top to bottom as he did in the first case, and then one card more.

4. Take the ten cards and fan them between your hands, face outwards, as you request the spectator to concentrate on his card.

Peek at the fourth card from the top, using the fan peek, and remember this card; it is the chosen card.

5. Give the spectator the cards and have him place the top card on the table, the next card at the bottom of the packet, the next card on the table, the next at the bottom, and so on until he holds only one card.

Say to him, "You took the ace of hearts, didn't you?" naming whatever card you peeked, and when he agrees ask him, "Do you know how I knew?" "No." "Look at the card in your hand." He does and finds that it is his card.

VI

THE KEY CARD

CENTURIES ago, when playing cards were rare and valuable objects owned only by the rich and powerful, the first tricks of legerdemain with cards were made possible through the use of the key card.

The principle is so obvious that there are few persons who are not familiar with it, and yet some of the finest and most deceptive card tricks, which have puzzled and entertained hundreds of thousands of persons, are made possible by the lowly key card.

We speak of the key card as "lowly" because among the uninformed it has fallen into disrepute because it is so widely known. Using it inartistically is a gaucherie. If used with finesse, it is one of the most potent artifices in the whole realm of conjuring with cards. In this, as in many other things, it is not the tool that is important but the personality, character, and intelligence of the person using the tool. Using the same tools, one artist produces an exquisite portrait; another, a meaningless daub. So it is with the key card; the dabbler performs a colorless trick, the competent conjurer presents a brilliant tour de force.

No doubt, before opening this book you were familiar with the principle that if you know the name of one card in the pack, and contrive to have an unknown card replaced either above or below it, you can unfailingly find the unknown card, no matter how many times the pack may be cut. This is the manner in which the dabbler at card tricks uses this principle.

But we shall show you how this same principle may be used in such a manner that even those familiar with it will be completely deceived. We shall give you the mechanics of tricks with the key card which make use of the principle in new and ingenious ways, and shall show you how the old methods may be used so that they appear new and different. Finally, we shall show you that use of the key card will enhance your reputation as a clever sleight-of-hand performer with cards, whose deceptions are entertaining and insolvable.

First, however, we must explain the key undercut and key undercut shuffle, two useful sleights which have been described, but not by name, in *Gray's spelling trick* (see page 63).

THE KEY UNDERCUT

This method of undercutting a pack is often used to place a key card above a chosen card, and we give it the above title to distinguish it from the regular undercut used in the overhand shuffle, with which it must not be confused.

1. Let us say that you have glimpsed the card at the bottom of the pack for use as a key card. Hold the deck by its sides at the tips of your left thumb and your middle and ring fingers. Draw out the lower half with your right thumb and your middle finger by grasping it at the sides near the inner corners.

2. Let the packet remaining in your left hand fall onto the palm and extend that hand for the replacement of the chosen card on top.

3. Immediately drop the right-hand packet on it and square the deck very openly, thus placing your key card above the chosen card. Be careful to hold the right-hand packet face downwards, and do not glance at it. Some performers take a glimpse of the bottom card at this time, a very bad practice widely open to detection.

KEY UNDERCUT SHUFFLE

The purpose of this shuffle is to mix the cards without separating the key card from the card which it keys. It should be used after the key undercut whenever possible.

1. Lift the whole pack and freely shuffle off about one-third of the cards, let another third of the cards fall in a block and then shuffle the remaining cards freely. Thus the two cards at the center must remain together.

A genuine overhand shuffle is not likely to separate the cards, but the above method makes their juxtaposition a certainty.

TRICKS WITH THE KEY CARD

Do as I Do

There are some tricks which stand head and shoulder above others. The trick now to be described has without doubt surprised and puzzled more people than any other trick conceived in the past two decades. It has everything a good trick should have— a good plot, ease of execution, and a terrific impact on those who see it. We have mentioned that the wise magician never reveals his methods to the curious, and in describing this trick we reiterate this counsel, for, once you have told how simple the trick is, you have lost the use of a superb feat of card magic.

The plot is this: A spectator thinks of a card and you think of one. You each show the card of your choice. They are the same!

1. You will need two packs of contrasting colors, say red and blue. Invite a spectator to choose one of the two packs. You take the other and shuffle it. "I want you to do everything I do. Please shuffle your cards." Turn your pack with the face toward yourself a little as you square it after shuffling, and remember the bottom card as your key card.

2. Hand the spectator your pack and take his. "I'll take your pack and you take mine," you say. Ribbon-spread your cards face downwards on the table from right to left and instruct him to do the same with his cards.

3. "Remember, you must do everything I do. First of all, each of us will take a card from his pack. You will take one from the pack which I shuffled, hence you cannot possibly know beforehand which one you will take. Similarly, I will take one from the pack which *you* shuffled, and I therefore cannot know which one I shall get." Run your right index finger back and forth over your line of cards and insist that he duplicate your actions exactly. After a moment, touch a card in the center of the spread and have him touch one in his spread. "Take out the card you touched, look at it, but don't let anyone else see it," you say. You say this because you do not want any of the others stand-

ing around to see the card *you* draw. Look at it but forget it, for it plays no part in the trick.

4. Place your card face downwards at the left end of your spread of cards and have him do the same with his card. Gather your cards without disarranging them and have him do the same with his. Finally, make one complete cut and have him do the same. His cut places the key card which you noted in step No. 1 above his chosen card.

5. "Let's exchange packs again," you say, taking his pack and giving him yours. "Now I'll find my card while you find yours." Run through the pack you now hold until you come to your key card, then take the card below it and place it face downwards on the table. Try to have your card on the table before he finds his card.

6. When he removes his card, have him place it face downwards on your card, but at right angles. Take the rest of his cards and place them at right angles on your pack, both groups of cards face downwards. Do this deliberately and neatly, adjusting the cards until you are satisfied that they are placed exactly as you want them. This is window dressing, but it is important.

Now recapitulate what has been done. "You will remember that you did exactly as I did. You shuffled my pack and I shuffled yours. We each took a card and remembered it. I have placed my card on the table and so have you. Would you be surprised if we both took the same card?"

7. The spectator admits that he would indeed be surprised. Do not say anything further, but slowly pick up the two crossed cards and drop them face upwards on the table. They are the same!

THE THREE PILES

The use of delay in performing a sleight is of great value to the conjurer. A moment's consideration will make it clear that to attempt to perform sleights at the start of a trick, when the attention of the onlookers is concentrated on your actions, is poor strategy and invites disaster. The element of surprise also is of inestimable value. This use of delay, to gain surprise, is applied here to the use of the key card, and the result is that even those who are familiar with it will fail to recognize its use.

Briefly the plot of the trick is that a card which has been merely thought of is discovered and revealed by the magician in a surprising fashion.

1. Have a spectator shuffle a pack of cards and cut it into three portions, about equal, while your back is turned. Instruct him to choose any one of the three piles, then to take it and, spreading its cards with the faces towards himself, select mentally any one card and commit it to memory. When he has done this, tell him to shuffle the cards he holds so that he himself will not know the position of his mentally selected card among the others.

2. Turn around and say, "I think your card is about twelfth from the top. Deal the cards face upwards and see if I'm right, but don't tell me where the card is if I'm wrong." Begin to turn away again but contrive to sight the first card the spectator deals, then turn away completely. This first card is your key card; remember it. Later, the spectators will forget that you turned around for a moment and will maintain that your back was turned all the time. This is the impression you wish to make.

3. When he has completed the deal, the spectator tells you that you were wrong. "Oh, well," you say, shrugging off your supposed mistake, "it makes very little difference."

4. Instruct the spectator to place his pile on the table, take the other two piles, and shuffle them together; cut the packet, place his pile on the lower portion, and then replace the cut. Finally, tell him to square the pack and make as many complete cuts as he likes.

5. Turn around, take the pack, and run over the faces as you make some casual remark, such as, "Well, you certainly mixed the cards thoroughly," or, "I forgot to notice if the joker is in this deck." In reality, you find your key card and count five cards below it and casually cut the pack at this point. Your key card will now be the sixth card from the bottom of the pack. Put the deck on the table face downwards.

6. Review briefly what has been done—a card merely thought of, the pack shuffled and cut several times, and all done while your back was turned. Then add ruminatively, "You will re-

member that I failed to name the card's correct position in the deck. I don't understand that . . . just how far down was it?" This question does not seem important and your tone and inflection imply mild interest only. Actually the spectator's reply tells you the present position of his card.

7. If he states that its position was sixth, then the required card is now at the bottom of the deck; if seventh, at the top. In such instances you bring the trick to a surprising finish at once by showing either the top or bottom card. If the position was from the first to fifth, take the pack in position for the glide and remove cards from the bottom. When you come to the spectator's card, glide it back and continue to deal cards until the spectator calls "Stop!" Remove his card and place it face downwards on the table. Have him name the card he thought of, then slowly turn that card face upwards.

If, however, the position was higher than seven, spread the cards and run your forefinger over them, hesitating now and then, and finally stopping at the right card.

Merely producing a card that was thought of makes a surprising finish to the feat, but it will afford the student excellent practice to devise more astonishing methods for revealing it.

The Twenty-Sixth Card

We have considered the use of key cards in close proximity to a chosen card; now we should like to tell you of a most ingenious application of the key card principle—that of the remote key.

1. You must know the name of the card twenty-sixth from the top of a pack of fifty-two cards. Let us say that this card is the four of spades. Place the pack before a spectator at A. Have him cut off about two-thirds of the pack and place these at B. Finally, have him cut off the upper half of B and place these cards at C. The four of spades, your key card, is somewhere in the middle of packet B.

2. Now instruct him to take packet C, and shuffle it well, then look at and remember its top card, replacing the packet at C. "Please remember that you first shuffled the cards and then looked at the top card. There is no possible way in which I can know the card of which you are thinking."

3. Next have him pick up the packet at A, shuffle it well, and place this on packet C. "Your card is lost," you point out. "I give you my word I do not know what it is or where it is at this moment."

4. Finally have him pick up the combined packet A-C and place it on B, then give the assembled pack one or two complete cuts.

5. Take the cards and run through them with their faces towards yourself until you come to the four of spades, your key card. Calling this card number one, count to the left until you arrive at the twenty-sixth card above it. Should your count take you to the top card before you reach the twenty-sixth card, continue the count from the bottom card. This card, the one twenty-sixth above your key card, will be the spectator's card.

6. Cut the cards at this point, taking all the cards above the spectator's card in your left hand and the remainder in your right hand, holding the hands widely separated. Glance from one packet to the other, shake your head a little, doubtfully, and move a step or so forward as you say, "I'll try to find it another way." At the same moment bring your two hands together, placing the cards in the right hand above those in the left and in this manner placing the spectator's card at the top of the pack.

7. Take the pack in your right hand, holding it at the ends between the fingers and the thumb, at the same time pushing the spectator's card at the top an inch off the pack to the right. "Please name your card." Raise your right hand and toss the pack into the left hand. As it falls, air pressure against the protruding top card will cause it to turn over so that when the pack drops into the left hand, the card will be face upwards. "There it is!" you exclaim. The effect is that you threw the deck into the left hand and the spectator's selected card somehow popped, face upwards, to the top.

A MEETING OF THE MINDS

Still another card trick in which the key card is distant from the card which it keys is this impressive feat, which may well pass as a demonstration of genuine mind reading.

1. Note the bottom card of the pack for use as a key card, and shuffle it to the top in the course of an overhand shuffle; then spread the cards from hand to hand, asking someone to remove a group of cards from the center and leaving to chance the number he will take. Square the remainder of the pack and place it to one side.

2. Take the spectator's packet of cards and pass them one by one from your left hand to your right hand, faces toward the spectator, asking him to think of one of them. Turn your head away as you do this but silently count the cards so that you know how many there are in the packet.

3. Hand the packet to the spectator, then move away a few paces and turn your back. Instruct him to remove his card and place it face downwards to one side, then shuffle the remainder of the packet and replace it on the deck and consequently upon your key card. Finally have him place his selected card on top of all.

4. Have him cut off about two-thirds of the pack, then place the cut to one side; take the lower portion, shuffle it, and place it on top of the other portion; make one complete cut.

5. Returning, take the pack and recapitulate what has been done in some such words as these: "You will remember that you have thought of a card and replaced it in the pack after shuffling and cutting. You are the only person present who knows the name of the card of which you are thinking. If you doubt this, say so at this time. You are satisfied that no one else can know the name of your card? Good. Therefore it is impossible that a confederate could transmit its name to me. I assure you that I have never found it necessary to employ confederates and would find it distasteful, but this trick is so amazing that some people afterwards think that this may have been the case. I mention it only to forestall such criticism.

"Others have claimed that I do not really succeed in the feat, but that the spectator who thinks of the card, through courtesy and a kindly desire not to embarrass me, agrees that the card I show is his when it is not. For this reason I shall ask you, sir, to write the name of the card of which you are thinking on a slip of paper or an envelope, being careful that no one sees the writing. In this way all of us will know whether I fail or succeed."

6. When this has been done, continue: "Finally, some persons have claimed that I study the expression of the person who thought of the card and by this means learn which is the proper card. To forestall this criticism, I shall turn my head away from you, sir, so that I cannot see you. Under these conditions, which are the fairest that I can devise, I shall show you the cards and when you see your card I will ask you to think 'That is my card,' and I will attempt to pick up your thought."

Turn your back and hold the cards well above your right shoulder so that everyone can see them. Push the cards off the face of the pack one by one with the left thumb, taking them in the right hand and allowing sufficient time for each card to be seen by the spectators. When your key card comes into view silently count the next card as *one* and count off as many cards as you counted in Step No. 2. The last of these is the spectator's card.

7. "I think I have your thought," you say, holding the card aloft. "This is your card!" The spectator acknowledges that this is so, and you have him hand the slip on which he wrote its name to someone, who reads it aloud and thus certifies to the success of your experiment.

Sincerely presented, the feat is most impressive.

The Non-Poker Voice

We have been considering the use of a single card as a key card which reveals the position of a chosen card, and now we shall describe still another use to which this stratagem may be placed.

Preparation. Remove from the pack and pocket any four cards, one of which is a heart. Place six cards of the heart suit at the top of the pack and the remaining six at the bottom.

Procedure. The steps are as follows:

1. Assert that you are convinced that there is no such thing as a poker voice; that, no matter how a person may school himself, he cannot keep the inflections which betray the inner emotion from his voice. You claim further that you can infallibly

determine which of a number of cards a person may be thinking of merely by listening to his voice as he calls out the names of the cards of a pack.

2. To offer proof of your assertion, hand someone the prepared pack of cards, turn your back and walk away as you request the spectator to deal six piles of cards, one by one from left to right in turn, thus secretly placing a heart at the top and bottom of each pile. This done, instruct him to remove any card from any one of the piles, show it to the others present, and drop it at the top of one of the other five piles. Next have him gather the piles in any order he likes (without disarranging the cards) and cut the pack two or three times, completing each cut.

When this has been done there will be six pairs of cards of the heart suit, side by side, spread at intervals throughout the pack. Between one of these pairs there will be an indifferent card, and this will be the chosen card.

3. Instruct the spectator to take the cards in his hands and, while you still have your back turned, to call out the names of the cards one by one. Warn him that although he may attempt to make his voice expressionless, you will detect the name of his card from the tone of his voice when he names it.

4. As he calls out the names of the cards, pretend to listen attentively. Whenever he names cards of the heart suit, note if a card of another suit intervenes; for example, he may call, "Nine of spades, ten of diamonds, *four of hearts*, seven of spades, *nine of hearts*." The intervening card, in this case the seven of spades, will be his card. Let him call off a half dozen cards more and then stop him.

"You have already named your card. That's right, isn't it?" you say.

"Yes."

"A few moments ago, when you named the spade suit, your voice quivered almost imperceptibly. Your card is a spade. That's correct?"

"It is."

"When you named the value of this spade card, your throat tightened. Do you remember? You were afraid that I would know that the seven of spades was the card. That's correct, is it not?"

He agrees that it is. You say: "A word of caution, sir. Be careful in poker games!" Take the pack from him, shuffle it absent-mindedly, and place it to one side, thus destroying any possible clues to your method.

INTUITION WITH CARDS

The key cards which have been discussed thus far have been those in which it is necessary to see the faces of the cards. There are many tricks in which this is not desirable, and we shall now explain how the key-card principle may be used when only the backs of the cards are seen.

Using a pack with a white border, take a soft pencil and place two small, light dots on the back of the card at the upper left and lower right corners (Fig. 47). You can find this card easily

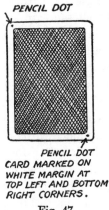

PENCIL DOT

PENCIL DOT
CARD MARKED ON
WHITE MARGIN AT
TOP LEFT AND BOTTOM
RIGHT CORNERS.

Fig. 47

and quickly in running through the pack, for you know what to look for. Your audience will never notice the dots.

The dotted key card may be used in place of the face key card in many tricks, and we leave it to your ingenuity to make use of the idea. The following feat is an example of the use to which it can be put:

1. Let us say that you are about to perform with a borrowed pack. Surreptitiously remove any two cards and place them in your pocket, then find an excuse to leave the room for a moment. Place the key pencil dots on the back of one of the cards and

write your initials on the face of the other. Remember the name of the latter card. Returning to the room, replace the cards at a propitious moment, with the dotted key card at the bottom and the initialed card just above it.

2. Riffle shuffle the pack without disturbing the two cards at the bottom. Place the pack on the table and have a spectator cut off a portion from the top. Take this packet and invite him to take the other packet.

3. Ask him to turn his back to you and to remove any card from the middle of his packet and place it face upwards at the top. Tell him that you will do the same thing and that both of you must synchronize your actions and thoughts if the test is to succeed. Instruct him to write his initials on the face of his card while you do the same with your card. Pretend, for the benefit of the others present, to initial your card but actually write nothing. The spectator, on the other hand, actually initials his card.

4. Next ask him to turn his card face downwards on his packet as you do the same thing with yours. Finally have him make one complete cut, as you also make a cut. His cut places his initialed card one card below the dotted key card.

5. Turn to face him and request him to visualize his card, explaining that you are forming a mental picture of your card. "This is an experiment in sympathetic action," you comment, "and if it is to succeed you must conscientiously try to make it succeed by obeying your first impulse from now on." Spread your cards face downwards on the table. "I will ask you to remove any card from my packet. Place your forefinger on any card and draw it from the spread." When he has done this, continue, "Now take that card and, without looking at it, thrust it in the middle of the cards you hold."

6. This done, tell him that you will remove one card from his packet. Take his cards and spread them ribbonwise, face downwards, from left to right. Pass your forefinger over this spread of cards, find the dotted key and drop your finger on the card to its left. This will be his initialed card. "I will take this card." Draw the card from the spread, thrust it face downwards in the middle of the cards you hold, without showing its face.

7. "Now," you say, "if our thoughts have been attuned, you have drawn my card, the four of spades—" (here you name the card you initialed) "—and I have drawn yours. Let's see if this is the case." Spread your cards face upwards and push out the card which he initialed. Have him spread his packet and he finds the card with your initials!

SLIDING KEY CARD

We have reserved to the last one of the finest and most deceptive methods of placing a key card above a chosen card. You will see at once that it can be put to use in some of the preceding tricks, but we thought it wisest to give you this method last, leaving it to your ingenuity to put it to good use.

In this sleight the key card is moved to any part of the pack at which it may be required. Let us suppose that you secretly glimpse the bottom card and you are about to use it as a key card.

1. Execute an overhand shuffle, retaining the bottom card in position. Spread the cards between your hands, and have a card freely selected.

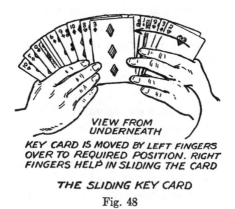

VIEW FROM
UNDERNEATH

KEY CARD IS MOVED BY LEFT FINGERS
OVER TO REQUIRED POSITION. RIGHT
FINGERS HELP IN SLIDING THE CARD

THE SLIDING KEY CARD

Fig. 48

2. Square the deck and overhand shuffle again in the same way while the spectator is noting his card.

3. Spread the cards between your hands for the return of the chosen card, but in doing so, with the tips of your right fingers underneath the spread, slide the bottom card to the right so that

it lies underneath the spread of the other cards and is hidden by them (Fig. 48).

4. Extend your hands, with the cards spread thus, toward the spectator and invite him to thrust his card into the deck. When he does this and the card is partially inserted, drop your left thumb on it, hold it and the cards in your left hand, and with your right hand remove all the cards to the right of it, *including* the key card. Thus the key card becomes the bottom card of the packet in your right hand.

5. Drop the right-hand packet on those in the left hand, and you have your key card above the selected card. Square the deck, and the most critical observer will be satisfied that he has replaced his card fairly and that you cannot know its position among the others.

VII

THE PALM

To PALM a card, in conjurer's language, means to take a card in the hand—generally the right hand—and hold it concealed there without its presence being suspected by the onlookers. The principle is a very important one in card magic, for many of the finest feats possible depend upon it. The best methods of palming cards are not difficult to learn. The reason that palming is neglected or badly done by cardmen is because of lack of confidence. The first thing a beginner is likely to say is that his hands are too small; he cannot conceive that he should hold so large an object as a playing card in his hand secretly. To show what a mistaken notion this is, test it in this way:

Take a card and lay it on your hand with the fingers extended in such a way that its outer left corner is at the outer phalanx of the little finger and its inner right corner against the ball of the thumb. Flex the fingers slightly and turn your hand over. You will find that the card is held (that is, palmed) securely, and so long as the fingers are pressed together it is completely hidden. Since one's hand always has a half-closed appearance when in repose, the position of the hand will appear to be a perfectly natural one, Fig. 54.

At first you will be so conscious of the presence of the card in your hand that you will want to drop it to your side or even put it behind your back. To overcome this self-consciousness, the best thing to do is to become so accustomed to having a card in your hand that you no longer take any notice of it. When you are reading a book or listening to the radio, place a card in your hand in the proper position, bend the fingers slightly, and then try to forget all about it. In a very short time you will become so used to it that you will be able to move your hand freely and naturally, always remembering, of course, that the back of your hand must always be outwards. Do not be afraid to bend the card; you cannot palm it naturally unless you do.

Practically everyone, when beginning to practice the palming of cards, will be careful to keep the fingers curved naturally but will overlook the importance of having the thumb lie in its natural position along the side of the hand. When the thumb extends at a right angle from the hand, a reflex action which must be overcome, its unnatural appearance at once attracts attention to the hand and arouses suspicion.

Top Palm, I (Single Card)

1. Hold the deck in your left hand by the sides between the middle, third, and little fingers, the tips of which are flush with the top of the deck, pressing the left side of the deck against the ball of the thumb. Bend the thumb at the outermost phalanx on the top card, with the tip resting a little below its middle, and place the tip of the index finger against the outer right corner (Fig. 49).

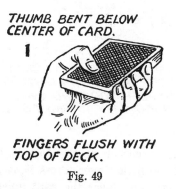

THUMB BENT BELOW CENTER OF CARD.

FINGERS FLUSH WITH TOP OF DECK.

Fig. 49

2. Bring the right hand over the pack as if merely to square it, the hand being well arched. Place the fingers, held close together, against the outer end, with the third (outermost) pha-

langes pressing against the outer end. Rest the tip of the thumb against the left inner corner (Fig. 50).

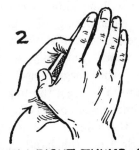

WITH RIGHT THUMB AT
LOWER LEFT CORNER, ALL
FOUR RIGHT FINGERS
COVER TOP END OF DECK.

Fig. 50

3. Straighten the left thumb pressing it on the top card and so push the card into the position shown in Fig. 51. (Right hand not shown.)

UNDER COVER OF RIGHT
HAND (NOT SHOWN HERE),
LEFT THUMB STRAIGHTENS
TO PUSH TOP CARD OVER
DIAGONALLY TO RIGHT SIDE

Fig. 51

4. The outer right corner of the top card is thus brought against the tip of the little finger. Press lightly downwards with the right little finger and lever the card upwards, at the same time bending the left thumb inward to its original position, and the card will be tilted upwards against the palm and the fingers (Fig. 52).

5. Draw the right fingers and thumb along the ends of the deck, squaring the cards. Grip the outer corners between the thumb at the inner end and the index and middle fingers at the

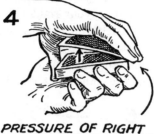

**PRESSURE OF RIGHT
LITTLE FINGER LEVERS
TOP CARD INTO PALM.**

Fig. 52

outer end, at the same time flexing the ring and little fingers (Fig. 53).

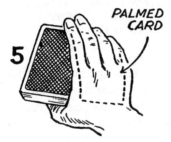

**PALMED
CARD**

**DECK HELD BY RIGHT THUMB,
FORE AND MIDDLE FINGERS
ON THE RIGHT SIDE. THIRD
AND LITTLE FINGERS BENT**

Fig. 53

The two essential points in the correct palming of cards are:

(a) The right hand must remain arched throughout.

(b) The right hand must retain the deck after the card is palmed, while the left hand moves away to make some appropriate gesture or natural personal action. For example, you may gesture to illustrate what you want done, which may be for a person to stand closer to you. Or you may brush the table clean of an imaginary speck, touch the corner of your mouth with the knuckle of your index finger, touch your chin as if in momentary thought—in other words, make some personal action that is natural and characteristic of you. Because of this, the transfer of the pack from your left to your right hand will seem to have no connection with the trick you are performing.

Do not make the mistake of trying to palm a card with the utmost rapidity, for all rapid actions of the hand arouse suspicion. The quickness of the hand does *not* deceive the eye. The

THUMB LIES ALONG
FOREFINGER. HAND
WITH PALMED CARD IS
NATURALLY BENT AND
RELAXED.

Fig. 54

palm must be made in exactly the same time as—neither more nor less than—in merely squaring the cards.

6. A moment later, take the pack from the right hand with the left and dispose of the palmed card as required by the trick.

Top Palm, II (Several Cards)

1. Hold the deck face downwards in your left hand between the second (top) phalanx of the thumb on one side and the third phalanges of the middle and ring fingers on the other, the index finger bent under the pack and the little finger free. Not only is this a very open and graceful method of holding the deck but it is also essential to the proper execution of the sleight.

2. With your right hand square the deck, and under cover of this action lift the inner ends of the cards to be palmed and insert the tip of the left little finger into the break thus made (Fig. 55).

3. Remove the right hand, making some appropriate gesture, then with it grasp the whole pack, with the fingers close together

at the outer end and the thumb at the inner end, which maintains the break. Move the left thumb and fingers inwards along the sides of the deck, squaring it. Press the tips of the thumb and fingers into the break, and in the outward squaring motion push

DECK HELD BY TIPS OF THUMB AND TWO MIDDLE FINGERS OF LEFT HAND.

1

LEFT FOREFINGER GOES UNDER THE DECK. TIP OF FREE LITTLE FINGER GOES IN BREAK READY TO RAISE THE TOP CARDS

Fig. 55

the separated packet of cards up into the right hand (Fig. 56).

4. Slide the right thumb and fingers along the ends of the pack, squaring them. Grip the pack between the thumb and the index and middle fingers, and flex the ring and little fingers a little, thus palming the cards securely. Remove the left hand,

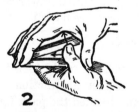

2

RIGHT HAND COVERS DECK AS IN SINGLE PALM. LEFT LITTLE FINGER AND THUMB RAISE TOP CARDS AT REAR END. THE THUMB MOVES TO FRONT OF DECK AS IT PUSHES CARDS INTO RIGHT PALM.

Fig. 56

holding the right hand stationary for a few moments. Use the left hand as you would when palming a single card, and a few moments later take the pack with the left hand again and dispose of the palmed cards as may be required.

PALM GLIMPSE

When a card has been palmed in the right hand, the mere act of handing the deck to a spectator affords a perfect glimpse of the card. Many performers prefer the palm glimpse to any other method of glimpsing a card. With a card palmed, a mere wave of the hand bringing the card within the line of vision is all that is necessary. The pack can then be placed in the left hand and the palmed card returned to the top in squaring the pack.

GLIMPSING PALMED CARD
Fig. 57

Note that when, having a card palmed in your right hand, you desire to hand the pack out for shuffling, it should be held by the lower left corners, thumb on the back and bent forefinger on the face, the other fingers curled inwards (Fig. 57). Hand the pack to someone on your extreme left.

REPLACING PALMED CARDS

The replacement of palmed cards upon the pack is much more difficult than is their secret abstraction. Let us say that you have palmed a card and handed the pack for shuffling. The shuffle completed, you ask for the return of the cards. If you take them with your right hand your awkwardness will betray the fact that you have a card palmed, and you will probably turn your hand so far that it will be seen. If you take the cards with your left hand, you must then have a good reason for placing your right hand over the pack. Moreover, since placing your right hand flat on the pack will tell your audience that you are replacing cards, how will you transfer them from the arched right palm to the flat pack?

First method. The palmed cards may be replaced as follows:

1. Extend your left hand, palm upwards, pointing to it with the forefinger of your right hand, and have the spectator place the pack on it. Hold the cards loosely as in Fig. 58.

2. Request the spectator to cut the cards. When he lifts the upper portion, bring the right hand over the remaining packet, the fingers slightly in front of it (Fig. 59), and grasp it with a little backward motion of the hand between the thumb and fingers. At the same time bend the index finger, pressing its nail downwards on the palmed card, flattening it and adding it to the packet (Fig. 60).

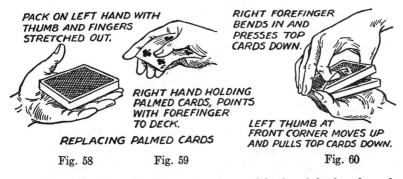

PACK ON LEFT HAND WITH THUMB AND FINGERS STRETCHED OUT.

RIGHT FOREFINGER BENDS IN AND PRESSES TOP CARDS DOWN.

RIGHT HAND HOLDING PALMED CARDS, POINTS WITH FOREFINGER TO DECK.

LEFT THUMB AT FRONT CORNER MOVES UP AND PULLS TOP CARDS DOWN.

REPLACING PALMED CARDS

Fig. 58   Fig. 59   Fig. 60

3. Immediately take the cards away with the right hand, and extend the left to take the spectator's cards. Drop those you hold in your right hand on top of those now in your left, saying, "You shuffled and cut the cards. Thank you."

This procedure is entirely natural, for, in assisting in making the cut, the right hand would move to the left to pick up the cards remaining in the left hand even if there were no sleight involved.

Second method. There are occasions when you will want to replace palmed cards and when it is not desirable to have the pack cut—as, for example, when performing the Card in Pocket, the next trick to be described. In such cases you use the procedure given in the first method, but the left hand with the pack is held at the center of the body so that the two hands come together naturally. The left hand places the pack in the right, which adds the palmed cards as already described.

To understand the importance of placing the pack in the right hand, rather than reaching for it and taking it with the right, stand on someone's left and hand him an object. Next offer him another object. He will move his left hand to his right, which will move very little, then place the first object in the right hand, and move his left hand back to take the second object.

In making the replacement, you simulate this natural action.

The best way to gain complete confidence in your ability to palm cards successfully is to do tricks in which the palm is used. In the feats which follow, the sleight is executed under such favorable circumstances—the attention of the spectators being directed elsewhere—that the student need have no fear of being detected if he times his movements properly.

TRICKS WITH THE PALM

CARD IN THE POCKET

In this feat the magician discovers a card which has been merely thought of, without apparently his having been given any clue to it. It is well, therefore, to introduce the trick as one that is done by mind reading.

1. It is necessary to have a spectator think of a small number; hence, instead of limiting him to numbers between, say, one and ten or twelve, ask him to think of his favorite hour. "For example," you say, "you may be an early riser and your favorite hour would then be six o'clock—although that certainly is not mine. Or you may favor your lunch hour, or the hour when you listen to your pet radio star. Any hour you please, but fix your mind on it and do not change it.

"I am going to hand you the pack and I want you to ascertain what card lies at your favorite hour from the top. For instance, four o'clock may be your choice—afternoon tea, you know. In that case you will lift the cards so, one by one, counting one, two, three, four. Look at and remember that fourth card, and put the cards back on top of the pack." Hand the pack to him. "Will you do the same thing, so that the matter will be quite clear to you?" See that the spectator counts and puts the cards back correctly.

2. "That's fine. Now shuffle the pack thoroughly, and cut it. Satisfied? Then I will turn my back while you count down to the number of your favorite hour, note the card at that number, and show it to all, finally replacing the cards on the top of the pack." Turn away. When the spectator announces he is ready, turn around and take the deck.

3. "Now, sir, you have thought of your favorite hour and you have noted the card at that number from the top of this deck which you shuffled and cut yourself. It is impossible for me to know where any particular card may be in the deck, but to make the test still more convincing I will place the cards behind my back." Do so.

"Now, sir, I want you to think intently of your favorite hour and the card you noted. Imagine you see a big picture of the number and the card on the wall. That's good. I believe I have it." Bring forward the bottom card of the deck, holding it facing you and not allowing anyone to get a glimpse of its face. Look at the card—it makes no difference what card it is—then at the spectators, and say, "Yes, I believe it's the one you are thinking of. Don't name it. I'll put this card in my pocket." Place it in your right trousers pocket and in doing so palm it as you thrust your hand to the bottom of the pocket.

4. You have the deck in your left hand. Bring your right hand from your pocket and place the pack in it, replacing the palmed card on the top by the second replacement method. Move the left hand away and gesture with it, saying, "If I have been successful I have your card here in my pocket." Pat the pocket with your left hand.

5. "Let me show you that your card is gone. What number was it? Don't name the card, just the hour. Six! Yes, I got the impression that you are an early riser." Have some appropriate remark for each hour. "Watch!" Deal five cards deliberately on the table face downwards. Take the sixth card and throw it down face downwards, saying, "Will you look at the card?" As he turns the card face upwards, and everyone's attention is centered on it, push the top card, which will be the spectator's

card, well over the side of the deck. Bring the right hand back in the natural reaction after the throw, palm the card flying so to speak, and immediately thrust the hand into your trousers pocket, saying, "Of course it isn't your card. I placed it here in my pocket."

6. Push your hand well down into the pocket, release the card, then bringing the hand upwards take the card by the extreme upper end and bring it up into view about three-quarters of its length out of the pocket. Its back will be toward the spectators. Hold it there and say to the spectator, "Please name your card." He does so and you turn the card slowly showing it to be that very card.

Do not move the right hand backwards swiftly to take the top card when making the palm. All eyes will be drawn to the card you have thrown on the table. Move it back at a natural pace, take the card by covering it with the full width of the hand, and continue the movement backwards to your pocket. By the time the spectators are looking toward your hand again it should actually be in the pocket.

This is one of the great card feats which has stood the test of time, and we urge the student to master it. Not only will it give him confidence in palming cards but he will also gain valuable insight into the importance of *timing* in the execution of sleights.

The palm described in step No. 5 is a special palm especially suitable for this particular trick and should not be confused with the top palm.

Now You See It!

Have a spectator select a card, note it, return it to the pack, and himself shuffle the pack. Announce that you will find the card if you are allowed four attempts. Accordingly you remove four cards from the deck without showing their faces. When, however, you do show the cards, not one of them is the chosen card. You replace them on the table, request the spectator to point to one of them, and—lo and behold—*it is his card!*

1. First of all, before you offer to show the trick, secretly note and remember the bottom card of the deck. Bring this card to

the top with an overhand shuffle. Let us assume that this card is the four of spades.

2. Holding the deck in your left hand, place both hands behind your back, saying, "I propose to attempt a surprising little feat under these conditions, with the cards held behind my back to prove that the result is inherent in the cards. I have nothing to do with it, it just happens as you will see." While saying this and still facing the audience, with your left thumb push the top card (the four of spades) into your right hand, its back against the palm and the slightly bent fingers. Turn this hand palm upwards and with it clasp the back of the left hand. In this position the card held in the right hand is concealed in a natural manner.

3. Turn your back to the audience and ask a spectator to take the pack and shuffle it. When he has done so, request him to replace it in your hand, *face downwards*. Failure to make this last stipulation would lead to an embarrassing result.

Continue: "You have shuffled the cards, and clearly I cannot know the position of any card. Now will you cut the pack at any point you wish?" When the spectator has removed the upper portion of the pack, turn around facing him and ask him, "Will you assure everyone that you cut the cards at a point of your own choice?" Seize this opportunity to place the card secretly held in your right hand on top of the remainder of the pack in your left hand and again grasp the back of the left hand exactly as before. Be careful not to move your elbows during this action.

4. Once more turn your back to the audience and with your left thumb push forward the top card of your packet. This is, of course, the four of spades which you have just secretly added, but the onlookers will be convinced that it is a card the name of which you cannot possibly know. Continue, "Please take the card at which you cut and show it to everyone."

Pause for a moment or two, then say, "Now replace the card on this packet and then place your packet on top of all. Finally, take the pack and shuffle it thoroughly so that none of us can have the slightest notion where your card may be in the deck."

5. When this has been done, face your audience, take the deck and say, "My feat is this. I shall remove four cards and one of

them will be your card—I hope!" Run through the cards, remove three as unlike the spectator's card as possible and put them on the table face downwards. Using our example of the four of spades as the chosen card, you would remove the seven of diamonds, the seven of hearts, and the eight of diamonds. Thus the spectator will know at a single glance at each of them that you have not found his card. Finally, remove the chosen card and place it on the other three.

6. Pick up the four cards and hold the packet face downwards in your left hand in position for the glide. Tip up the packet and show the face card—a red card—and ask, "Is this your card?"

"No."

Turn the packet face downwards, draw out the bottom card which you have just shown and put it on the table face downwards, tipping it up a little so that the spectators can get a glimpse of its face. Do this casually, not ostentatiously.

7. Draw out the card now at the bottom of the packet and put it on the top. Tip the packet upwards and show the card now at its face. "Is this your card?" you ask. When this is denied, turn the packet face downwards and perform the glide, thus drawing out the chosen card above it—in this case the four of spades. Place it face downwards on the table beside the first card. Be careful not to show its face.

8. Two cards remain in your left hand. Remove the lower one and place it on top of the other card. Tip up the packet and show the face card. "Then is this your card?" you ask. Upon receiving a negative response, drop your hand, remove this card, and place it beside the other two.

9. You now hold one card face downwards in your left hand and this card you have already shown. Turn it face upwards and ask, "Is this your card?" Immediately place it face downwards beside the other three, even before the spectator has a chance to reply. It was for this purpose that you chose three cards altogether unlike the chosen card in both suit and value. Using this precaution you will find that the audience will never notice you have shown the same card twice. In this case we have supposed that the chosen card was a black card, and you have shown three red cards only, so that the merest glance at each card

satisfies the onlookers that you have failed. They have no real interest in the cards you show and therefore do not study them closely.

10. You have placed the four cards on the table in a row, which extends away from the spectator, with the selected card second from the end nearest him (Fig. 61). Ask him to touch

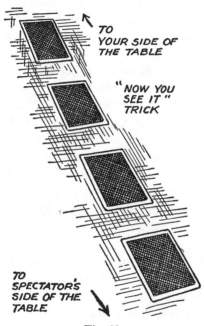

Fig. 61

one of the four cards. He will in nineteen cases out of twenty point to the second card, the chosen card!

Pick up the other three cards, show them casually and drop them on the deck.

"What was the name of your card?" you ask.

"The four of spades!"

Wave your hand over the one card remaining on the table. Then slowly turn it face upwards. It is the chosen card.

You will ask, "But what shall I do if the spectator points to one of the other cards?" In that case you would resort to a stratagem known as the *equivoque*. If he points to one of the other cards, you continue, "And one of the other cards, too, if you please." If, now, he touches the chosen card, you remove *the other two cards* and place them on the deck. But if he points to another of the indifferent cards *you remove and discard them both*. Thus you interpret his choice with your own end in view. The spectator does not know *why* you have asked him to point to a card and therefore cannot object to your actions. In either case two cards will be left on the table, the chosen card and another.

Now say, "Please point to one of the two cards."

Again you interpret his choice as suits you best. If he points to the chosen card, remove the other one and drop it on the pack. But if he points to the indifferent card you discard it. This Hobson's choice must always bend the spectator to your will and bring the trick to a successful conclusion.

All feats in which cards transpose or change are especially effective, for they appear to be the most baffling to laymen. Of these the foregoing is one of the most brilliant.

Grab-Bag Card

This is an ingenious use of the palm which is made when all attention is diverted from the pack and from your hands. For that reason, this is a good trick for you to use while gaining confidence in your ability to palm.

1. Ask someone to step forward to assist you in your next feat, and when some obliging soul has done so have him shuffle the pack and remove any card, showing it to everyone. Take the pack, and in having the card replaced control it to the top by means of the overhand shuffle control.

2. Hand the deck to your assistant, saying, "Kindly deal ten cards into my left hand, then place the remainder of the pack to one side." Count the cards as he deals, so that all may be assured that there are no more and no less than ten. Hold the ten cards high as he discards the pack, but with their backs to the audience so that no one can see the chosen card at the bottom of the packet; then place it in your outer right coat pocket with the

face card innermost, thus bringing the chosen card nearest your body.

3. Say: "I'll wager you haven't taken a chance on a grab-bag in years, sir. Let's try it tonight with the ten cards in my pocket. Here's how we'll do it." Dip your right hand into your pocket and remove the selected card at the bottom, placing it face downwards in your left hand and being careful that no one sees its face. "I'll take a card, number one. Now you take a card from my pocket—any card—from the top, the bottom, or the middle, just as you like." When he removes one, count, "Number two," and have him keep the card.

4. "You see how simple it is? You don't know what card you'll get, and neither do I." Remove another card, counting, "Number three!" and slide it face downwards under the one you already hold in your left hand.

5. Have him remove another card, counting "Four." Dip your right hand into your pocket to remove another card and as you do so turn the two cards in the right hand face upwards by tipping them over with the thumb. Do not make a sleight of this; everyone will be watching your right hand and in any event what you do with the cards in your left hand does not seem important. Count "Five," as you place the card *face upwards* on those already in the left hand.

6. Have the spectator remove another card, urging him always to take any card he likes. Count it as six; then remove one yourself, counting it as seven.

7. As your vis-a-vis is removing the eighth card, palm the selected card from the top of those you hold. This is an easy palm as you naturally turn your right side forward to enable everyone to see him remove his card, and your hands are forgotten. Count "Eight," as he adds his card to those he holds.

8. Place your hand with the palmed card in your pocket, and drop the card. Take the other two remaining cards, square them, and remove them as one card, counting "Nine." Place them on those you already hold.

9. Have the spectator name his card. "Let me point out that you have had a perfectly free choice as to which cards you would remove from my pocket," you recapitulate. "Yet if our

grab-bag has been a success, the last card remaining in my pocket must be your card!"

Have him remove the last card. It is his chosen card!

GOOD-LUCK CARD

Since your purpose in presenting card tricks is to entertain your audiences, you should have in your repertoire plenty of feats that will cause both amazement *and* amusement. In the following trick, which can cause much laughter, a spectator thinks of a card and discovers, much to his surprise, that you are sitting on it.

1. Seat yourself farther away from the table than you would normally, for a reason we shall explain later, saying, "I haven't played a game of bridge or poker for six years. If you will pretend to be me—" (address this request to one of the onlookers) "—I'll try to show everyone why I quit those innocent pastimes."

2. Take the pack, give it an overhand shuffle, and deal three poker hands of five cards each. "I was playing poker one night with two friends—one of those kill-time games—and this is what happened. Which one of these three hands shall be mine?" you ask the spectator. He points to one of the three, which you pick up and spread with the faces of the cards toward him. "I picked up my hand and noticed in it a card that has always brought me good luck. Since you're playing my part, sir, will you think of one of these cards? Don't name it, merely think of it."

3. Drop the five cards on the pack, then pick up the other two hands and place them on the pack also. Shuffle, using the overhand shuffle control, retaining top stock (see page 10) to keep the fifteen cards at the top of the pack. As you make this shuffle you say, "My story doesn't really become interesting until about two weeks later, when I was in a five-handed poker game." Deal five hands from the top of the deck. The spectator's card will be the third card in whichever hand he finds it in. Hold the remainder of the deck in your hand, saying, "On the very first deal, the dealer gave me my good-luck card. Since you know which card it is, sir, and I don't, will you tell me if it is in one of these hands?" Show each hand in turn until he tells you that he sees his card. Drop this hand on one of the other hands, pick

up both and drop them on a third, then pick up the three hands and drop them at the top of the pack. Finally pick up the two remaining hands and place them on top of all. Do this casually, saying, "Do you see what was happening to me? My good luck card was following me around!"

4. Undercut the pack, run one card onto the cards remaining in the left hand, injog the next card, and shuffle off the rest. Undercut at the injog and drop the undercut on top. You have returned the first fifteen cards to the top, with one extra card above them, thus placing the spectator's card fourteenth from the top. As you do this, explain, "This is all background so that you will understand what happened next, when I was playing bridge. And I don't mind saying that even now I don't believe it could have happened."

5. "On the very first hand the dealer gave me my thirteen cards." Deal thirteen cards, push them over to him and say, "See if your good luck card is in the hand." When he has picked up the cards to look at them, palm the top card of the remainder of the pack, which will be the spectator's card, and lay the rest of the cards on the table. In a natural manner, adjust your chair by seizing the edge between your legs with your right hand, at the same time dropping the palmed card on the chair seat as you rise a little to draw the chair closer to the table. When you are again seated, the card is well under you.

The assisting spectator announces that his card is not among those you dealt him. "Amazing!" you exclaim. "It's happened again! Tell me, what was the name of the card of which you thought?"

When he names his card, you turn to the others. "Ladies and gentlemen, I ask you to bear witness to what has happened here tonight. All that my friend has done is think of a card, nothing more nor less. He tells us now that it is the four of diamonds—" (or whatever the card is) "—and I say that it could not possibly have been the four of diamonds, because I have been sitting on that card all evening!"

Get up, lift the chair for all to see the card, and jerk it onto the table. It is the spectator's card!

Do It and Fail

The trick which we now give you is one that has challenged the wits of many thousands of persons. It is especially suitable for use after dessert, when the company is relaxed, the talk is general, and everyone is in a congenial mood. It is not a trick for a set performance.

The trick is one that people remember. One famous magician, while making an ocean voyage, performed it at the dinner table every night at the insistence of his fellow voyagers, and years later shipboard acquaintances would remind him of the trick and ask him to explain it. Such a trick is a good one.

The effect is that the magician does a trick, explains it, and then allows the spectators to do it, or fail utterly, at his will.

One sleight only is used, the palm, but it is done at favorable moments and, since you present the trick as a puzzle, no one thinks of sleight-of-hand being used.

1. Take a pack of cards, turn it face upwards, and, saying that you will use a few cards of each suit in order to save time, take out seven cards of the same suit as the face card. Do not openly count them or give anyone else a chance of doing so; square them and put the packet down. Do the same with each of the other three suits, thus making a packet of twenty-eight cards. Secretly, however, you have slipped one card of each suit to the top of the remaining twenty-four cards. Lay these aside.

2. Arrange the twenty-eight cards in seven rows of four cards each, the first row consisting of a card of each suit, taking no notice of their values. The second row must begin with a card of the same suit as that with which the first row ended, then continue with the suits in the same sequence as the first row. The same rule applies to the remaining rows. For example, if the first row consists of a club, a heart, a spade, and a diamond, the layout will be

<pre>
C H S D
D C H S
S D C H
</pre>

and so on for the succeeding rows. The cards of each vertical row must overlap each other by half.

3. Pick up the fourth vertical row, that on the extreme right, by sliding the cards together from the top down. Lay the packet on the bottom card of the third row and pick all up in the same way. Do the same with the last two rows.

4. Place the assembled packet before someone and have him make as many *complete* cuts as he pleases. Then deal the cards face downwards into four hands, one card at a time from left to right. Turn the packets face upwards and show that each one consists of cards of one suit only. *Always* deal face downwards and turn each packet face upwards in turn to show this result.

5. Explain fully how the trick is done and have a person on your left take the cards and do it. While he is doing this and all are watching the process, take the remaining packet of twenty-four cards casually and palm the four cards at the top in your right hand. No one will take any notice of you at this stage. Lay the packet down again.

6. When the spectator turns each of his four packets face upwards and it is seen that he has succeeded in dealing each suit into a separate pile, reach out with your left hand and turn the packet farthest away from you face downwards. Draw it towards you and pick it up with your right hand, adding the four palmed cards. Turn the other packets over and assemble the whole into one pack and square it. Shuffle the cards, now thirty-two in number, and lay them down.

7. "A very easy trick when you know how it's done, isn't it?" you ask the spectator. He agrees and you continue, "You understand, of course, that one mistake in laying out the cards would spoil the trick?"

"Yes."

"But you are sure that you know the proper procedure?"

"Yes."

"And you are positive that you could do the trick again?"

"Of course."

"Do you think that by mental control only I could cause you to make a mistake and ruin your trick?"

"No."

"Very well," you say. "Try again. This time I'll make you fail."

8. The spectator confidently lays out the cards and, as he does so, you keep up a running fire of comment, assuring him that he will make a mistake, and you appeal to the onlookers to make no remark when they see an error, and so on.

9. When he has completed the layout and the packets have been assembled, have a third person make as many complete cuts as he wishes and then have the spectator deal the four hands *face downwards.* Say to him, "You really believe that you laid out the cards exactly as before? You do? That's strange! Turn over the cards yourself." To his consternation he finds cards of every suit in each packet.

Most likely he will want to try again. Let him do so. Carry on the same bluff of causing him to make an involuntary error. The result is the same, there are mixed suits in every packet. In showing them and reassembling the thirty-two cards, contrive to get one card of each suit to the top and palm the four cards. Lay the packet down.

10. Apparently the trick is over. Casually pick up the other packet, adding the palmed cards to it; then lay it aside. After a moment or two, you say to your victim, "You don't believe I really caused you to fail, do you? Well, I'll prove it. This time I'll allow you to succeed." He goes through the same procedure as before, so he thinks, and this time, when the hands are turned over, there are the four suits segregated, each in its own pile!

That is your climax and you'll find it a good one. Gather up the cards and add them to the remainder of the deck, thus allowing no opportunity for anyone to determine exactly how many cards were used.

Presented under proper conditions, this trick will cause more talk and be remembered longer than many more ambitious card feats.

GATHERING OF THE CLAN

It is always advisable to use a number of tricks which do not require the choice of a card. In this trick, the four aces, placed in different packets, gather mysteriously in one of them.

1. Let us say that you have just done the *poker player's picnic* (see page 16) and that the four aces are lying on the table. Gather the other cards and, under cover of squaring them with the right thumb, lift the inner ends of two cards at the top and insert the tip of the left little finger under them.

2. Pick up the four aces one by one and place them face upwards on top of the pack. Do not look at your hands; concentrate your attention on those about you. Immediately lift off the face-up aces, together with the two face-down cards below them. Hold the six cards neatly squared into a packet with its outer end sloping downwards.

As though struck with a sudden thought, say, "Here's an interesting thing you may like," and place the pack on the table. If you have played your part well, the spectators will not realize that the aces have even approached the pack.

3. Take the packet in the left hand by the sides, between the thumb on one side and the fingers on the other. Indicate the top ace of the packet, calling its name. Remove it, turn it face downwards, and place it at the bottom of the packet. Do the same with the next two aces, but after calling the name of the last ace turn it face downwards on top. Thus you have not only shown the four aces but you have secretly arranged the two indifferent cards second and third from the top.

4. Place the packet on top of the deck, and pick up the deck. Deal the first four cards in a row from left to right, casually allowing the onlookers to get a glimpse of the faces of the first and fourth, which are aces, but being careful not to show the two indifferent cards.

5. Announce that you will place three indifferent cards on each of the four aces. Push off the top card of the deck into your right hand, taking it between the thumb at the inner end and the fingers at the outer end, counting "One." In the same way push off and take the next card underneath and, overlapping the first card, count "Two." Take a third card in exactly the same way and count "Three." Square the three cards by pushing them against the side of your left thumb and in so doing let the third card drop back onto the pack. Carry away two cards only, as if they were still three, and place them on the ace at the extreme

left of the row. These two cards, you remember, are aces, so that three aces are now together in this packet.

6. Push off three more cards in the same way, counting them into the right hand and squaring them against the left thumb. Place the packet of three indifferent cards on the second (supposed) ace. Do exactly the same with the third and fourth cards of the row. You have thus made three packets of four cards and one packet of three (aces).

7. Push the packet at the extreme left, the three aces, a little to one side. Pick up the next packet by cutting half the deck, dropping the cut on the packet, picking all up, and replacing the cut. Cut about a third of the deck, drop it on the third packet, and add all to the deck. Pick up the fourth packet and drop it on top of the deck. Execute an overhand shuffle, retaining these four cards at the top.

8. It is necessary now to get the fourth ace, which is fourth from the top, to the top of the deck in order to palm it. To do this very simply, say: "You remember what we did? I dealt an ace on the table, so" (deal one card face downwards). "On it I dealt three cards, so" (deal three more cards). "And I did that four times. Is that right?" All agree. Pick up the packet and place it on the deck. You have the ace on the top.

9. Square the deck and. under cover of the movement and talking, palm the top card—the fourth ace. Hold the deck in your right hand as you say, "The aces are very clannish. They hate being separated. Remember that there are three aces in the deck—" (take it with your left hand and place it on the table in front of a spectator) "—and one ace here." Place your right hand on the packet of three aces, adding the palmed ace and picking all up by drawing the cards towards you. "Place your hand on the deck, please. No matter how tightly you hold the cards you cannot stop the gathering of the clan, but you may feel them go."

10. Tap the back of his hand with your packet, then take it, still squared, in your left hand. Take the deck with the right hand and spread it face upwards on the table with a flourish. "No aces there!" you exclaim. "Here are all four!" Turn the packet in your left hand face upwards and slowly spread the four aces.

Spring Catch

The flourish *springing the cards* (see page 45), when used in conjunction with the palm, affords a most effective climax to a program of feats with cards. Let us say that you have secretly brought a spectator's card to the top of the pack. Proceed as follows:

1. Palm the card in your right hand.

2. Hold the pack face upwards in the right hand, bending it strongly as for the spring flourish.

3. Let the cards fly upwards in a stream. Rapidly thrust your right hand among the cards in the air, and produce the palmed card at your finger tips by bending the top phalanx of the middle finger on the back of the card, then extending the fingers and placing the thumb on the inner right corner. The card is then held between the tips of the thumb and forefinger as if just caught from the air.

Simple as this sounds, the feat makes a brilliant finish to a series of card discoveries, but it must be done with dash and showmanship.

A Vested Interest

A chosen card vanishes from the pack and is found under the performer's shirt, both vest and shirt having to be opened to bring it out.

The only requirements are a pack of cards and two pencil stubs. Have the latter in your upper left vest pocket.

1. Have the cards shuffled and allow a spectator to select one card freely. When he has noted it and has shown it to the others, have it returned and control it to the top.

2. Shuffle the pack again, keeping the chosen card in the same position, then in squaring the cards palm it in your right hand. Give the pack to the spectator for him to shuffle also.

3. As he does so, say, "Oh, I forgot that in this experiment the card should be marked for identification." Reach under your coat to your vest pocket and under cover of getting the small pencil stub, slip the end of the palmed card under the edge of your vest at the armhole, then bring out both stubs. Continue, "Will

you find your card and place a small mark on its face?" Hand the spectator one of the stubs.

4. Replace the second stub in your vest pocket, at the same time reach out with your fingers and pull the card inwards under the vest as far as possible.

5. The spectator fails to find his card and tells you it is not in the pack. "Your card has disappeared, you say? That's strange, very strange! What card was it?" The spectator names his card. "Ah, that accounts for it. That card is the biggest prankster of the lot, always playing tricks on its own account. I feel something tickling me. Allow me, please." Unbutton the second and third lower buttons of your vest and open your shirt at that place. Thrust your right hand into the opening, your thumb going under the shirt and your fingers between the shirt and the vest. Pull the card down with the tips of your fingers, then quickly seize it between the thumb and fingers, and draw it out smartly, apparently from under the shirt.

"There it is, the playful little rascal. It was tickling me to let me know where it had got to!"

The only plausible plot would seem to be the one indicated, namely, that the cards indulge in unexpected antics of their own accord.

PIANO TRICK

Announce that you will try to show a simple card trick of pure skill, and ask the company to pay particular attention to your movements, for your success will depend on whether or not they detect your sleight. Make this statement as a sincere challenge, for its purpose is to condition those present to look for a sleight which you never perform and thus divert them from the real explanation. "If at any time I make a false movement," you continue, "I want you to stop me immediately and say so."

1. Hand a pack of cards to someone for shuffling and, when he is satisfied that they are well mixed, take them back and invite him to assist you. Have him place the tips of the fingers and thumbs of both hands on the table, the hands arched as if playing the piano. It is from this position of the hands that the trick takes its name.

2. Take any two cards from the pack, show them, and say, "Here are two cards, a pair, even. I place them between your fingers in this manner." Place them in the space between the person's ring and little fingers, the sides of the card résting on the table, and have the person grip them in that position.

3. Take two more cards, saying, "Two more cards, another pair, always even." Place them in the space between the ring and middle fingers, adjoining the first pair.

4. Show a third pair and repeat the phrase, "Two cards, a pair, always even," and place them between the person's index and middle fingers.

5. Now take one card only and place it between the thumb and index finger as you say, "One card only, odd" (Fig. 62).

SINGLE
PAIRS

THREE PAIRS BETWEEN
FINGERS. SINGLE CARD
BETWEEN THUMB AND
INDEX.

THE PIANO TRICK

Fig. 62

6. Continue by filling the four spaces of the other hand with pairs of cards, being very careful each time to lay stress on the words *even* and *pair*. You do *not* place an odd card between the thumb and index finger of this hand. The peculiarity of this arrangement always attracts attention and arouses much curiosity as to what you are going to do.

7. Proceed by taking away one of the pairs of cards, showing them. "Two cards," you say. "A pair, even." Take one card in each hand and lay them apart, face downwards, on the table. Take a second pair, repeating the formula, "Two cards, always even," and place one on each of the first two cards. Proceed in

exactly the same way until you have laid all the pairs in two piles.

8. "Now," you say, "we have made two piles, each of which contains an even number of cards. That is right, isn't it?" The reply is always in the affirmative, strange as that may seem when you know the trick.

"Very well," you continue, "if I place this odd card—" (you remove the single card from between the person's thumb and index finger) "—on either heap, it must make that heap odd. Correct?" Again there is universal agreement. "Very well. On which of the two heaps shall I put this odd card? This one? So now this heap becomes odd while the other remains even. I warn you, you must watch very closely, for I am about to attempt a very difficult sleight. If you catch me at it, I want you to say so. If you don't—I'll be happy. I place one hand on this heap, now become the odd one, as chosen by you. I place my other hand on the even pile and I keep them well apart, as you see.

"My trick is this. I shall pass one card from one heap to the other, so that this odd pile will become the even pile and the even pile the odd one. Remember, if you see the card as I throw it across, I want you to say so. Ready? Watch closely! Pass!"

9. Suiting your actions to your words, you have placed your hands palms downwards on the two packets, keeping them about eighteen inches apart. At the word "Pass" you make a quick sidewise motion of each hand an inch or two and at once rather excitedly exclaim, "Did you see it go?" Of course they didn't, and you say happily, "Then my trick is a complete success. This heap, which was odd, is now even." You pick up and count the cards by pairs—"two, and two, and two, and two—even. While this one, which was even, is now odd—two, and two, and two, and one—odd, isn't it?"

Do not be misled by the apparent simplicity of the trick. Presented as described above, it has a really astonishing effect, but remember that the presentation is everything.

VIII

THE BACKSLIP

THE backslip is an easy and useful sleight in which the pack is cut, and in the action the top card is slipped secretly to the top of the lower portion.

1. Hold the pack face downwards in the left hand, the thumb extending along one side, the index finger at the outer end, the other fingers at the other side.

2. Grasp the upper half of the pack at the ends with the right fingers and thumb (Fig. 63), and open it in book fashion.

1

THE PACK IS OPENED BOOKWISE.

Fig. 63

3. Press against the top card with the tips of the left middle, ring, and little fingers.

4. Lift upwards all the cards held by the right hand except the top card. Fold this card down on the top of the lower portion with the left fingers.

Smoothly performed, the slipping of the card cannot be seen, but care must be taken to make the fall of the card noiseless.

This is the basic sleight. Nate Leipzig, the late great American card conjurer, devised the following procedure to hide the transfer of the card: In making the action in step No. 4, turn both hands at the same time so that the cards they hold are face upwards. Point to the face card of the packet in the right hand with your extended left index finger and make some appropriate remark about this card (Fig. 64).

BOTH HANDS TURN OVER.

Fig. 64

BACKSLIP FORCE

Let us say that you have a card at the top of the pack which you wish to force. Riffle downwards with the thumb at the left side of the pack and ask someone to stop you whenever he likes. Stop the riffle at this point and remove the cards above the thumb with the right hand, backslipping the top card onto the lower portion. Extend the left hand and have this card removed.

This is an easy and deceptive force used by many performers.

BACKSLIP CONTROL

1. Grasp the pack in readiness for the backslip and open the pack bookwise with the right hand as you request that a chosen card be replaced.

2. When it is placed on the lower portion, move the right hand with the upper portion outwards in a gesture, at the same moment backslipping the top card onto the lower portion above the chosen card.

3. Say, "Let's be sure that your card is lost in the pack," and with the left thumb push off the top card of the lower portion—the card which everyone believes to be the chosen one—and thrust it flush into the center of the packet held in the right hand.

4. Hand this right-hand packet to the spectator to shuffle while you shuffle the remainder, sending the top card, the chosen card, to the bottom and back to the top.

5. Reassemble the pack by placing the spectator's packet below yours. The chosen card, apparently completely lost, is now the top card of the pack.

TRICKS WITH THE BACKSLIP

Lightning Card

There are few tricks from which so much entertainment can be got as from the trick about to be described. A spectator sees his chosen card among a number he holds, and a moment later it vanishes to appear elsewhere!

1. Take a shuffled pack and ask someone to think of a small number, larger than five but less than fifteen. "A long trick is a dull trick," you explain. "We'll keep this one brief."

2. Holding the pack upright and facing the spectator, thumb cards from the left hand into the right without reversing their order, counting them aloud. Have the spectator remember the card which falls on his number. Count to fifteen and replace these cards on the pack.

3. Cut away the top half of the pack with the right hand, and in doing this backslip the top card onto the lower portion, which you place at your right.

4. Riffle the upper portion and ask the spectator if he sees his card. He says that he does but, unknown to him, it is now one card higher in the packet than he thinks it is.

5. Hand him this packet. "Your card is among those you now hold?" you ask.

"Yes."

"If you're not absolutely sure of that, look again."

"No. I know it's there."

"Very well. Now, what was the number of which you thought? Not the card, just the number."

"Nine."

"Better and better," you exclaim. "You couldn't have thought of a more fortuitous number!"

6. "You have your packet of cards with your card among the others," you say. Tap your packet of cards on the table at your right. "I have my packet over here." Pick up the top card of

your packet. "I'll count to your number in my packet, you count to it in yours." Place the card face downwards in your left hand, counting "One."

Extend your left hand and have him place the top card of his packet on top of your card. Remove the next card from your packet, placing it on those in the left hand, counting "Two," and similarly have him place a second card in your left hand, all the cards being face downward.

7. Continue to do this until you reach the number that is one less than the number he named, which in the illustration we have cited would be eight. The last card he places in your left hand will be his chosen card, although he believes that it is the top card of those he still holds. You say, "The next card, the ninth card, is your card. Kindly place it face downwards on the table." When he does this, no matter how he places it, have him turn it so that it is at right angles to its original position, as if this were important, which it is not.

8. As everyone's attention is misdirected to the adjustment of the card on the table, place your right hand casually over the cards you hold in your left hand and palm the top card, the spectator's card. "Ah, I think the trick will work," you exclaim. "You have placed the card absolutely correctly! What is the name of that card?"

9. He names his card, and you say, "I don't think it is. Will you turn it face upwards?" As he turns the card and all attention is misdirected toward it, move your right hand with the palmed card at a normal speed to the packet at your right, drawing it inwards and adding the palmed card. Rest your fingertips on the center of the card and continue, "You see, it isn't your card. You thought you saw your card among those you were holding, but actually it has been at the ninth position in *my* packet all the time. Look—here is my ninth card!"

Turn the top card of your packet and show that it is his card.

THE TANTALIZER

In this trick there is an element of sly humor which should be capitalized upon. A card is selected and returned to the pack. The whole pack is dealt into two piles, one of which you keep.

The spectator cannot find his card among those dealt him, hence you deal your pile into two piles in the same way as before; but he still cannot find his card among those given him. This continues until what you are doing dawns on him—and, sure enough, when only one card remains this is the chosen card.

1. Glimpse the bottom card of the pack and bring it to the top in the course of an overhand shuffle. Spread the pack and have someone remove a card and show it to everyone; as this is being done, cut the pack, backslipping the top card, your key card, onto the lower portion. Keep your gaze averted from the pack.

2. Have the card replaced upon the lower portion, and replace the upper portion. Shuffle the cards, using the Key Undercut Shuffle, which will not separate the key card from the chosen card; then have someone make as many complete cuts as may be desired.

3. Take the pack and run through the cards as though searching for the card. Find your key card; the card above it is the spectator's card. Counting his card as one, count twenty-two cards to the left, and cut any cards over twenty-two to the bottom. If there are not enough cards to bring you to twenty-two, continue the count from the bottom and cut the required cards to the top.

In either case, the spectator's card is placed twenty-second from the top.

4. "I'll do this trick a little differently," you say, and deal the pack into two piles, one for the spectator and one for yourself. In this, and in every subsequent deal, always give him the first card, and always deal the cards face downwards.

5. Ask the spectator if he sees his card among those he holds. He will not. Have him discard his cards.

6. Take your pile, which you have dealt neatly to keep the cards in order, and deal two more piles. Ask him if he sees his card in his pile. He will not. Have him discard his pile.

7. Take your pile, deal two more piles, and ask if he sees his card, which he will not. Have him discard his cards.

8. Take your pile and deal two more piles. He will not find his card among those he holds.

9. You now have three cards in your hand. Deal two more

piles, in which he will receive two of the cards and you will receive one. Ask him if his card is one of the two he holds. It will not be.

10. Glance at him wryly and say quizzically, "Well?" You now both know that the card face downwards before you is his card, and usually your audience will be amused. Have him name his card, turn over the one before you and show that is his card.

UNDER YOUR HAT

Five cards are sealed in an envelope before one of them is chosen. Although the envelope remains in view at all times, propped against a borrowed hat, the chosen card vanishes from the envelope and is found under the hat.

1. Borrow a pack of cards, a sheet of paper, two felt hats, and an envelope. Place the hats, crown downwards, on the table and

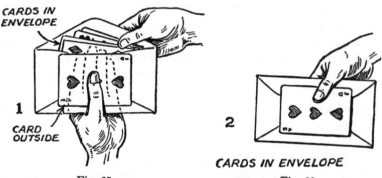

CARDS IN ENVELOPE

1

CARD OUTSIDE

2

CARDS IN ENVELOPE

Fig. 65   Fig. 66

stand to its left. Tear the paper into five slips and hand them and the cards to a volunteer spectator, instructing him to have five spectators each freely select one card, to give each of these spectators a slip of paper, and then to lay the pack aside.

Request the spectators to write the names of their cards on the slips of paper. This done, have your assistant collect the five cards and hand them to you.

2. Take the envelope in your left hand and hold it as in Fig. 65. Apparently slide the five cards into it, but actually allow four only to enter, keeping the face card—which you note (say it is

the two of diamonds)—on the outside under your left thumb (Fig. 66).

3. Seal the envelope naturally and pass it, with the card concealed behind, to your right hand, dropping them into one of the hats. You must not be hasty or furtive in doing this. There is no reason why anyone should suspect what you are doing.

4. Walk away a few paces, pause, and turn back. Remove the envelope from the hat, then turn the hat over and place it, brim downwards, on the table, the card dropping onto the table top where it is concealed by the hat. Saying, "I'll place the envelope here in this makeshift easel," stand it upright in the crease of the hat, which you deepen to accommodate it.

5. Instruct your assistant to take the other hat and collect the written slips after they have been folded or crumpled. Next invite him to reach into the hat and mix them thoroughly, pick one at random and hand it to you. Casually open it and, regardless of what is written on it, ask, "Will the gentleman who wrote the two of diamonds—" (or whatever your glimpsed card may be) "—step up and take the envelope?" *Do not add to or change the wording in any way.*

Without showing the slip to the spectator (unless by chance it bears the name of the card you glimpsed), direct him to take the envelope and open it. As he does this, unhurriedly and absently put the slip in your pocket, concentrating all your attention upon the spectator.

6. Tell him to take the five cards from the envelope and call their names. He finds four cards only—the two of diamonds is missing.

7. You look at him, smiling, then turn to the audience and say, "The card has vanished!" Turn back to the spectator, saying, "Perhaps it's under the hat." He lifts the hat and finds the missing card!

By the law of averages, once in five times the name of the glimpsed card and the name written on the slip will coincide. When this happens, hand the slip to the spectator when he comes forward, saying, "That is your handwriting?" and when he confirms this, continue with the trick. The feat is strengthened immeasurably when this occurs.

THE OVERHAND SHUFFLE, II

Injog and Break

THE drawback to the undercut and throw, after jogging a card in the overhand shuffle, is that frequent repetition would reveal to a keen observer the fact that only half of the deck is being shuffled. To obviate this difficulty, recourse is had to the formation of a division between the jogged card and the cards below it, which are to be kept intact and returned to the top of the pack. This division is termed a *break*, and the method of forming it is as follows:

1. Undercut half the cards, injog the first card, and shuffle off in the manner already explained.

2. Preparing for a second overhand shuffle, pat the upper side of the deck square with the flat right fingers, then place the right thumb against the end of the jogged card and the right middle finger against the outer end. Press the thumb *upwards* and inwards, bending the protruding end of the jogged card upwards as it enters the pack, thus making a division or break between it and the cards below it.

3. Grip the whole pack firmly between the right thumb and middle finger, lift it, and begin another overhand shuffle in the usual fashion. Shuffle freely until the break held by the thumb is reached, then throw the whole of the packet below it on the top in one block.

Thus the same result follows as that obtained by the undercut; apparently the deck has been freely shuffled twice.

We have found that most beginners cannot learn this sleight from a printed explanation, whereas an ocular demonstration enables them to do it in a few minutes. The difficulty seems to be in understanding the action of the thumb on the jogged card, with the result that it is pushed flush with the other cards and so lost. To avoid this fatal error, let the tip of your thumb touch the end of the jogged card and rest it there for a fraction of a second. Then, as you press your middle finger against the outer end of the deck, push the end of the jogged card upwards and inwards, and the break will be formed automatically under the thumb as it presses firmly against its end of the pack.

OVERHAND BREAK CONTROL

This method of controlling a card returned to the pack is the same as the overhand shuffle control already given, save that in this case the injog and break is used in place of the undercut.

1. After a card has been selected, begin an overhand shuffle and, when about half the cards are in the left hand, extend that hand and have the chosen card placed on top of those you hold.

2. Run three cards flush on top of the chosen card, injog the next card, and shuffle off.

3. Perform the action described in step No. 3 of the injog and break; that is, form a break under the jogged card with the right thumb, by bending the protruding end of the card upwards as the right hand takes the pack.

4. Shuffle off the cards above the break, and drop the cards below it on top. The chosen card is four from the top.

5. If your trick requires the placement of the chosen card at the top, you can shuffle the four top cards to the bottom, injog the next card, and shuffle off. Form a break at the injog, shuffle down to it and throw the four bottom cards on top—in other words, repeat the overhand break control shuffle.

OVERHAND LIFT SHUFFLE

To a certain extent the same objection that we have noted with regard to the undercut and throw method applies to the use of the break. If used constantly without any variation it would be possible to detect the fact that a portion of the deck is kept intact. The lift shuffle obtains the same result as both the preceding methods in *one shuffle* and is therefore the most perfect partial false shuffle extant. Here is the method:

1. Let us suppose that a small number of cards, up to say eight or ten, must be retained intact on the top of the pack in the course of an overhand shuffle.

Begin by lifting the whole pack with the right hand, holding it by the ends between the third (top) phalanges of the thumb and middle finger.

2. As the first movement of the shuffle, pull off these cards into the left hand. Bring the deck down on top of this packet (A) and pull off another packet (B) with the left thumb. *At the same moment* that the deck strikes the left palm, press the tip of the right ring finger against the end of the first packet (A), pressing its inner end against the right thumb at the second joint and thus holding it firmly.

3. After releasing packet B, lift the right hand, carrying away the remainder of the deck *and* packet A gripped between the

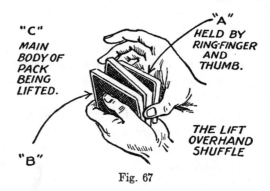

"C" MAIN BODY OF PACK BEING LIFTED.

"A" HELD BY RING-FINGER AND THUMB.

THE LIFT OVERHAND SHUFFLE

"B"

Fig. 67

ring finger and the thumb. Packet B completely conceals this move (Fig. 67).

4. Continue the shuffle until all the cards between the middle finger and the thumb have been shuffled off, then drop packet A intact on top of all the cards in the left hand.

A few minutes' practice will enable you to make this lift of the special packet smoothly and imperceptibly. We know of no other sleight in the whole range of card conjuring which is so valuable and so easily learned. A judicious mixture of the shuffle and undercut (overhand shuffle control), the shuffle and break (overhand break control), and the shuffle and lift (overhand lift shuffle) will baffle the keenest and most skeptical observer.

Naturally the top card can be controlled in this way just as easily as can a small number, but this is only one of the several uses to which the sleight can be put.

A very effective use is for gathering several chosen cards and retaining them on the top of the deck, although they are replaced separately and the pack is shuffled each time. To do this, start with the deck in the left hand. Undercut the bulk of the cards with the right hand, and thrust forward the left for the replacement of the chosen card on top of that packet. Then execute the lift sleight in the first movement of the overhand shuffle, and finally drop the lifted packet on top of all. Repeat the moves for the remaining cards, and you have all the chosen cards on the top of the pack. Remember, however, that the order they are now in is the reverse of that in which they were replaced.

LIFT SHUFFLE FORCE

It is often necessary to compel a spectator to take a certain card. This is termed *forcing*, and there are a number of ways in which it can be done, some of which will be discussed later. It must always be borne in mind that a force is only successful when the spectator is convinced that he has had a free choice. If he has any suspicion that he has been made to take a certain card, then the glamour of its later discovery is tarnished. The lift shuffle affords a method of forcing that is not only easy but also convincing.

1. Have the card to be forced on the top of the deck; shuffle it to the bottom and back to the top.

2. Tell a spectator that you are about to shuffle the cards, and request him to call "Stop" at any moment that he pleases. Execute step No. 2 of the overhand lift shuffle.

3. Continue the shuffle without pause, taking off cards with the left thumb in small packets. At the moment the spectator calls stop, bring the right hand down and release the lifted packet on top of the cards already in your left hand, as you say, "Here? Very well."

4. Extend your left hand to him to take the top card of that packet, that is to say, the card to be forced.

The action is so natural that many of the best cardmen use this force in preference to any other. It should not be necessary to reiterate that you must not look at the cards while shuffling. Keep your gaze fixed on the spectator, watch his lips, and you will note the exact moment he is about to call stop and act accordingly.

By having several cards that are to be forced on the top of the deck, you can force them in rapid succession in the same way. When the first card has been taken, place the cards in your right hand under those in your left, and simply repeat the procedure with a second and third spectator.

SPREAD AND BREAK

A modern and inartistic way of controlling a card after its replacement in the pack is to cut off half the cards with the right hand and thrust out the left hand for the spectator to place his card on the left-hand packet. The cut replaced, the tip of the left

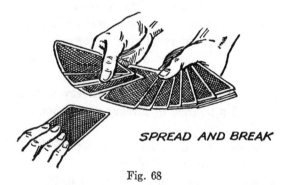

SPREAD AND BREAK

Fig. 68

little finger is inserted secretly between the two packets, that is, above the chosen card. This method is bad, first, because the spectator is given no choice as to position in the placing of his card, and, second, because the bending of the little finger is generally noticeable.

Instead, spread the cards fanwise with both hands, in the same way as when offering the pack for the selection of a card. Move your hands toward the spectator as you ask him to replace his card. At the moment he is about to do this, make an opening in the middle of the spread (Fig. 68), reach forward and *take* his card as with a forceps, by closing the cards on it and immediately drawing your hands back. The insertion of the left little finger between the packets will be covered completely in the action.

Holding a Break

When a break is made by the insertion of the tip of the little finger, a common error is to hold the break in the same way, that is, by keeping the little finger tip inserted between the two portions of the pack. The correct procedure is this:

When the break has been formed by the insertion of the little finger tip, square the deck with the right hand, the fingers at the outer end and the thumb at the inner end. Grip the pack momentarily with the right thumb and fingers, holding the break

HOLDING THE BREAK. LITTLE FINGER IS NOT INSERTED IN PACK BUT HOLDS AGAINST BREAK

Fig. 69

with the thumb, and withdraw the little finger. Immediately press it against the side of the deck as in Fig. 69.

It will be found that the break can be held quite securely in this way, and the right-hand side of the deck can be shown freely as well as the outer end. The holding of the deck, therefore, appears to be perfectly regular. This is most important, since the break is of great use in card conjuring and to hold it correctly is essential to clean manipulation.

When a chosen card has been returned to the pack and a break above it has been secured by the left little finger, it can be brought to the top of the deck easily and quickly in the following manner:

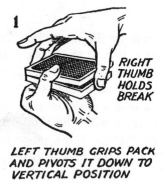

RIGHT THUMB HOLDS BREAK

LEFT THUMB GRIPS PACK AND PIVOTS IT DOWN TO VERTICAL POSITION

Fig. 70

1. Square the ends of the pack with the right hand, then grip it firmly between the right thumb at the inner end and the fingers at the outer end, the thumb holding the break (Fig. 70).

RIGHT THUMB STILL HOLDS THE BREAK

Fig. 71

2. Change the grip of the left hand by seizing the left side of the deck at the middle, near the edge between the tip of the left thumb on the back and the tips of the fingers on the face.

3. Maintain the pressure of the right thumb and fingers on

the ends of the pack, and with the left hand turn the left side of the deck downwards to the regular position for an overhand shuffle (Fig. 71).

4. The break will be retained by the pressure of the right thumb, and you go at once into an overhand shuffle. Shuffle freely until the break is reached, then throw the remainder of the deck on top, bringing the chosen card to the top of the pack.

TRICKS WITH THE OVERHAND SHUFFLES

THE SEVENS

The following trick, a good one, makes use of the overhand shuffle to force a card and to bring a number of required cards to the top of the pack so that they can be used in the course of a "coincidence" trick. Four cards are selected, apparently by purest chance, and the cards prove to be the four seven-spots, a remarkable violation of the laws of probability.

1. To prepare for the trick place the four sevens secretly on the top of the pack, then force the top card (the first seven) on a spectator by means of the lift shuffle force. Have the spectator place that card face downwards on the table, without looking at it, and place his hand on it. As he does this, place the packet in your right hand under those in your left, so that the remaining three sevens are on the top of the pack. Shuffle by running off two cards into the left hand, drop the pack on them, and pick up the whole pack. One seven will now be on the top and two at the bottom.

At once continue the shuffle as in step No. 2, *retaining top and bottom cards in position*, (see page 6) thus keeping the sevens in the same position, two at the bottom and one at the top.

2. Spread the entire deck face downwards on the table in a neat row, and request the spectator to touch any card. Remove the card and turn it face upwards. Whatever its value, gather up the remainder of the deck and deal beside it, face downwards and in an orderly pile, cards to correspond in number. For example, if the card is an eight-spot, deal eight cards. If the card is a picture card, announce that you will count all such cards as tens

and treat them as such. Thus you have a seven-spot at the bottom of this pile.

3. Repeat the same overhand shuffle, retaining one of the other two sevens on the bottom and bringing the other one to the top of the pack. The position now is that you have a seven on the top and the fourth seven on the bottom.

4. Spread the cards on the table again and request another spectator to touch a card. Remove it, turn it face upwards, gather up the remaining cards and deal beside it, as before, the number of cards to correspond with its value.

5. Shuffle the cards once more, this time simply bringing the bottom card (the fourth seven) to the top. "You will notice," you say, "that your choice of cards is entirely fair. Neither you nor I can know the value of the cards you will select."

6. Have a third spectator touch still another card after you have spread the deck on the table, and proceed in exactly the same way as before. There will then be three piles of cards on the table, and at the bottom of each of them, unknown to the spectators, there is a seven-spot.

7. Turn now to the spectator whose hand still rests on the seven spot which you forced on him at the start of the feat. "Will you, sir, turn up your card and show it to all of us?"

He does so and it is seen to be a seven-spot.

"The vagaries of chance are inexplicable," you observe thoughtfully, "for here we have four cards selected by four different persons in the fairest possible way. The probability of each selecting a card of the same value is so remote as to be practically impossible. And yet—" (slowly turn each of the packets face upwards and show, at their faces, the three remaining sevens!) "—that is exactly what has happened."

The student will be gratified, upon performing this feat, to notice the astonishment which it arouses. This is caused largely because the spectators were not told beforehand just what you proposed to do and for this reason did not scrutinize your preliminary actions so closely as they might have had they known your objective.

This is one of the psychological advantages which the good card conjurer keeps to himself. He does not tell in advance what he proposes to do. If he forewarns his audience, their vigilance will be aroused and they will study what he does to determine how he does it. Since they do not know his purpose, however, they are not alerted and later, when they attempt to reconstruct what has been done, their memory fails them.

This should also make clear why the expert card conjurer rarely if ever repeats a trick for an audience, no matter how great their importunity.

There are two good rules to remember:

1. Never tell your audience the effect of a feat until all the preliminary actions which make it possible have been completed.

2. Do not repeat a trick unless you can produce the same effect by a different method.

Obliging Aces

"I wouldn't want to play cards with you!" is a statement inevitably addressed to a good cardman at some time or other. A good trick to use after someone has made this remark is the following easy feat, which has all the appearance of great skill.

Preparation. Secretly place any nine-spot at the ninth position from the top, with the four aces immediately following it. To do this while openly toying with the cards and carrying on your part in the general conversation, spread the cards with the faces towards you. Spot an ace and cut the pack to bring it to the top. Then run through the cards and slip each of the other three aces to the top in turn.

Next find any nine-spot and slip that to the top. Turn the deck face downwards and shuffle overhand thus: Undercut about two-thirds of the deck, run four cards, injog the next card, and shuffle off. Undercut to the jog and throw on top. Repeat the same shuffle, and you will have placed eight cards on top of the nine-spot and the aces will lie in the tenth, eleventh, twelfth, and thirteenth positions as required for the trick.

Procedure. Now we are ready for the feat itself:

1. Presuming that the conversation has been about gamblers and poker playing, offer to give a little demonstration, under very strict conditions, by having the spectators themselves name the numbers at which certain cards are to be found. Shuffle overhand,

using the overhand break control to return the arranged cards to the top of the pack.

2. Invite a spectator to call any number between ten and twenty. Suppose fourteen is called. Deal fourteen cards face downwards in a pile, and lay the remainder of the pack aside. Pick up the fourteen cards. "You named the number fourteen," you say. "One and four make five so I shall take the fifth card." Deal four cards face downwards, take the fifth card and lay it aside face downwards.

Drop the cards remaining in your hands on those just dealt, pick up all, and replace them on the remainder of the deck.

3. Overhand shuffle again, using the injog and break, and again bring the arranged cards into the required position. Ask a second spectator to name another number between ten and twenty. Proceed in exactly the same way as in step No. 2, using the new number. Place the card thus arrived at with the first, also face downwards.

4. Have a third spectator name a number and so arrive at a third card. Place it with the other two.

5. "I want one more card," you say. "This time I'll leave the choice of a number to pure chance." Shuffle overhand again, using the overhand lift shuffle this time but being careful to have more than nine cards in the first packet. This shuffle will return the nine-spot to the top of the pack, and the ninth card under it will be the fourth ace. Turn the top card, the nine, then deal and place the ninth card with the other three cards you have found and laid aside.

"In spite of the fact that you named any numbers you pleased and that the last card was determined by chance alone, look what has happened!" Turn the four cards face upwards with a flourish. They are the four aces!

LEAPFROG

Here we have a rather striking discovery. A selected card leaps into view over the backs of the others.

1. Following the usual routine a card is freely selected, noted, returned to the pack, and controlled to the top.

2. Shuffle the card to the bottom and retain it in that position.

3. Key undercut about one-third of the deck, and place the

packet on top so that about one-third of its length protrudes outwards, being careful not to expose the bottom card in making the cut.

4. With the tip of the left forefinger pull down the outer end of the selected card at the bottom of the upper packet until it is bent almost at right angles (Fig. 72). "If there is one game the cards love, it's leapfrog. Watch!"

5. Have the chosen card named, and instantly let all the cards of the upper packet escape from your left thumb and fingers and press the forefinger hard against the end of the bent card. All the

1
FOREFINGER BENDS THE
CHOSEN CARD DOWNWARD
FORMING
A SPRING.

Fig. 72

2
GRIP
RELEASED
ON TOP
CARDS
WHICH ARE
SHOT ON TO
THE TABLE.

Fig. 73

cards of this packet will fall upwards and outwards, turning face upwards as they fall on the table, except the bottom card, the chosen card, which will also turn face upwards but will be retained against the bottom card of the deck by the left forefinger. Fig. 73.

6. Raise your left hand and display the card thus extending face outwards from the top of the pack, which faces you.

SPECTATOR'S CARD TRICK

Sooner or later you will meet the man who insists upon taking the pack in his own hands and then challenges you to do a trick. The following feat is useful on such occasions:

1. Secretly glimpse the top card of the pack, which we will

say is the four of hearts. False shuffle the cards, retaining the four of hearts at the top.

2. Hand the pack to a spectator, saying, "It is curious that so many people suspect a magician of conniving and subterfuge. I assure you that the things I do simply happen—I have no control over the cards. To show you what I mean, let's pretend that you are the magician and I am the spectator. First of all, you must spread the cards and invite me to remove one."

3. Remove a card and glance at the card guardedly. You do not care what card it is since it plays no part in the trick, but a good satiric impersonation of a canny spectator can be amusing. "Now," you say, "tell me to replace my card." When he does so, cautiously insert the card about halfway down in the pack and push it flush. Have him square the cards. "You see how simple it is? Now all you have to do is find my card and produce it in some surprising manner."

4. Your assistant will be forced to admit that he cannot do this. "Then you must appeal to others," you say. "Ask this gentleman. Have him name some number, say between ten and twenty, and no doubt my card will be at this number."

5. Someone names a number, say fourteen. Have your assistant deal fourteen cards face downwards, reversing their order. "My card was the four of hearts," you say, naming the card you glimpsed in step No. 1. "Look at the next card." He looks at the card at the top of the rest of the pack, but it is not your four of hearts. Have him turn it face downwards and replace the dealt cards on the pack.

6. "Horrible experience, wasn't it?" you say sympathetically. "It has happened to me, too. But when something goes wrong, always blame it on the spectator. Tell him he wasn't concentrating. Then ask someone else to name a number, say a number between twenty and thirty."

7. Have a second spectator name such a number. Let us say it is twenty-five. Have your assistant deal twenty-five cards face downwards, thus reversing their order, and look at the next card on the pack. It still is not your four of hearts. Have it turned face downwards and the dealt packet replaced.

8. "Well," you say, "you've not done very well, have you?

I'm afraid I'll have to take over." Take the pack from him and give it a little shake. "I think that will do it," you comment. "Now, I believe in the happy medium. The first number was fourteen and the second was twenty-five, and the difference between the two is eleven. To find my card I will deal eleven cards, like this—" (here you deal off eleven cards) "—and the next card is my card, the four of hearts!" Turn this card face upwards and show that it actually is the four of hearts.

The trick is entirely automatic if the above procedure is followed. It is only necessary to have the first spectator name a number between ten and twenty, the second a number between twenty and thirty.

A POKER PUZZLE

"Can you deal a good poker hand?" is a question which is almost certain to be asked after you have shown your prowess with cards. The routine which follows has been arranged to convince the questioner that you can.

1. "Can I deal a good poker hand?" you repeat. "The answer to that is—yes and no. I'd better show you what I mean. No doubt you've read articles on the methods used by the gamblers —everyone has heard of second dealing and bottom dealing, although very few persons have seen these sleights performed. In poker, the gambler arranges to get the high cards of course. Let me show you the usual method. I'll use the four kings." As you are talking in this vein, run through the cards with the faces toward yourself and, as you come to each king or ace, slip the kings to the bottom and the aces to the top of the pack. Do this casually without explaining what you are doing.

2. Take off the four kings and show them. "Four kings make a good hand," you say, "so the gambler places the cards he wants on the bottom of the pack." Place the four kings on the bottom.

3. "We shall suppose it is a five-handed game. The gambler deals four cards, but when he deals one to himself he pulls off the bottom card, so." Do this openly, laying the king face downwards before you.

4. Continue the deal in the same way, each time pulling out a king for yourself as you explain that by years of tedious prac-

tice the gambler can make this false deal imperceptibly. When you have dealt yourself the four kings from the bottom, deal the next five cards in the ordinary way. You have dealt five hands of five cards each and you show that you have the four kings.

5. "That is the gambler's method," you say. Gather up the other four hands carelessly in any order but without disturbing their sequence, and drop them on top of the pack. Do not expose the face cards, which are the four aces. Drop your own hand with the four kings on the pack last of all. The deck is now stacked to give you the four aces on a deal of five hands.

6. False shuffle the pack by undercutting not more than twenty cards, injogging the first card and shuffling off. Form a break at the injog, shuffle to the break, and throw the cards below it on top, thus returning the top thirty cards to their original position.

"That is the way a gambler does it," you explain. "However, you asked me if I could deal a good poker hand, and I must remind you that I am not a gambler and therefore never use the gamblers' methods. If I did try to deal myself a good hand I'd use magic, like this. Watch my hands and see if you can find any fault with the way I deal."

7. Deal five hands of five cards each in the regular way. "Did you notice anything unusual with the deal?" you enquire. "Of course not. Yet I dealt myself the four kings. Look!" Pick up your hand and, holding it well squared, turn it face upwards, showing a king at its face. "The four kings!" Remove the top card, exposing an ace. "Ah, something's gone wrong!" you exclaim disgustedly. Pause for a second, then brighten, saying, "Oh, well! I imagine that four aces are good enough!"

Spread the other four cards you hold showing that they are the aces.

X

FALSE SHUFFLES AND CUTS

OPTICAL SHUFFLE

WE HAVE already studied one overhand shuffle by means of which the whole pack is kept in a prearranged order while apparently becoming well mixed. The same effect is obtained with the optical shuffle, so called because for deceptiveness it depends upon an optical illusion.

1. Begin an overhand shuffle by undercutting about two-thirds of the deck.

2. Bring the right-hand packet down in front of the packet remaining in the left hand, its lower side striking against the left palm. Raise the left thumb in the usual action of drawing off cards from the right-hand packet, but actually do not remove any; simply slide the thumb over the back of the uppermost card as the right hand lifts its packet away intact.

3. Tilt the left-hand packet back against the left thumb with the left fingers. Drop a packet from the top of those held by the right hand against the face card of the left-hand packet.

4. Let the cards in the left hand fall forward onto the left fingers, and repeat the action in step No. 2.

5. Repeat step No. 3, and continue until the cards in the right hand are exhausted.

At first thought this pretense of removing cards with the left thumb appears to be too audacious, but when it is smoothly done the illusion is perfect, as a few trials before a mirror will show.

CHARLIER SHUFFLE

This shuffle is also called the "haymow" shuffle. It is unique among card sleights in that neatness of execution is not required;

in fact, it is most effective when done rather clumsily. Although expert cardmen affect to disdain it for that reason, the wise operator values it for its effect on laymen, to whom it is the most convincing false shuffle extant. The shuffle, though apparently thoroughly mixing the cards, really leaves them in the same condition that a simple complete cut would do. The moves are:

1. Hold the pack face downwards in the left hand, as for dealing. Push off a small packet, some five or six cards, with the left thumb and take it in the right hand between the thumb on the back and the fingers on the face (Fig. 74).

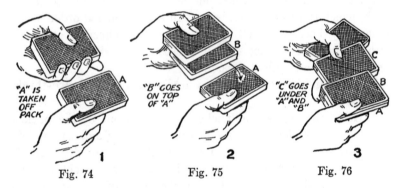

Fig. 74   Fig. 75   Fig. 76

2. Raise the left hand slightly and with the left fingers push out a small packet *from the bottom* of the deck. Take this packet in the right hand *on top* of the first packet, by lifting the right thumb and then dropping it on top (Fig. 75).

3. Lower the left hand a little, push off another small packet *from the top* with the left thumb, and take it with the right fingers *underneath* the cards in the right hand (Fig. 76).

4. Push out another small packet *from the bottom* with the left fingers, and take it *on top* of the cards in the right hand.

5. Continue as above until all the cards have been transferred to the right hand.

As has already been stated, this shuffle leaves the deck in the same condition as it would be after one complete cut. By jogging the first packet from the bottom of the deck—that is, by making it protrude inwards from the packet in the right hand—a break can be formed at the jog at the end of the shuffle, and a single cut will return the pack to its original condition.

This shuffle is especially useful for keeping a small packet of cards in sequence, for which purpose neither the overhand nor the riffle shuffle is suitable.

We would emphasize the need for making the shuffle rather slowly and roughly, with great emphasis on the fact that it *mixes* (do not use the word "shuffle") the cards thoroughly.

THE CUT

It is the invariable rule in games of cards to have the deck cut after it has been shuffled. How far back the custom arose it is

FALSE CUT

**BOTTOM HALF IS PULLED OUT.
TOP HALF DROPS ON LEFT PALM.**
Fig. 77

impossible to tell, but it is easy to account for the origin of such an exhibition of good faith. "Trust ivvrybody but cut the ca-ards," as the Irish cynic said. The magician, therefore, must prove his good faith by cutting the cards, which he does—but in such a way as not to disturb the arrangement he has already made. In other words, he uses a false cut. False cuts are made in different ways according to whether the whole deck is to remain in the same order or whether a small packet of cards is to remain intact on the top or on the bottom of the deck.

First Method: *Retaining the Whole Deck in the Same Order.*

1. Hold the deck in the left hand, face downwards and near the outer corners, between the third (top) phalanges of the thumb on one side and of the middle finger on the other. The tip

of the forefinger rests against the middle of the outer end, and the ring and little fingers rest free.

2. With the right hand seize the lower half of the deck near the inner corners, between the thumb on one side and the middle finger on the other, the forefinger extended and resting on the back of the top card near the middle of the outer end (Fig. 77).

3. With a rapid backward and then upward movement of the right hand, pull out the lower half of the deck—the right forefinger sliding on the back of the top card without moving it—and place the packet on the table.

4. With the right hand take the remaining cards in the same way, with the same backward and upward movement, and place them on top of the other packet with a slight slap.

Properly timed—that is to say, when you are addressing some quick remark to a spectator and looking at him—this false cut is undetectable.

Second Method: *Retaining the Whole Deck in the Same Order.*

1. Place the deck on the table at A.

2. Cut off a small packet and place it at B, not far from A. Continue in the same way, cutting packets from A and placing them at C, D, E, and F.

A   B C D E F

3. Pick up packet B and place it on C, pick up BC and place the combined packet on D, and continue in exactly the same way with packets E and F.

4. Leaving a few cards at A, place the rest of the cards in your left hand. Begin to square the deck, then pretend to notice that you have overlooked the packet A. Drop all the cards you hold on it, then pick up and square the whole deck.

The action keeps the cards in the same order throughout and is completely deceptive to the uninitiated.

Third Method: *Retaining a Small Packet of Cards on the Top of the Deck.*

1. Hold the deck in the left hand by the sides, near the ends, between the thumb and middle finger near the corners, with the

forefinger on the back and the ring and little fingers resting free.

2. With the right thumb and middle finger at the far end cut off from the top a packet consisting of a few more than the cards to be retained, and place it on the table in front of you.

3. Take hold of the free end of the deck with your right thumb and second finger, and with both hands place the pack on the cut. Let the outer sides of both packets come flush, but hold a break at the inner sides with the left thumb tip (Fig. 78).

FALSE CUT
Fig. 78

4. Draw both packets toward you, the action enabling you to get a firm grip of the packets; then lift the whole pack.

5. With the right thumb and second finger draw off small packets from the top, letting them fall to the right, one on top of the other, until you reach the break. Finally take the last cards intact and drop them on top of all the rest.

This is one of the easiest and most deceptive false cuts extant. The whole of the action is done by the thumbs and middle fingers only, the cards being held as openly as possible. An even pace, not a rapid one, should be maintained. The break will be found by the right thumb solely by the sense of touch; there is no need to look at the cards.

Fourth Method: *Retaining a Small Packet of Cards on the Bottom of the Deck.*

1. Hold the deck in the same position as for the third method.

2. With the right thumb and second finger draw off about two-thirds of the pack and place it in front of you.

3. Take hold of the free end of the packet in your left hand,

between your right thumb and second finger. Place the packet on top of the cut, the outer sides flush, but holding a break at the rear sides as explained in step No. 3 of the third method.

4. Draw off the top packet to the break and drop it on the table. Continue drawing off small packets and dropping them one on top of another until the pack is exhausted.

This method of cutting is called a *running cut* and is in common use among card players. The action should be timed at the same pace as the preceding sleight. It is so well covered that the keenest observation from the front will fail to detect any irregularity.

PALM CUT

Retaining a Small Packet on the Top of the Pack. Let us suppose that you have the four aces on the top of the pack and, having executed the overhand break shuffle and retained the aces in that position, you wish to cut the pack yet keep the aces on the top. Make these moves:

1. Hold the deck in your left hand, as for dealing, and square the ends with the right thumb and fingers. Palm the aces in your right hand by the second method. It is not necessary to take off only the four aces; just make sure that you lift five or six cards in making the necessary break.

2. With the right thumb and fingers cut off about half the deck, and drop the cut in front of you on the table.

3. Bring the right hand back squarely over the remainder of the deck in the left hand; grasp these cards, adding the palmed packet, and drop all on the tabled packet.

Immediately after the palmed packet has been added to the cards in the left hand, it is essential that the forefinger be bent inwards so that its tip rests on the middle of the back of the added packet as seen in Fig. 60.

TRICKS WITH THE SHUFFLES AND CUTS

AN INCOMPREHENSIBLE DIVINATION

The old war horses, as we have mentioned, are good tricks, if only because they have survived the passage of time. This feat is one of the most satisfying in the whole range of card magic, it is easy of accomplishment, utterly baffling to one unfamiliar with its mechanics, and has a simple plot that is easily understood.

To perform the trick, quietly remove the following cards in sequence, using any suits: A-2-3-4-5-6-7-8-9-10-Joker. The ace is the top card, the joker the bottom card.

1. Holding the cards face downwards, you apparently mix the cards well but actually perform the Charlier shuffle. In squaring the cards secretly sight and remember the top card, which let us say is a 4.

Tell a spectator that you want him to think of a number between 1 and 10 and that, while you turn your back, you want him to transfer this number of cards, one by one and silently, from the top to the bottom. Illustrate by transferring three cards from top to bottom, which will make the new top card a 7. Subtract this number from 12, and remember 5 as your key number.

2. Turn your back as the spectator follows instructions, and when he is finished turn back and take the cards. Spread them and without seeming to count, run through the packet and cut the card at your key number, the 5th from the top in this case, to the top. Request the spectator to name the number of which he thought, and when he does so turn the top card face upwards and show that its value corresponds to his number.

3. Turn the top card—which let us say is a 6—face downwards, and again subtract its value, 6, from 12, arriving at a new key number of 6.

"This time I want you to think of a number, and I also shall think of a number," you remark. "Take the cards and transfer as many to the bottom, one by one, as the number of which you are thinking."

4. Turn away until he has completed the transfer; then take the cards, saying, "I am thinking of the number 6," naming whatever key number you arrived at before giving him the cards. Transfer one less than this number to the bottom (5 in this case), and turn the 6th card face upwards at the top. It will have the same value as the number of which he thought. Turn the card

face downwards and deduct its value from 12; if the card is a 9, then 3 will be your new key number.

5. "Now I shall name a number while you think of one," you continue. "Let me see . . . well, I'll take the number 3," naming the key number. Turn your back once more as the spectator transfers as many cards to the bottom as the number of which he is thinking. Take the cards, saying, "I named the number 3." Transfer one less than your key number, in this case 2 cards, and turn the next card face upwards at the top; its value again corresponds to the number of which he thought.

6. Note the value of this number as before, and deduct it from 12. If the card is an 8, your new key number will be 4. Hand the cards to the spectator, turn away, and have him think of a new number and transfer that number of cards from top to bottom. Turn back and, standing a short distance away, request him to deal cards onto the table. When he has dealt one less than the key number, in this case 3 cards, request him to stop the deal. "What is your number?" you ask, and when he has named it, you say, "Turn up the next card." He does so and again its value corresponds to that of his number.

Occasionally someone will attempt to confuse you by refraining from transferring any cards. In such a case, when you count down to your key number the joker will be turned up, and you say, "There's a joker in every pack, and there's also a joker in every gathering. You're the joker in this case; you didn't think of any number at all," and the spectator will be forced to admit that this is the case.

When the joker is the top card, consider its value to be 11, which when deducted from 12 tells you that your next key number will be 1, the top card. Take advantage of the circumstance by taking the packet, giving it a little shake, having the spectator name his number, and turning the top card to show that its value corresponds.

CIRCUS CARD TRICK

In the old days this trick was used by cardsharpers to fleece the unwary. It is an amusing swindle for use with a small group when presented as legitimate entertainment.

1. Have someone shuffle the pack, and in taking it back glimpse the bottom card for use as a key card. Spread the cards and ask a spectator to remove one, having him show it to everyone. This is important, for later you may need witnesses.

2. Have the card replaced, and place the key card above it by using the key undercut method. Shuffle the pack by means of the key undercut shuffle, which will leave the chosen card and the key card somewhere near the middle. Next have someone make *two* complete cuts.

3. Take the pack and assert that you can find the spectator's card unfailingly by sense of touch alone. Deal the cards face upwards, watching for your key card. When it falls, the next card dealt is the chosen card. Deal this card, maintaining an impassive expression; remember its name and deal a half dozen cards more.

4. Finally push a card off the pack, feel its face with your right index finger tip, hesitate, and feel the card again. Glance up triumphantly, tapping the card. "I'll wager you a nickel that the next card I turn over is your card!"

5. Having seen you deal the chosen card, and mistakenly believing that you will turn over the card at the top of those you hold, some people will gleefully accept your wager. You then say, "My grandfather was right. He said that you should never bet on a sure thing!" Reach out and turn the chosen card *face downwards*, thus living up to your promise to turn this card *over*.

The trick causes a good deal of laughter, and since this was your objective you naturally refuse to permit the loser to pay his debt.

Black Jack, Detective

A chosen card and the jack of clubs, which you introduce as Herlock Sholmes, a detective card, are placed in different parts of the pack; yet, after several cuts, when the cards are dealt the detective card and the chosen card come out together.

1. Have a card freely selected from a shuffled pack, and leave it in the spectator's hands.

2. Run through the pack to find the jack of clubs, and as you do this note and remember the top card, which let us say is the ace of hearts. Remove the jack of clubs and place it to one side.

3. Square the cards and hold them face downwards in the left hand. Using the key undercut, strip out the lower half of the pack with the right hand, and have the chosen card replaced on top of the cards remaining in the left hand, which will place it above the key card, the ace of hearts.

4. Hand the other packet to a second spectator, inviting him to take about half the cards, place them on top of the chosen card, and square the cards.

5. Have a third spectator place the jack of clubs on top of these, and then have the remaining cards of the cut placed on top of all.

6. Finally have a fourth spectator make two complete cuts, which will more or less bring the pack back to about its original order.

7. Holding the pack as for the glide, patter about the marvelous accomplishments of your detective card, the jack of clubs, and order it to find and arrest the chosen card. Deal from the bottom, placing the cards face upwards until you deal the ace of hearts, your key card.

8. Glide back the next card, the chosen card, and continue the deal with the cards above it until the jack of clubs appears. Now draw out the glided card and place it face downwards on the face-upwards jack.

9. Have the chosen card named and then with the jack flick the other card over, showing that your Herlock Sholmes has succeeded in his mission.

XI

THE DOUBLE LIFT AND TURNOVER

WHEN used in moderation and properly done this sleight is one of the most useful and deceptive of modern card sleights. Unfortunately many card men do it badly and far too often. We would caution the student first to learn to execute the sleight perfectly and then to use it sparingly and discreetly.

As the name implies, the sleight consists of lifting two cards as

DOUBLE LIFT
Fig. 79

one, turning them over on the deck, and then turning them face downwards again. The moves are as follows:

1. Hold the deck face downwards in the left hand, practically in the position for dealing but with the left thumb extended against the left side. With the right hand square the ends, and at the same time wedge the pack slightly by pressing back with the tips of the last three fingers on the outer edge, the tip of the index finger resting on the back near the outer end.

2. With the tip of the right thumb lift the inner end of the

top card and then the inner end of the second card about a quarter of an inch (Fig. 79). The wedging of the pack enables you to do this with ease and certainty. Press the tip of the left little finger against the side of the second card to hold the break thus made. Do not insert the tip of the finger into the break.

3. Make another squaring motion with the right hand, and then remove it to make some gesture appropriate to your patter.

4. To lift the two cards as one, turn your right hand palm upwards and seize the inner right corners between the tips of the thumb above and the index and middle fingers below. Turn the hand over to the left and lay the two cards face upwards on the

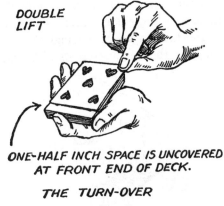

DOUBLE LIFT

ONE-HALF INCH SPACE IS UNCOVERED
AT FRONT END OF DECK.

THE TURN-OVER

Fig. 80

deck so that the lower ends protrude inwards about half an inch (Fig. 80). Move the right hand away toward the right, running the tip of the thumb along the ends of the two cards. This is done to make certain that the ends of the two cards will be perfectly aligned. The pressure of the left fingers on the cards, forcing them against the ball of the thumb, will insure the sides being flush.

5. The second card having thus been shown, turn the two cards face downwards again as follows: With the right hand palm upwards, seize the index corner, turn the two cards face down, and lay them flush on the pack.

Done properly, the sleight is a very easy one. The two cards must be made ready and the hands separated before the lift and turnover is made. Too often the move is made immediately after fumbling in getting the two cards separated at the inner ends. To attain an easy and natural action in performing the sleight, first turn a single card in the manner described, and then turn two cards as one, copying the action closely.

DOUBLE-LIFT GLIMPSE

The double lift affords a subtle method of glimpsing a chosen card when it is on the top of the pack. Ostensibly to show that the card is not at the top, make a double lift, showing the second card and naming it. Replace the two cards, then show the bottom card and call its name. Turn the pack face downwards and lift the top card, holding it so that only you can see its face, and again name the second card. Note what it really is and replace it. Miscalling a card can often be used to good advantage.

DOUBLE-LIFT CARD REVERSES

One of the most effective climaxes for a quick trick is that in which a chosen card is found face upwards when the deck is spread face downwards on the table.

The following methods of secretly reversing a card make use of the double lift:

(A) *Top Card Reversal.* In this method the top card is found reversed in the center of the pack.

1. Hold the pack face downwards in the left hand, as for dealing, with the chosen card at the top.

2. Double-lift the two cards at the top and turn them over as one card, placing them face upwards on the pack. Square the pack and call attention to the card face upwards at the top.

3. Turn the left hand palm downwards, thus turning the pack face upwards. Shift the grip of the left hand, so that it holds the pack as for the glide. Tap the face card and call attention to it.

4. Draw off the top card, now the lowermost card, which was originally second from the top. It will be face downwards. Turn it face upwards, mention its name again as if refreshing your memory, and thrust it into the center of the pack.

5. Make a single complete cut with the face-up pack, and the chosen card is reversed at the center.

Note that the chosen card may be glimpsed by tilting the pack a little toward yourself in making the cut.

In this and the next two methods, cards with a white border should be used.

(B) *Second Card Reversal.* In this method the chosen card is second from the top.

1. Hold the pack face downwards in the left hand, as for dealing. Turn the top card face upwards, and square it on the deck. As you do this, secretly push the second card a little off the pack to the right, and slip the tip of the left little finger under it. Call attention to the card face upwards at the top.

2. Grasp the two cards at the ends, near the right corners, between the right thumb and middle finger. The break under the two cards held by the little finger makes this easy. Slide them to the right as one card, until their left side rests on the left finger tips.

3. Drop the left thumb under the pack and flip this over to the right so that it falls face upwards upon the two cards held by the right hand. Call attention to the card at the face of the pack.

4. Square the pack and make one complete cut, placing the chosen card at the center in reversed position.

(C) *Second Card Reversal.* The chosen card is second from the top.

1. Hold the pack face downwards in the left hand, as for dealing. Turn the top card face upwards and square it on the deck, at the same time secretly pushing the second card to the right with the left thumb and slipping the left little finger tip under it.

2. Grasp the two cards above the little finger tip at the ends, near the right corners, between the right thumb and middle finger. Slide them to the right so that their left edges rest on the left finger tips.

3. Push the third card, which is face downwards, off the pack with the left thumb. Flip it face upwards on the pack with the two cards held by the right hand. Calling attention to it, push it off the pack with the left thumb and take it squarely under the two held in the right hand. This hand now holds three cards,

the middle of which is face downwards, although the audience believes that only two cards are held.

4. Replace these cards on the pack, flipping them face downwards. The chosen card is face upwards below the top card. Make one complete cut to carry it to the center of the pack.

This method differs from the others mainly in that the pack is not turned over.

TRICKS WITH THE DOUBLE LIFT

RAPID TRANSIT

Two cards taken at random, one held by a spectator and the other by the magician, change places instantly. Any deck can be used and there are no duplicates.

1. Have a spectator shuffle the deck to his own satisfaction.

2. Take the cards, square them, and under cover of that action prepare for the double lift by raising the inner right corners of the two cards at the top of the pack and holding the break with the left little finger.

3. Making a gesture toward the spectator with your right hand, say, "Neither you nor I can possibly know what this top card is, hence I will use it for my experiment. Let's see." Lift the two cards as one and turn them face upwards on the deck—showing, say, the king of spades. Let everyone see this card plainly.

4. Turn the two cards as one, face downwards, on the deck and with the left thumb push off the top card onto the table close to you. This is an indifferent card the face of which the onlookers never see. You say, "I'll take this king of spades."

5. Square the deck again with the right hand and get the next two cards ready for the double lift. Then touch the card on the table with your right forefinger tip, saying, "Remember, this card is the king of spades." Turn the next two cards face upwards on the deck—showing, let us suppose, the eight of hearts. Name it as you allow everyone to see its face plainly, then turn the two cards face downwards as one.

6. Reach out toward the spectator with your left hand and thumb off the top card, the king of spades. Have him place his

hand on it. "Now, sir," you say, "you have the eight of hearts, and I have the king of spades." Lift up the indifferent card, look at its face without allowing any one else to see it, and lay it on the top of the pack. In the meantime you have pushed the top card off the pack to the right a little and have taken a little finger break under it, the eight of hearts, so that you are ready to make another double lift.

7. Continue, "It was an Irishman who said that, not being a bird, he could not be in two places at the same time. Einstein says that no material object can do that, but these poor philosophers know nothing of magic. Watch!" Wave your right hand over the cards and say "Arbadacarba—that is abracadabra backwards, the most powerful magic spell extant—and here I have your eight of hearts—" (make the double lift showing that card) "—while you have the king of spades!" The spectator turns his card and there it is.

Turn your two cards face downwards on the pack and shuffle casually thus disposing of the indifferent card.

Mastery of this feat will convince the student of the great value of the double lift and turnover. Again we urge that it must not be used too often but only for certain tricks which depend upon its use.

THE TREY

Bits of byplay are useful when interspersed among more pretentious card tricks. The following is amusing:

1. While running over the faces of the cards, as if merely toying with them, spot a trey. Look up and make a remark to someone, at the same time dividing the deck at that card, taking it and those to the right of it with your right hand. Separate your hands a foot or so, making a gesture with your right hand, for example; then bring your hands together again, but this time with the right hand *under* the left. The three-spot will now be at the top.

2. Make the double lift and turnover, calling attention to the card thus brought into view, whatever it may be.

3. Turn the two cards face downwards and remove the top card, the trey. Holding it face downwards, ask someone, "Would

you like to see me turn this card into a tray?" Receiving an affirmative answer, take a cigarette and knock the ash onto the back of the card. "You see, it's an ash tray!"

4. Continue, saying, "Really, that's more than a pun!" and turning the card over show that it is a *trey*.

AMBITIOUS CARD

A favorite trick with audiences is that in which a card, placed in the deck, mysteriously comes to the top over and over again. The feat is suitable for either intimate or platform work, and when done with good humor it is very amusing and intriguing.

Preparation. Run through the cards and cut the eight of clubs to the top, then find the nine of clubs and place it above the eight.

Procedure. Part One:

1. Shuffle the pack overhand, retaining the eight and nine of clubs at the top. Explain that you have found that in every deck there is one card that is more ambitious than the others. It likes to be "top dog" and always pushes its way to the top of the pack.

2. Make the double lift and turn over, showing the eight of clubs; then turn the two cards face downwards as one, saying, "Apparently the eight of clubs is the ambitious card in this deck."

3. Remove the top card, the nine of clubs, and without showing its face thrust it into the outer end of the deck at the center, leaving about an inch of the card protruding. Put the tip of your right middle finger on the face of the card, covering the index, and tip the pack upwards so that the face of the card is "accidentally" exposed. With the index concealed, the nine will appear to be the eight.

4. Push the nine flush into the pack. Tap the top card, turn it over, and show the eight of clubs. Be sure to turn the card in exactly the same way as you did in making the double lift. Pause a moment for the effect to sink in, then turn the eight face down.

Part Two:

1. Undercut the pack for an overhand shuffle, run one card, injog the next, and shuffle off. Form a break at the injog, shuffle to the break, and throw the remainder on top. This action places the eight of clubs second from the top.

2. Continue, "Let's try with another card." Make the double lift and turnover, and again show the eight of clubs. Pretend to be surprised and then recall that it is the ambitious card. Turn the two cards downwards as one, remove the top indifferent card, and thrust it into the center of the deck. Do not allow its face to be seen.

3. Tap the top card, turn it face upwards with the same action as before, and show the eight of clubs once more.

Part Three:

1. Shuffle overhand, running the top card to the bottom and shuffling off onto it. Retain this card at the bottom during a second shuffle.

2. Tap the top card, saying, "It isn't here." Turn it, show it, and turn it face downwards again.

3. Turn the pack face upwards and say, "Here it is! On top of the bottom," showing the eight of clubs.

Part Four:

1. Holding the pack face upwards, prepare for a double lift. Take the two cards as one, face upwards, and thrust them into the center of the deck at the outer end. Call attention to the eight of clubs, which protrudes for about half its length.

2. Grasp the pack by its inner end, between the right thumb on its face and the fingers on the back, and turn it face downwards. Place it in the left hand, taking it by the sides—between the thumb on one side and the middle, ring, and little fingers on the other—with the forefinger curled underneath.

3. Tilt the pack upwards a little to show that the eight is actually in the center, then slope it downwards slightly. Grasp the protruding cards with the right hand—the thumb at the top, the forefinger pressing against the outer edges, and the middle

finger on the face—and push the two cards, always as one, into the deck about half an inch. Draw the upper card outwards again, so that the tip of your left forefinger can engage the outer end of the lower card, and push it flush into the deck. This action is hidden from the spectators by the upper card and by the sloping position of the pack.

4. Push all the cards under the protruding card inwards half an inch. Grasp a few cards at the top of this packet with the right thumb and middle finger at the inner end. Draw these cards away inwards, then drop them on the top of the pack as you say, "We'll put the eight of clubs a little deeper in the deck." Actually this action has brought the eight of clubs to the top of the pack.

5. Push the protruding card, supposed to be the eight, flush and square the pack.

6. Tap the top card, turn it face upwards, showing that it has arrived on the top again. After a moment, turn it down again.

Part Five:

1. Shuffle overhand by undercutting the deck, injog the first card, and shuffle off. Undercut below the injog and throw on top, returning the eight of clubs to the top of the pack.

2. Take the lower half of the deck in your left hand. Give it to a spectator, asking him to shuffle the cards. As he does this and while all attention is on him, palm in your right hand the top card of the portion you still hold, and hold the packet in that hand. A moment later take these cards with your left hand and give them to another spectator *on your left*, asking him to shuffle them.

3. "Let's see if the eight of clubs will be ambitious when you handle the cards," you say. Have each of the two spectators turn the top card of his packet. Neither of the cards is the eight.

4. "The eight wouldn't perform for you because you didn't treat it with kindness. You shuffled too roughly altogether," you say. "Another reason is this: Here's the card!" Place your right hand with the palmed card under your coat on the left side and produce the card at its finger tips as if you drew it from your vest pocket. "I told you—it's an ambitious card."

THROUGHTH AND CONSEQUENCES

Although the handling of the cards in this fine trick, in which a chosen card reverses itself in the pack, is not that of the orthodox double lift, the principle involved is the same and for that reason we include it in this section.

1. Have a card drawn from a shuffled pack and, when it is returned, control it to the top by means of the overhand break control.

2. Hold the pack in the left hand, as for dealing, and place the right hand over it, with thumb and fingers at the ends. Under cover of the hand, push the top card a quarter inch off the pack to the right. Insert the tip of the left little finger under it and square the cards. Thus you have a little-finger break under the chosen card.

3. Riffle the outer end and remove any card from the center of the pack, placing it face upwards at the top. Square this card with the one face downwards under it, by running the right fingers and thumb along the ends of the pack, saying: "Is this your card?" As you say this, lift the two cards above the break as one, with the right second finger and thumb at the ends near the right corners. Hold them about an inch above the pack, and press down on the top card with the right index finger, thus bending the cards and preventing them from spreading.

4. Simultaneously drop the left thumb under the pack and turn the pack face upwards on your left palm, saying: "Then is the card at the bottom your card?" Receiving a negative response, place the two cards held by the right hand on the face of the pack.

5. Turn the pack face downwards, and make a complete cut as you say: "In the past ten years science has made such enormous strides that few laymen comprehend its achievements. The theory of *throughth* is one of these new findings. Formerly it was believed that if I were to turn this pack face upwards, like this—" (here you delicately turn the pack face upwards, holding it in the left hand) "—every card in the pack would be turned face upwards. Scientists have now discovered that this need not be so. By utilizing throughth, the new dimension, I will

turn the pack face downwards, like this—" (and you turn the pack face downwards) "—and no doubt you are certain that every card in the pack is facing downwards. Actually every card *but one* was turned. One card remained face upwards, while the others rearranged their molecular structure, disintegrating for a fraction of a second, and passed through the throughth card.

"This concept is so revolutionary that the average person cannot grasp its implications. For this reason, I offer proof."

Spread the pack face upwards on the table. The chosen card lies face downwards among the cards. Delicately push this card forward with the right forefinger. Have the spectator name his card, and slowly turn it over. "One card did not turn with the others. That card was your card. You see, I applied throughth —and that's the consequence."

INSIDIOUS DR. FU LIU TU

In this urbane feat the celebrated Chinese magician, Dr. Fu Liu Tu, comes to your rescue and reveals the name of a chosen card.

Preparation. Secretly purloin one of the aces from the pack which you will use for this trick, and upon it ink a half dozen Chinese characters, copying some *real Chinese writing*. Do not trust to your imagination and draw some nondescript hiero-glyphics which you think look like Chinese.

Since the trick is such a good one and you will do it often, it would be a good plan to have an extra ace thus prepared. Carry it in your wallet and when occasion arises secretly add it to your deck. Place this card at the bottom of the pack, face upwards.

Procedure. The steps are as follows:

1. Ribbon spread the cards face downwards on the table, bunching the bottom cards so that the reversed card will not be seen (see situation B of the spread and turnover, page 44). Have someone draw a card and show it to all.

2. Gather the pack and hold it in your left hand in position for an overhand shuffle, holding it so that the reversed card cannot be seen. Undercut about half the pack and begin an overhand shuffle, inviting the spectator to replace his card wher-

ever he likes. When he places his card at the top of the portion in your left hand, drop the cards remaining in your right hand on top of all, placing the reversed card above the selected card.

3. "Here's a curious thing I stumbled onto the other night," you say, spreading the cards from your left into your right hand. "There's a card in the pack . . . ah, here it is!" When you come to the reversed card, cut all those above it to the bottom. Remove the card with the Chinese characters with your right hand, holding it face upwards with its outer end sloping toward the floor so that all can see the cryptic characters.

4. Turn the left-hand back upwards and point to the writing with the index finger, at the same time glimpsing the chosen card, which is now at the top by means of top card glimpse No. I. "That was written by the celebrated Chinese conjurer, Dr. Fu Liu Tu, and it reveals the name of your card." A little anxiously, ask: "Do you read Chinese?" The spectator assures you he does not. "Ah, that's a shame!" you say. "Well, I'll have to translate for you. It says that the card you chose is the ten of diamonds!" Here you name whichever card you just glimpsed.

5. Insert your left little finger under the top card (the chosen card). Casually drop the "Chinese magician's" card face upwards on top of it. Grasp the two cards, as one, at the ends between the right thumb and middle fingers. Lift the two cards about an inch, then drop the left thumb under the deck and flip the deck face upwards on the left fingers. Place the two cards at the face of the pack, cut the pack, and the chosen card is reversed at the center.

Little attention is being paid to what you do, for so far as the spectators are concerned the trick is over. Now you say: "Do you know how Dr. Fu Liu Tu knew the name of your card?" When there is a general disclaimer, spread the pack face downwards in a long ribbon, showing the chosen card face upwards at the center of the spread. "Very simple. The card is standing on its head."

XII

THE PASS

T HE first exposition of the principles of card magic was published in 1769 by the French writer Guyot, and he it was who first laid down the dictum that mastery of the pass is the first requisite of the art of conjuring with cards. His actual words were: "Before risking an attempt at these kinds of Recreations, you must know how to make the pass."

All succeeding French writers on the subject followed his lead and insisted that the pass is the first essential. Professor Hoffmann, whose book *Modern Magic*, published in 1876, was the first scientific treatise on magic in the English language, took most of his material from the French authors and followed their example in this respect. He described the pass as "the very backbone of card conjuring," and for years this statement was accepted as gospel by all our other writers, who reiterated without exception that, "without the pass, card magic is impossible."

The pass is a very difficult sleight to master, and this insistence on its indispensability makes it easy to understand why the would-be card conjurers of the last century, after a prolonged and vain struggle with the intricacies of this sleight, finally decided that conjuring with cards was not for them and turned to some easier hobby.

After all, the principal use of the pass is to bring a chosen card from the middle of the pack to the top, or vice versa; but it was not until the turn of the century that card conjurers freed themselves of this inhibition and devised easier methods of attaining the same objective.

We have shown in the preceding pages that the pass is not

153

absolutely essential to card conjuring and that any trick can be performed without using it. Any intelligent person who really has the urge to perform good tricks with cards, and to do just that in the shortest possible time and with the simplest possible methods, has been shown how it can be done. The methods which have been given are simple, but always in conjuring the simplest methods are the most effective. By mastering the simple, natural ways of making all necessary moves which we have given you, you will have made great progress in a surprisingly short time.

Although we have relegated the pass to the role of a subsidiary sleight, we do not wish you to think that it is unimportant. When it is done *well* it is the most important sleight in card magic; but, because it is so difficult to master, it should be the last sleight which the novice should be called upon to learn. We can think of no good reason why you should not be performing good card magic in the months it will take you to learn to do the pass well; we do not want you to wait until you have learned this difficult sleight.

And if you never do learn this sleight you still will be able to perform mystifying, amusing, and deceptive tricks of card magic by using the other methods which we have given you; these you will continue to use in any case, even when you have mastered the pass.

THE PASS

The Grip:

1. Hold the pack, back upwards, in the left hand as for dealing, but with the thumb flat against the left edge of the cards (Fig. 81).

2. Insert the little finger tip between the two portions of the pack to be transposed.

3. Place the right hand over the pack, the fingers at the outer end and the thumb at the inner end (Fig. 82).

Left-Hand Action:

1. Grip the upper packet firmly, by pressing down upon it with the first phalanx of the left ring finger, thus gripping it

firmly between that finger and the little finger. Press the first phalanges of the index and middle fingers on the top of the pack.

2. Straighten the left hand so that the fingers, between the first and second phalanges, are parallel with the back of the left hand. The upper packet will be carried to the right between the left little and ring fingers, which continue to grip it firmly.

Right-Hand Action:

1. Now press upwards against the outer end of the lower portion with the right middle finger, which bends inwards to exert

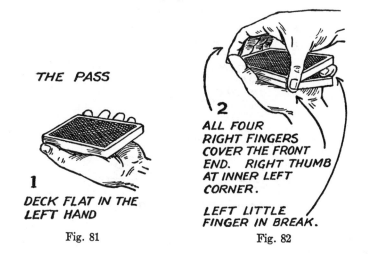

THE PASS

1
DECK FLAT IN THE
LEFT HAND

Fig. 81

2
ALL FOUR
RIGHT FINGERS
COVER THE FRONT
END. RIGHT THUMB
AT INNER LEFT
CORNER.

LEFT LITTLE
FINGER IN BREAK.

Fig. 82

that pressure upwards. This pivots the lower portion between the middle finger and the thumb of the right hand, slanting it upwards to the right, until it moves above the other packet (Fig. 83). Note particularly that the left thumb remains pressing against the left edge of the packet.

2. Close the left fingers into the palm, carrying the upper packet below the other, where it rests on the left palm.

3. Close the packet originally at the bottom on top of the other portion, and square the pack. Do not extend the left forefinger in the action. This is a very common and serious fault.

The classical pass just described requires a cover of some sort, and in general the advice given is never to do it immediately after a card has been returned to the deck or while the eyes of the spectators are fixed on the performer's hands. There are certain covers, however, which allow one to do just that; since they are known to very few, we shall set them forth here. The first and one of the best follows.

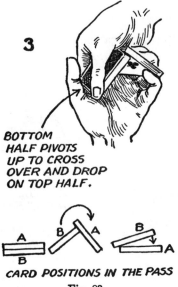

BOTTOM
HALF PIVOTS
UP TO CROSS
OVER AND DROP
ON TOP HALF.

CARD POSITIONS IN THE PASS

Fig. 83

RIFFLE PASS

1. A card having been returned to the deck, preferably somewhere above the middle, and a break having been secured above it with the little finger, square the cards so that the outer end of the deck, visible to the spectators, is perfectly regular.

2. Riffle the outer ends of the cards with the right middle finger, the hands moving slightly upwards and separating in the action. This is the feint.

3. Bring the right hand over the deck to repeat the riffle; the moment the hands begin to move upwards, make the pass and immediately riffle the ends of the original lower packet, which is still held between the right middle finger and thumb, the cards falling upon the original upper packet, now at the bottom.

4. Finally riffle the whole deck and square up.

Smoothly done, the transfer of the upper packet to the bottom appears to be a part of the riffle.

SPREAD PASS

Make the pass in the usual way, but, as soon as the upper part of the deck has been transferred to the bottom, spread the cards of that packet with the left thumb on the fingers of the left hand, stretched out flat for their support. At the same time make a short quick remark, such as, "You see your card remains in the middle of the deck!" Close the spread smartly and execute an overhand shuffle, controlling the card as may be necessary.

A slight swing of the hands from left to right will help to make it appear that the spreading of the cards is all that has taken place.

SPRING PASS

The idea behind this cover is the same as that in the riffle pass—the distraction of the attention of the spectators by a secondary artifice.

1. With the pack held flat in the left hand, the left little finger holding a break above the chosen card, with your right hand lift the greater part of the cards above the break between the tips of the thumb and middle finger at the ends and spring them onto the cards in the left hand.

2. Square the deck and repeat the same action.

3. Square the cards again, make the pass, and immediately lift the packet now held between the right thumb and middle finger and spring these cards onto the cards in the left hand.

Correctly executed, the pass is quite invisible. The spectators have become used to the fall of the cards into the left hand, and this maneuver covers the actual movement of the pass.

TRICKS WITH THE PASS

OFF AGIN, ON AGIN, FINNEGIN!

When the student has progressed to the point of making the transposition of the two packets fairly smoothly, the following feat will afford excellent practice:

A spectator shuffles the deck, which is then placed on the magician's left hand. The magician cuts at any point indicated by the spectator, and the spectator removes the top card of the lower packet, notes what it is, and replaces it. By simply tapping the back of the card with the packet he holds, the magician causes the noted card to vanish and the spectator verifies the fact by examining the packet.

The cards are replaced on the magician's left hand and he taps it once more making the missing card reappear.

1. Have a spectator shuffle the pack and then place it face downwards on your left hand.

2. Have him indicate the point he wishes you to cut at, and lift off the cut, taking the cards between your right thumb and middle fingers. Invite him to lift off the top card of the remainder, note it, and replace it.

3. Announce that by merely tapping the back of that card with the other packet you will make it vanish. Strike downwards with your right hand, so that the packet it holds will hit the top card of the left-hand packet near the edge of its right-hand side, and count "One!"

4. Repeat the blow, but this time press the tips of the left fingers against the top card of the packet in the right hand and backslip the card onto the lower packet as the right hand moves smartly upwards. Thus the backslipped card is instantly and imperceptibly folded onto the back of the top card of the lower packet, the noted card. Count "Two!" and rapidly repeat the blow with your right hand, counting "Three! Off agin, Finnegin!"

5. "Would you believe it," you say, "your Finnegin card has vanished. Look!" The spectator removes the card on the top of your left-hand packet; the moment his eyes travel to its face, make the pass, but retain your grip of the lower packet with your right thumb and forefinger and carry it away, leaving the original top half of the deck lying on your left hand. All eyes will be on the card the spectator removes, and by the time they are looking at your hands you have the chosen card snugly on top of the packet in your right hand.

6. "Your Finnegin card has vanished completely, as you can see." Holding the packet upright, spread the top cards with your left thumb; or you may allow the spectator to take the packet and run through the cards.

7. Square the packet on your left hand as before. Repeat exactly the same actions as in steps Nos. 3 and 4, counting and saying, "On agin, Finnegin!" Have the card named and have the spectator turn it face upwards himself.

Note that, when a spectator removes the added card, your hands should be close together, but, immediately the pass is made, move the right hand away a foot or more.

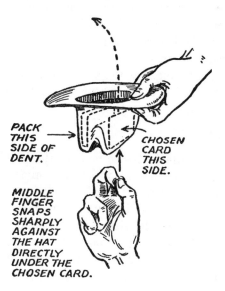

PACK THIS SIDE OF DENT.

CHOSEN CARD THIS SIDE.

MIDDLE FINGER SNAPS SHARPLY AGAINST THE HAT DIRECTLY UNDER THE CHOSEN CARD.

THE KANGAROO CARD
Fig. 84

Kangaroo Card

Magicians refer to tricks that are quickly performed and have a strong element of novelty as "quick tricks." Here is such a feat which can be performed anywhere that a man's felt hat is available:

1. Have a card selected and returned to the deck, forming a

break above it as described under the spread and break (see page 120).

2. Ask, "Who has a felt hat?" at the same time riffling the cards; then make the riffle pass, immediately afterwards executing an overhand shuffle and retaining the chosen card at the top of the pack.

3. Take the hat proffered to you. If it does not have a lengthwise crease in the crown, put one in it. Place the pack in the hat and, the moment your hand is out of sight of the spectators, push the top card into the pocket at one side of the crease and drop the pack into the pocket on the other side (Fig. 84).

4. Ask a spectator to assist you, and have him hold the hat by the brim above the level of his eyes.

5. "I call this the kangaroo card trick," you explain, "because some of the cards jump like kangaroos." Snap the crown of the hat with your index finger at the side which contains the chosen card (Fig. 84), making it fly up out of the hat very much like a startled kangaroo.

RIGHTING A WRONG

This is one of those feats—so dear to the hearts of all audiences, and all magicians—in which the mystifier apparently himself becomes the mystified. He fails but in the end turns the tables in striking fashion. Nothing pleases an audience more than to catch the infallible wizard in an apparent failure. They enjoy his discomfiture for the moment, then are amazed and intrigued when he emerges triumphant.

1. Have the pack shuffled, take it back, and have any card removed and noted.

2. Have the card replaced and pass it to the top.

3. Shuffle overhand, running seven cards above the chosen card, which becomes the eighth card from the top.

4. Invite the spectator to name his card, which let us say is the ace of hearts, and instantly say, "Eight cards down!"

5. Deal seven cards and prepare for a double lift, as you say, "Will you name your card again?" Turn over the two cards and show an indifferent card, which let us call the nine of clubs.

6. Appear disconcerted by your failure, and turn the two

cards face downwards as one. Remove the top card—the spectator's ace of hearts—and toss it face downwards on the table to one side. "Let's get rid of that nine of clubs," you say grimly. "Don't worry. I'll find your card, if it takes all night."

7. Shuffle overhand, running seven cards above the top card as in step No. 3. The nine of clubs, which is supposed by the audience to be on the table, is now eighth from the top.

8. Weigh the cards in your hand, as if making a calculation, and say in a puzzled tone, "That's very curious. I still get a vibration of eight. Perhaps your card is at eight this time."

9. Deal seven cards and say, "This card *could* be any card—except, of course, the nine of clubs, which is on the table—but my vibrations tell me that it is your card."

10. Turn the eighth card and show that it is the nine of clubs. "Curiouser and curiouser!" you say. "This can't be the nine of clubs. I put it on the table. Unless . . .!" Turn over the table card and show that it is the spectator's ace of hearts.

BLINDFOLDED PACK

Matter through matter has been a favorite subject for the stage illusionist. The same effect is had in this trick employing a pack of playing cards and a borrowed handkerchief. It was an especial favorite with the late Nate Leipzig.

Preparation. Secure a small quantity of diachylon (lead plaster) from your druggist. If he does not have it in stock he can secure it for you. Work a small pellet of the lead plaster until it is tacky, and affix it to one of the buttons of your left sleeve, where it is readily accessible. You will also need an opaque linen handkerchief.

Procedure. The steps are as follows:

1. Take a shuffled pack; have a card removed and noted by all. Have it replaced in the pack and secure a left-little-finger break above it as described under the spread and break. Glance about you and ask for the loan of a handkerchief. Make the pass, bringing the chosen card to the top as you advance to accept a proffered handkerchief. If it does not appear to be opaque, say, "On second thought, I'll use my own," and remove it from your pocket.

2. Hold the pack in your left hand and draw back the left sleeve a little with the right hand, grasping it at the wrist and securing the pellet of wax on the right second finger. As you do this say, "Let's find a good place to do this trick. The floor is probably best." If it is not desirable to sit on the floor, move toward a near-by table. In either case, affix the wax to the back of the chosen card near the middle.

3. Let us say that you sit cross-legged on the floor. Still holding the pack in your left hand, show the handkerchief on both

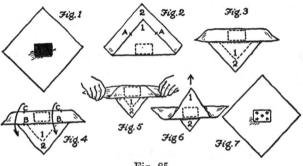

Fig. 85

sides. Drape it over the pack and in arranging it press down on the wax through the cloth, which will make the card adhere firmly to the fabric. Place the pack on the floor before you (as shown in Fig. 85-1), with the handkerchief centered *over* the pack. Corner No. 1 is nearest you.

4. Fold corner No. 1 over toward corner No. 2. As you do this and the following arrangement, you say, "I used to do a trick in which I was blindfolded and found the chosen card, but this became very tiring. Now I do the trick the easy way. I blindfold the pack instead."

5. Grasp both layers of the handkerchief at the points marked A-A (Fig. 85-2). Lift the handkerchief and the card, which adheres to it, upwards between the thumb and middle fingers of each hand, and corners Nos. 1 and 2 will fold downwards over the chosen card on the side away from you, concealing it from the audience (Fig. 85-3).

6. Place the folded handkerchief on the pack (as shown in Fig. 85-4), with the hidden card directly over the pack.

7. Using both hands, place the thumbs at B-B and the fingers at C-C (Fig. 85-5), and fold the cloth over inwards toward yourself once. Replace the folded handkerchief over the pack.

8. Draw corner No. 1 from under the folded handkerchief on the side away from you (Fig. 85-6).

9. "In this trick I don't tell you the name of your card. The pack itself, even though blindfolded, will reveal your c. d." Grasp corners Nos. 1 and 2 and pull them in opposite directions. The handkerchief unfolds and the card seems to melt through the fabric to appear face upwards (as in Fig. 85-7). "You see? Your card has popped straight up through the handkerchief. A very clever pack, don't you think?"

The folding of the handkerchief, once learned, is done in a matter of seconds.

Double Speller

A trick which can be performed in a minute or two—and one that has strong elements of surprise—is valuable for the early part of an impromptu performance. The following is an excellent feat of this type, both in technique and effect:

1. Have a card drawn, noted by all, and replaced in the pack, securing a little finger break above it by means of the spread and break. Make the pass, bringing the card to the top, as you say, "Everything in nature is vibration. Since this is so, cards also vibrate, and to find your card I have only to measure the vibration of each card."

2. Place the pack to your left ear, ruffle the cards, and say, "Hmmm," in a thoughtful tone. Shuffle the cards overhand, placing one card above the spectator's card so that it is second from the top.

3. Again ruffle the cards at your ear, saying, "I think I have it. A very definite plus-nine vibration." Push the two cards at the top of the pack to the right a little with the left thumb. Grasp the top card, an indifferent one, and turn it face upwards on the pack. In squaring the cards, slip the tip of the left little finger under the second card in preparation for a double lift.

4. "Your card?" you enquire. Receiving a negative response, say apologetically, "Of course, I didn't really think it was. The cards don't really vibrate, you know." Grasp the two cards above the little finger break at the ends near the right corners, and perform the double-lift card reversal, method (b) described on page 144.

5. Square the pack, and the chosen card is reversed at the top; that is to say, it is the lowermost card as you hold the deck face upwards in the left hand. Explain your action in turning the pack by saying hopefully, "I know it isn't the bottom card, either . . . but, on the other hand, it *might* be. *Is* it?" The spectator naturally says that it isn't.

6. Look a little woebegone, cluck a little, and then brighten. "I'll find it another way!" Rap the pack on the table as if to square it, with the faces of the cards toward the spectator, at the same time glimpsing the reversed card at the top, which will be facing you. Let us say it is the ace of hearts.

7. Hold the pack face upwards in your left hand, and thumb through the cards as if in search of the proper one. Actually, push one card into the right hand for each letter of the name of the card you just glimpsed—*a-c-e o-f h-e-a-r-t-s*, taking them one under the other and not reversing them. Place these cards at the top of the pack, that is to say, underneath the reversed card.

8. Note the card now at the face of the pack—say the four of spades—and push one card into the right hand for each letter in its name as in step No. 7, transferring these cards to the top as before.

9. Turn the pack face downwards, saying, "Just as I thought. A very difficult trick, but I have succeeded at last. I give the pack a tiny shake and your card rises to a new position in the pack, which enables me to do this." Deal one card for each letter as you spell aloud the name of the second card—*f-o-u-r o-f s-p-a-d-e-s*—and turn up the last card, showing the four of spades. "There you are—the four of spades!"

10. Seem very happy about the trick and act as though you had finished. Someone will be sure to tell you that you haven't found the correct card. "Not the right card?" you exclaim. "Why, I

was positive . . . ah, now I remember! This trick won't work for a magician. *You* should do the spelling!"

Hand him the pack and have him deal one card for each letter in the name of his card, in this case the ace of hearts. When he completes the deal, his card lies face upwards on the pack, staring him in the face.

XIII

MISCELLANEOUS FLOURISHES

COLOR CHANGE

THE name given to this sleight is a misnomer; it really is the mysterious change of one card for another regardless of suit. The sleight has been termed the *color change* for so long, however, that we shall continue to use the name for the sake of conformity.

Almost all methods of performing the sleight involve the palming of cards. The method we give you is one of the easiest and best.

1. Hold the pack in the left hand, the card faces toward the audience, with the thumb at the top side, the middle, ring, and little fingers at the lower side, and the index finger curled behind the pack and out of sight.

2. Raise the right hand; cover the pack for a moment, curling the top phalanges of the fingers over the outer end; remove and drop the hand. Repeat this once or twice as you comment on the curious properties of this particular pack. These are *feints* to cover the palm which you will make in a moment.

3. Cover the cards with the right hand once more, and at the same time push out the rear card a quarter of an inch with the left index finger (Fig. 86).

4. Curl the right fingers over the outer end as before, and grip the edge of the protruding card in the top phalanx of the middle finger (Fig. 87).

5. Move the right hand outwards and downwards, taking the rear card with it. Close the right middle, ring, and little fingers slightly, and the card will buckle into the palm, where it can be retained while the right forefinger points to the face card of

the deck. At the same moment place the left index finger at the outer end of the pack, squaring it should this be necessary.

6. Bring the right hand up to the pack, simulating the action of your previous *feints*, depositing the palmed card at the face of the pack. Without hesitation, move the right hand downwards, as though wiping the cards, and reveal that the card at the face has mysteriously changed. Neatly done, the illusion of a transformation is perfect.

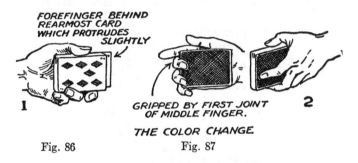

FOREFINGER BEHIND
REARMOST CARD
WHICH PROTRUDES
SLIGHTLY

GRIPPED BY FIRST JOINT
OF MIDDLE FINGER.

THE COLOR CHANGE

Fig. 86   Fig. 87

7. A very amusing bit of byplay which always evokes laughter is to move the right hand to the right side of the body after the change, curling the fingers awkwardly and extending the thumb at right angles from the hand. The audience assumes that you have palmed a card from the face of the pack and sometimes demands that you show the right hand. When this happens, affect to misunderstand, raise your right hand with its palm outwards, and point with the forefinger at the face card, saying, "You see the card has changed," as if you thought they hadn't noticed it.

You should never appear deliberately to *sell* the onlookers. They don't like it and may take their revenge on you at an awkward moment.

DOUBLE COLOR CHANGE

In this transformation, two cards change simultaneously.

1. Take the pack in your left hand, holding it as for the color change with the faces of the cards to the spectators.

2. Move the upper half so that it projects for about half of its length beyond the lower portion.

3. Call attention to the two cards, the faces of which can be seen. Place the right hand over the cards, concealing both packets, once or twice.

4. Palm the bottom card of the upper packet as described under the color change, bring the right hand downwards below the pack, and again call attention to the two face cards. Fig. 88.

5. Bring up the right hand and deposit its card on the face of the upper packet. At the same moment engage the rear card of the upper packet with the tip of the left index finger and

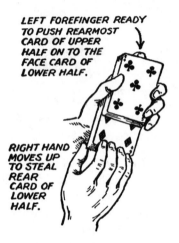

LEFT FOREFINGER READY
TO PUSH REARMOST
CARD OF UPPER
HALF ON TO THE
FACE CARD OF
LOWER HALF.

RIGHT HAND
MOVES UP
TO STEAL
REAR
CARD OF
LOWER
HALF.

DOUBLE COLOR CHANGE
Fig. 88

push this card inwards until it is flush with the lower packet.

6. Remove the right hand and show that *both* cards have changed.

THE CHANGING CARD

In this intriguing conclusion to a trick, one card changes to another before the spectator's eyes. The change is useful when concluding a "location" feat.

1. Have a selected card replaced, and control it to a position second from the top of the pack, using any method of control which has been previously described.

2. Facing left, hold the pack in the left hand face outwards

as for the color change, the sides of the pack parallel to the floor. Draw the top card inwards toward yourself with the right thumb and fingers, so that about half its length projects and everyone can see its face. Secretly engage the outer end of the second card, the spectator's card, with the tip of the left index finger.

3. Tap the projecting card with the tips of the right fingers and claim that it is the spectator's card. When this is denied, move the right hand back to grasp the protruding card at the points marked X in Fig. 89.

REARMOST CARD PULLED OUT HALF
WAY TO BE HELD AT EXTREME END
EDGE BY RIGHT HAND FINGERTIPS.
LEFT FORE FINGER READY TO PUSH
THE NEXT REAR CARD ON TO THE
FACE OF RIGHT HAND CARD.

THE CHANGING CARD

Fig. 89

4. An instant before the extreme tips of the right fingers and thumb grasp the protruding card, push the second card inwards toward yourself and flush with the protruding card, by a *swift* thrust of the left index finger. Close the right fingers and thumb on both cards at their ends, keeping them in alignment. Instantly withdraw the right hand a few inches so that the full face of the changed card is visible. The effect is that the protruding card *visibly* changes into the chosen card.

5. Place the cards, as one card, face outwards on the face of the deck.

SELF-CUTTING DECK

1. Hold the pack in the left hand with the tips of the middle, ring, and little fingers at one side and with the thumb at the other. Place the index finger against the lower half of the pack

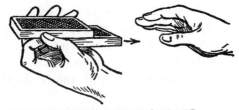

LEFT FOREFINGER SHOOTS LOWER
PACKET BACK TOWARDS RIGHT HAND
WHICH ADVANCES AND CATCHES THE
PACKET QUICKLY.

SELF CUTTING DECK
Fig. 90

at the outer end (Fig. 90). Hold the pack with its sides parallel
to the floor.

2. Snap the index finger inwards sharply, propelling the lower
portion into the right hand, which is held against the body about
six inches from the pack, back upwards, thumb and fingers
separated ready to catch the flying packet.

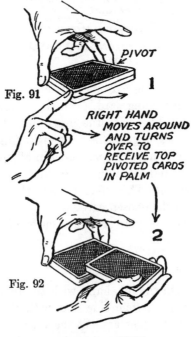

PIVOT

Fig. 91   1

RIGHT HAND
MOVES AROUND
AND TURNS
OVER TO
RECEIVE TOP
PIVOTED CARDS
IN PALM

2

Fig. 92

A PRETTY CUT

A Pretty Cut

1. Hold the pack in the left hand, between the middle and ring fingers at one end and the thumb at the other. The cards are held from above, the palm arching above the pack.

2. Place the right index finger at the inner right corner (Fig. 91). Lift and swing the upper half in a semicircle outwards, the other end pivoting on the left second finger, continuing the movement until the packet drops into the right palm (Fig. 92). Drop the other packet on top.

This is a genuine cut and a pretty one.

Pop-Up Card

Here is an amusing way of revealing a chosen card which has been brought to the top of the pack.

1. Hold the pack in the left hand, face outwards, with the thumb lying flat along the upper side, with the middle, ring, and little fingers at the other side, and with the index finger curled up against the top card at the rear.

FOREFINGER PUSHES THE
REARMOST CARD BACK
AND UP.

THE POP UP CARD
Fig. 93

2. Separate the end of the top card from the other cards with the tip of the left index finger. Request that the chosen card be named; when it is, snap your right fingers, saying, "Card, rise!"

3. Press inwards and then upwards on the card with the left index finger, making it turn between the ball of the thumb and the pack until it swings into the position shown in Fig. 93.

A Bit of Byplay

Incidental bits of business that are done offhand are sometimes remembered when more pretentious effects are forgotten. For this reason, minor byplay should be used whenever possible. You should always give the impression that you do these things on the spur of the moment.

The following is a good trick of this type:

1. Double-lift the two cards at the top of the pack and show them as one. Replace them on the pack, take the top indifferent card, and without showing its face thrust it into the center of the pack.

2. Hold the deck in the left hand in readiness for the color change. Tap the card at its face. Pass the hand over the pack once or twice, and finally make the color change, depositing at the face of the pack the card which should be in the middle.

A trick of this type should be played down. In other words, such occurrences are so common with you that you do not even think this one important enough to comment upon.

Charlier Cut

The Charlier cut is often treated as a fancy flourish, for it has an undoubted fascination for the layman. It is of far greater

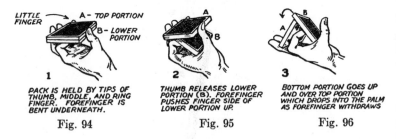

LITTLE FINGER
A - TOP PORTION
B - LOWER PORTION
1
PACK IS HELD BY TIPS OF THUMB, MIDDLE, AND RING FINGER. FOREFINGER IS BENT UNDERNEATH.
Fig. 94

A
B
2
THUMB RELEASES LOWER PORTION (B). FOREFINGER PUSHES FINGER SIDE OF LOWER PORTION UP.
Fig. 95

B
A
3
BOTTOM PORTION GOES UP AND OVER TOP PORTION WHICH DROPS INTO THE PALM AS FOREFINGER WITHDRAWS
Fig. 96

value, however, when used as a method of openly controlling cards, and we shall discuss it in that light. To perform the cut:

1. Hold the pack in the left hand at the sides, between the tips of the thumb and the ring and middle fingers, with the tips of the index and little fingers pressing up against the face card (Fig. 94).

2. Allow the lower half to fall from the thumb onto the palm of the hand (Fig. 95). Press upwards against this packet with the tips of the index and little fingers, moving the pack into the position shown in Fig. 96.

3. Allow the other portion to sink down onto the palm by slightly extending the middle and ring fingers, with the index finger at first supporting it but moving out of the way as the packet nears the palm and the original lower portion folds downwards on top of it.

4. Square the cards by moving the index finger beyond the outer end.

This sleight is usually referred to (improperly, we think) as the Charlier pass.

ACROBATIC ACES

The Charlier cut is put to good use in this surprising feat with cards.

1. Place the ace of hearts at the bottom and the ace of diamonds at the top of the pack, then spread the pack face upwards, showing that there are only the two red aces in the pack.

2. Gather the cards, turn them face downwards, and in squaring them bend them rather sharply downwards; or you can spring them into your left hand if you prefer. Seize the pack between the right fingers and thumb at the ends and riffle the upper half upwards, at the outer end, commenting that the cards are well mixed and showing them. What you have done is bend the lower portion downwards, the upper portion upwards, for a reason which will be apparent in a moment.

3. Hold the pack in position for the Charlier cut and with the right fingers draw away the bottom ace and hold it up for all to see, but as you do this make the Charlier cut without completing it, holding the original bottom packet up a little with the left thumb. You will do this unnoted, because you have misdirected the attention of everyone to the ace which you show. Drop this ace face downwards on top of the original upper portion, and allow the original lower portion to fall on it, squaring the cards.

If you will glance at the pack at this point (as you practice) you will see that there is a crosswise *bridge* in the deck, which you placed there when you bent and riffled the cards at the start. If you now make a second Charlier cut, the pack will split at this bridge.

4. Now take whatever card is at the top of the pack and hold it up with its back to the audience, miscalling it the ace of diamonds. As you do this make another Charlier cut, splitting the pack at the bridge. Prevent the lower packet from dropping on the upper packet as you did before. Saying, "The ace of diamonds also goes somewhere in the middle," drop the indifferent card on the lower packet, and allow the other packet to drop off your thumb and onto it, squaring the pack.

"Now my trick is this," you continue. "The aces have been placed somewhere in the middle of the pack, but they are acrobatic aces and if you give the pack a little shake like this—" (Here you take the cards by a corner and give them a shake) "—they somersault back to their original positions."

5. Lift the top card and show that it is the ace of diamonds, then turn the pack and show the ace of hearts back at the bottom.

Once the Charlier cut has been mastered, the trick itself is practically self-working.

PART TWO

XIV

THE REVERSES

THE revelation of a card face upwards in a face-down deck is a favorite feat with the card conjurer, and a few of these tricks have already been explained. A card reversed in the pack is also used as a secret artifice which makes possible many puzzling feats. There is one cardinal condition that applies to all the tricks in which a card is reversed in the pack—the fact that the principle must never be used with cards having an over-all back pattern. The reason is obvious, for with such decks the slightest spreading of the cards reveals part of the white face of the reversed card.

Cards with a white margin on the back allow for a spread of about three-sixteenths of an inch between cards without exposing any part of the back patterns. In fact, with a card face upwards in the deck, the cards can be spread in a fairly large fan without any risk of exposure.

We have already discussed methods of reversing a chosen card under the double lift (see page 143). Before explaining the best feats in which reversed cards play the leading role, other ways of secretly reversing a card or cards at the top or bottom of the deck must be considered.

First Method

One of the best and easiest ways of reversing a single card, either at the top or the bottom of the deck, is this:

1. Hold the deck in the left hand, turn half left, and at the same time let the left hand drop to the side.

2. Push off the top card with the left thumb so that its side strikes against the side of your leg (Fig. 97). Move the hand

downwards, the thumb still pressing on the back of the card which will make a half revolution. With the fingers press it flush with the other cards and replace the thumb on the top of the pack (Figs. 98, 99).

The whole action takes but a second, and the fact that the left hand is out of sight momentarily will never be noticed.

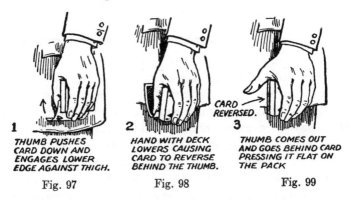

1 THUMB PUSHES CARD DOWN AND ENGAGES LOWER EDGE AGAINST THIGH.

2 HAND WITH DECK LOWERS CAUSING CARD TO REVERSE BEHIND THE THUMB.

CARD REVERSED.

3 THUMB COMES OUT AND GOES BEHIND CARD PRESSING IT FLAT ON THE PACK

Fig. 97   Fig. 98   Fig. 99

Second Method

1. Under cover of squaring the pack, palm the top card.

2. Keep the grip of the first phalanges of the right thumb and forefinger on the right-hand corners of the deck, and turn the hand to a vertical position.

3. Extend the left fingers and insert their tips under the lower side of the palmed card. Flex them and thus draw the card flush against the bottom of the deck, back downwards.

The action is masked by the back of the right hand, which then squares the cards again and is removed.

Third Method

This method makes use of the artifice already mentioned in *throughth and consequences* (see page 150).

1. Hold the pack in the left hand, and secure a break under the top card with the left little finger, conversing as you do so.

2. Withdraw the bottom card and place it face upwards at the top. Give the impression that you are toying with the cards.

3. With the right thumb and middle finger at the ends, lift the

two top cards, as one, about an inch above the pack. Drop the left thumb under the pack and turn it face upwards on the left palm.

4. Place the two cards held by the right hand on the face of the pack. Turn the pack face downwards, withdraw the bottom card, and thrust it into the center of the pack.

The card at the bottom is now face upwards.

FOURTH METHOD

This method may be used to reverse a chosen card in the center of the pack, or to reverse any card at the bottom.

1. Let us say that you have a chosen card at the top of the pack and wish to reveal it reversed at the center. Hold the pack face downwards in your left hand. Place the right hand over it, thumb and fingers at the ends, and lift the inner end of the top card, holding a break under it by pressing inwards with the ball of the thumb.

2. Cut off the top half of the pack with the right hand, still holding the break with the thumb.

3. Drop the left thumb under the packet remaining in that hand, flip it face upwards, and place it on top of those held in the right hand.

4. Place the left hand under the deck, and drop into it all the cards below the break held by the right thumb. Move the left hand away, drop the thumb under this packet and flip it over, face upwards, on the palm.

5. You now hold a packet face upwards in each hand. Ask if either of the face cards is the chosen card. Receiving a denial, place the left-hand packet *under* that in your right hand and square the pack.

6. Ribbon spread the cards on the table and show the reversed card.

To reverse a card at the bottom for use in a reversed-pack trick: Hold the pack face upwards and follow the above through step No. 4. Place the left-hand packet *upon* those held by the right hand. Spread the cards from hand to hand, showing the faces of about three-fourths of the pack but preventing the lowest cards from spreading. Do not explain why you do this. Your reason is that you want everyone to notice that the cards all face in the same direction.

REVERSED LOCATION

It is a wise magician who varies his methods for obtaining his secret objectives, and it is a still wiser magician who sets apart certain methods for certain objectives for use in set tricks. For example, it is not good policy to use the same method for controlling a card twice in one routine. By allocating a certain method to a certain trick and always using that same method in that trick, not only is there less chance of the onlookers detecting your secret operations but your work will be so much the easier and smoother for you than if you made up your mind on the spur of the moment as to which method you would use.

The location by means of a reversed card is excellent for use as a variation of method, but it should not be used more than once in the same routine. The action is simplicity itself:

1. Secretly reverse the bottom card. There is no need to glimpse it first.

2. A card having been chosen and noted by a spectator, and the cards having been shuffled by you while retaining the reversed card at the bottom, use the key undercut method to place the reversed card above the spectator's card when it is replaced in the pack. Slope the packets downwards so that the reversed card cannot be seen.

3. Square the pack very openly, and the onlookers must be convinced that the chosen card is lost, buried among the other cards.

4. To obtain control of the chosen card, turn half left and begin an overhand shuffle. As the middle of the deck is reached, run the cards singly until you see the reversed card, which will be facing you. Immediately thumb it off the deck, letting it fall to the floor. Stop the shuffle, drop the cards in your right hand on top of those in your left hand; apologizing for your clumsiness, stoop and pick up the fallen card. Push this card into the deck and you have the chosen card at your disposal on the top of the deck.

In connection with this affected clumsiness: There are two classes of card conjurers. One class takes every opportunity of parading dexterity by using flashy flourishes and showy shuffles throughout their performance, whereas the other class handles the cards just as any card player would—indeed, sometimes affecting a little clumsiness by dropping a card or the like. In the first case the reaction of the onlookers is that they are not surprised by the results of the tricks, since the "quickness" of the performer's hands has literally been thrown at them. His work is dismissed with the remark, "He's clever with his hands," and forgotten almost at once. In the second case, when the spectators see the cards handled with perfect fairness and without sleight-of-hand, as they think, then the results simply seem to happen of their own accord. The magician's feats thereafter make a lasting impression on the minds of the onlookers and will be seen by them with pleasure over and over again.

TRICKS WITH THE REVERSES

SPELLBOUND

This feat has been devised for the purpose of showing the use of the reversed card as a locator and the reversal of a card against the performer's leg. In effect, a chosen card is unmistakably buried in the deck and then discovered by the spectator himself in a mysterious way.

1. Have a card freely selected by a spectator, and have him show it to everyone as you turn your head. Take the opportunity of secretly reversing the bottom card. It is not necessary to note what card it is.

2. Turn to the spectator, key undercut the pack for the replacement of the card, and thus place the reversed card above it at the center. Square the pack very openly.

3. Turn half left and shuffle overhand, thumbing off the reversed card as explained above under reversed location. Drop the cards remaining in your right hand on those in your left, and pick up the fallen card with your right hand, at the same time reversing the chosen card on your leg. Show the card you dropped,

asking, "This doesn't happen to be your card?" The answer, of course, is "No." Thrust the card into the deck.

4. Turn your left side to the front and, holding the pack in your left hand, with the bottom card facing the audience, say, "I want to show you that your card is not anywhere near the bottom." The chosen card is now facing you; suppose it is the seven of clubs. Pull cards off the face of the deck with the left thumb, rather rapidly, but showing the full face of each card; at the same time mentally spell *s-e-v-e-n o-f c-l-u-b-s*, taking one card for each letter. Stop on the *s* and ask, "Have you seen your card?" "No." Drop the cards in your right hand in front of those shuffled off onto the left hand, run two or three more cards onto the left hand, and drop the right-hand cards behind these. The chosen card, the seven of clubs, is now in position to be spelled out from the top of the pack and to appear *after* the last letter in the spelling.

5. The next move is a bold one, but in the many times the feat has been performed it has never been challenged. Turn the deck face downwards in the left hand, take off a bunch of cards— seven or eight—and fan them face outwards, asking the spectator, "Is your card among these?" These cards have already been shown, but that is never noticed and the answer again is "No." Replace these cards on the top of the pack.

6. Hand the pack to the spectator, instructing him to hold it in his left hand behind his back. "Now, sir, you must think intently of the name of your card, the full name. For example, the king of hearts or whatever it may be, and don't forget the 'of.' Your concentration will put a spell on the cards, and you must spell the card's name mentally, bringing forward with your right hand one card from the top of the pack for each letter. Will you do that, please?"

7. The spectator acts accordingly, bringing forward one card at a time, and you keep check as he does so. When he has brought forward the card for the last letter he stops. Nothing has happened, and you affect to be a little embarrassed. "You have spelled the name of your card?" you ask. He assents. "Very strange!" you say. "I wonder what has happened. What was the name of your card?" He names it. "Kindly bring the pack for-

ward!" He does so and there face upwards on the deck staring him in the face is his card, leaving him spellbound. "The cards will have their little joke," you remark.

A Tipsy Trick

A chosen card is found reversed in the deck under peculiar circumstances. The trick is an amusing one and is used by many of the best card conjurers in their intimate performances.

1. "Magicians often have disconcerting adventures. I would like to show you something that happened to me the other night. To illustrate the mishap exactly, will you select a card?" Offer the deck to a spectator and have a card chosen.

2. "Remember that card, please. Better show it to the others so that they can enjoy the fun. Right? Replace the card, please." Control the chosen card to the top by the overhand shuffle control.

3. "At this point I always hand the cards out to a spectator to be shuffled. Generally they shuffle like this." Shuffle overhand, running the chosen card to the bottom and back to the top. Then make another overhand shuffle, retaining the card there. "That is called the overhand shuffle, and with long practice it is easy to follow the movements of the chosen card among the others.

4. "Sometimes the cards are shuffled like this." Split the deck and execute an end-to-end riffle shuffle, finishing with the waterfall flourish retaining the chosen card at the bottom. "That is somewhat more confusing, but with a keen eye the gyrations of the card can still be followed.

5. "On rare occasions someone will use the Chinese shuffle, like this." Spring the cards from hand to hand and bring the hands together with a loud slap. "That really is confusing, but nothing to what happened to me the other night. I offered the deck to a lady to shuffle, and a man just behind her reached out and grabbed the cards. 'Here, I'll migsh 'em up for you,' he said. He'd evidently had several drops too many, so I knew I was in for it. This is what he did."

6. Holding the deck face downwards in your left hand in dealing position, with the left thumb push off a small packet of cards, say half a dozen, over the side of the deck. Turn your right hand

with its back upwards, and take the packet with the thumb underneath and the fingers above; then turn that hand palm upwards, bringing the cards it holds face upwards.

7. Push off another small packet with the left thumb, and take them with the fingers of the right hand *underneath* the face-up packet it holds. Turn the right hand with its back upwards, and take another packet with the right thumb. Again turn the hand, this time palm upwards, and take some more cards with the fingers. Do this rather rapidly.

8. Continue these actions until one card only, the chosen card, remains in the left hand. Slap this card face down on the top card in the right hand, which will be face upwards. Throughout these movements simulate the actions of a slightly tipsy individual. Handle the cards sloppily and keep talking: "I'll migsh 'em up. Fash up, fash down, fash up, fash down, thash the way to migsh the cards," and so on.

9. "Finally he tried to square the deck." Do so, holding it in your left hand, the outer end between the thumb and middle finger toward the onlookers. The result of all the apparently higgledy-piggledy mixing has been simply to divide the deck into two portions, one face upwards and one face downwards; thanks to the bend given to the cards by the spring flourish, there will be a break between them at the inner end of the deck.

10. Seize the lower half by the end with your right hand, between the thumb and middle finger; draw it out with a little upward flourish and hold it face downwards against the table top. Follow this action with your gaze. Immediately move the left hand toward the right, turning it back upwards in the action, and place it beside the right hand in position for making a riffle shuffle. Both packets are now face downwards, whereas the chosen card is face upwards at the bottom of the left-hand packet. Riffle shuffle, dropping the chosen card first, and cover the shuffle with your hands so that no one can see that the cards are all turned one way.

11. Square the deck, turn it over so that the single face-down card is uppermost, then cut at about the middle and complete the cut. The audience will be convinced that the cards are really face up or face down indiscriminately. " 'There,' he said as he

handed the deck back. 'The cards are migshed. Lash shee what you can do with 'em.' Well, he had me in a fix. The most skillful card conjurer living could not have followed the movements of the chosen card. Luckily I called to mind an emergency spell. 'Arbadacarba,' I muttered. That's abracadabra backwards and the most powerful incantation we have. Be very careful how you use it. If it has worked for me, all the cards will have righted themselves, face upwards, while the chosen card will remain face downwards. What was your card? The seven of diamonds? Let's see."

12. Spread the cards ribbonwise with a flourish, and they are seen to be all face upwards except one card in the middle, which is face downwards. With the tip of your right forefinger push this card forward out of line. Turn it slowly face upwards. It is the selected card!

The feat is one of the most amusingly effective tricks that can be performed for an intimate group.

DOUBLE REVERSE

You will get great satisfaction from this trick, for its simplicity, ease of execution, and strong climax make it one of the best of the self-working feats.

1. Secretly note the bottom card and reverse it, so that it is face upwards in the face-down pack. Let us say that it is the ace of diamonds. Spread the cards between your hands as if to have one drawn, then change your mind and square the pack. This shows that the cards are all face downwards without your stressing the fact.

2. Invite someone to cut off the top half of the pack and retain it. Hold the lower portion in your left hand, being careful not to expose the reversed card at the bottom. Have the spectator remove a card from the center of his portion, look at it, and remember it. You do the same thing, but actually you only pretend to remember the card.

3. Say: "Let me put my card in your packet," and do so, pushing it flush into the center of the cards he holds. As you do this, drop your left hand with its packet and turn it over, so that the single reversed card is at the top. Everyone is watching you insert your card in the spectator's packet, and the reversal goes unnoticed.

4. Take the spectator's card and without showing it say, "Even Stephen is fair play, isn't it?" Thrust his card, face downwards, into your half of the pack. Do not spread the cards when you do this. Because of the reversed card at the top, your packet appears to be face downwards and the audience will be satisfied that his card is lost in your packet.

5. Reach for his packet, saying, "This is the fairest trick I know, up to this point. From now on I cheat!" Drop your left hand to your side as you say this, again turning over your portion and returning the reversed card to the bottom.

6. Place his packet on top of yours and square the pack. "Did you see what I did?" you ask. "Nothing. Not a single solitary thing."

7. Make one complete cut, saying, "You surely saw what I did then? Nothing. Just a perfectly honest cut. At this rate, it won't be much of a trick, will it?"

8. "But I did cheat a little, just the same, when you blinked. My card was the ace of diamonds—" (here you must give the name of the card you reversed at the bottom in step No. 1) "—and yours—what was your card?" The spectator names it. "The seven of hearts! Just as I thought. Let me show you how I cheated."

9. Spread the cards face downwards on the table in a long ribbon, and the two cards, amazingly enough, are seen to lie face upwards in the spread.

MENTALIVITY

In this puzzling feat the card of which one person thinks is found at a number thought of by a second person. You cannot have known either number beforehand.

1. Have the pack shuffled and returned to you.

2. Request spectator A to think of a number between one and ten and, as you count the first ten cards, to remember the card which falls on his number. Show him one card at a time, counting them aloud, until you have shown ten cards. Replace them on the top in the same order.

3. Invite spectator B to think of a number between ten and twenty. Gaze at him intently, nod your head knowingly; then turn and gaze at spectator A, as if divining his thoughts. Again you indicate that you have succeeded in an abstruse calculation.

4. Place the pack behind your back. Silently remove the top twelve cards and place them at the bottom but in reversed position, that is to say, in the same order but face upwards. As you do this, explain, "I shall attempt to read your thoughts and prove that I have done so beyond a shadow of a doubt."

5. Bring the pack forward, its outer end sloping downward so that the reversed cards at the bottom cannot be seen, and ask spectator A to name the number of which he thought. Let us say that he thought of six. Deal five cards face downwards on the table and show the sixth card, saying, "Your card is no longer in the sixth position."

6. Turn next to spectator B, saying, "Kindly name the number of which you are thinking." When he names it—say it is fifteen—nod affirmatively. "I thought so." You now make a simple calculation, in which you deduct six from fifteen, giving you a key number of nine. Whatever may be this key number, which you arrive at by deducting A's number from B's, you must deal this number of cards from the top of the pack, turn the deck over, and continue the deal to the required number with the cards then at the top.

You do this in the following manner: Say to spectator B, "I was confident that you would think of the number fifteen, and I have placed this gentleman's card at your number." Deal the key number of cards from the top of the pack (nine in our illustration), counting each one aloud. Pause, pick up the last card dealt, turn it face upwards, saying, "The ninth card sometimes ... that isn't your card, is it?" to spectator A. You do this to supply misdirection. While all eyes are on this card drop your left hand to your side, place your thumb under the pack and turn it over, This brings the reversed cards at the bottom uppermost.

7. Now continue the deal with these cards until you come to spectator B's number, fifteen. Remove this card, saying, "This is the card at the number of which you are thinking. That is correct?" He states that it is. Turn to spectator A: "Now, for

the first time, will you name the card of which you are thinking?"
He names the card, say the ace of clubs.

8. Recapitulate briefly what has been done: "You will remember that you thought of a card at a certain position in the pack. This gentleman thought of another number and I have placed the card at his number before all of us. Would you be surprised if this card should prove to be your ace of clubs? You would. Then let us see if it is."

9. Turn the card face upwards showing that it really is the required card.

To right the reversed cards which are lowermost in the pack, pick up one of the packets of dealt cards and drop them face upwards on the table as you talk with those about you. Drop the pack on them in an absent-minded manner. In a moment, pick up all the cards. Remove *all* the reversed cards at the bottom, right them, and replace them. It will seem that in gathering the pack you absently made an error and corrected it.

MOUNTEBANK MIRACLE

Someone thinks of a card without touching it. When you deal the cards a moment later the card appears reversed in the pack.

1. Have the pack shuffled and placed on the table, saying, "In a moment I shall ask you to think of a card under conditions which will convince you that chance alone dictates the card of which you will think. When I turn my back, cut off any small number of cards, about ten or twelve or so. You will not know how many cards you have cut and neither will I. Count the cards, remember how many there are, and put them in your pocket."

2. This done, turn back and take the rest of the pack. "You have a number arrived at by chance. As I deal the cards, kindly remember the card which falls on your number." Deal fifteen cards, counting each one aloud, lifting each so that its face can be seen, and dropping the cards face downwards in a neat pile. This action reverses their order.

3. Pick up the dealt packet and replace it at the top of the deck, then remember that he still has some cards in his pocket. Turn away and have him replace these on top of the pack.

4. Deal cards face downwards rather swiftly, dropping them

about a foot before you. Silently count the cards and when you deal the sixteenth card, which will be the spectator's card, flip it face upwards, lengthwise, and continue the deal for two or three cards without the slightest pause. The effect is that the card was reversed in the pack and that you simply dealt it, for the spectators watch the cards as they fall on the table and not your hands. The effect of showing the mentally selected card reversed in the pack makes this a fine quick trick.

XV

THE HINDU SHUFFLE
AND OTHER CONTROLS

THE shuffle which goes by this interesting name is an excellent sleight which serves a number of purposes. It may be used as a genuine shuffle, as a method of controlling a card or a number of cards, as a force, or as a glimpse. It is not difficult and it is genuinely deceptive.

1. Hold the pack in your left hand between the top phalanges of the thumb and the middle, ring, and little fingers. Place the index finger at the outer end. Hold the pack a little toward your left side, at about waist level, the outer end sloping downwards.

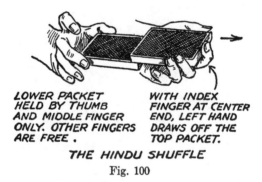

LOWER PACKET HELD BY THUMB AND MIDDLE FINGER ONLY. OTHER FINGERS ARE FREE .

WITH INDEX FINGER AT CENTER END, LEFT HAND DRAWS OFF THE TOP PACKET.

THE HINDU SHUFFLE

Fig. 100

2. Grasp the inner end of the pack by its sides between the outermost phalanges of the right thumb and middle finger, with the index finger resting lightly on the top and the ring and little fingers free.

3. Move the left hand outwards, taking with it a few of the top cards gripped between the thumb and fingers (Fig. 100).

When these cards are clear of the pack let them drop onto the palm.

4. Move the left hand back to its original position, grasp another small group of cards from the top of the pack in the same way as before—that is, between the thumb and the fingers—then move the left hand outwards and let this packet fall on the first cards drawn off.

5. Continue these movements until you have drawn off all the cards held by the right hand.

Do not move the right hand during the shuffle; the left hand does all the work. After a little practice you will be able to draw off a few cards at a time. The slanting position of the pack slides the cards against the left index finger, which acts as a stop and neatly squares them.

To repeat the shuffle at once: Grasp the lower half of the pack at the inner end by the sides, between the right thumb and second finger, and draw the upper half outwards with the left thumb and fingers. Let the upper half fall into the position described in step No. 3 above. Now continue the shuffle exactly as described until you have used all the cards held by the right hand.

Hindu Shuffle Control

Single card. Proceed as follows:

1. Have a card drawn by a spectator. When he has shown it to everyone, begin the Hindu shuffle as described above.

2. After you have drawn off several small packets from the top into the left hand, extend the hand and have him place his card on top of these cards.

3. Move the left hand back to the right hand to continue the shuffle, placing its cards directly under those held by the right hand so that the outer ends of both packets butt against the left forefinger. Press firmly against the side of the top cards of the lower packet with the tip of the right thumb, which extends below the upper packet, and pick up a card or several cards, holding a break (Fig. 101). Immediately draw the left hand outwards, drawing off a few cards from the top of the upper packet and letting them fall on the cards which remain in the left hand.

The right hand thus retains its own cards *and a few of the top cards of the left-hand packet,* the topmost of which is the chosen card. These are separated from those above them by a small break held by the right thumb. The outer ends and the right sides of both packets are flush, and the pack presents an ordinary appearance.

THE THUMB PICK-UP
Fig. 101

4. Continue the shuffle in the regular way until the cards above the break have been shuffled into the left hand, then drop those remaining in the right hand on top of all, thus bringing the chosen card to the top.

There should be no hesitation in securing the card from the top of the left-hand packet in step No. 3 above, since it does not matter whether one, two, three, or even more cards are picked up by the thumb.

Several Cards. This procedure is much the same as that used to control a single card:

1. Let us say that three cards have been drawn and noted by three persons. Begin the Hindu shuffle by drawing off several packets into the left hand. Extend the hand and have one of the cards replaced on them.

2. Continue the shuffle as described in step No. 3 of the single card control, picking up the chosen card and one or two more in the first action of the shuffle, and approach the second person, who holds the second card. Draw off several packets into the left hand; in the next movement, however, do not draw off any cards from the top, but instead let all the cards below the break drop onto those held by the left hand, which you immediately move outwards toward the spectator.

3. Have him place his card on top of those you hold in your left hand, thus placing his card above the first man's card.

4. Repeat this procedure exactly—that is, begin the Hindu shuffle, picking up a few of the cards at the top of those held in the left hand between the right thumb and second finger, holding a break with the thumb. Draw off several packets from the top with the left hand as you approach the third person, and when you reach him let the cards above the break fall upon those in the left hand, without drawing any from the top with the left fingers. The third card is thus placed above the second.

5. Finally, continue the shuffle by drawing off a packet from the top with the left fingers and at the same time grasping between the right thumb and second finger a few of the top cards of those in the left hand, holding a break above them with the thumb as before.

6. Continue the shuffle until all the cards above the thumb break have fallen into the left hand. Drop those that remain on the cards in the left hand; the three chosen cards will be at the top of the pack, but in reverse order to their replacement; that is, the first man's card will be the third from the top.

By using the Hindu shuffle to control a number of cards you save time, an important item, and you also convince those present that the cards are really scattered throughout the pack. This is important, because we must reiterate that, unless you have convinced everyone that the cards really are lost, the most brilliant subsequent discovery will not be impressive.

HINDU SHUFFLE FORCE

As we have seen, forcing a card is making a spectator draw the card you want him to take and at the same time convincing him that he has had a free choice. The Hindu shuffle enables you to make a most convincing force.

1. Place the card to be forced at the top of the pack.

2. Begin a Hindu shuffle by drawing a packet from the top into the left hand in the regular way. In drawing off the second packet, grasp in the usual way a few of the top cards of those now in the left hand, by gripping them between the right thumb and second finger, holding a thumb break.

3. Continue the shuffle as usual by drawing off small packets from the top. Invite a spectator to stop the shuffle whenever he pleases. When he says "stop" bring the outer end of the right-hand packet against the left forefinger, flush with the outer end of the packet in the left hand, saying, "Right here." Drop the cards below the break onto those in the left hand. Extend this hand and ask the spectator to remove the card at the top.

This force is completely deceptive. It may be used to force several cards if these are placed at the top of the pack.

HINDU SHUFFLE GLIMPSE

Let us say that you have taken a shuffled pack and wish to learn the name of a card before forcing it.

1. Begin the Hindu shuffle and, after several packets have been drawn off the top into the left hand, turn the cards held by the right hand so that they face you and are at right angles to those held in the left hand. Rap the inner end of the other packet with these cards (Fig. 102), as if to square them, glimpsing the bottom

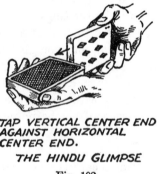

TAP VERTICAL CENTER END
AGAINST HORIZONTAL
CENTER END.
THE HINDU GLIMPSE

Fig. 102

card at the same time. Continue the shuffle, and drop this card at the top, last of all. This is a natural way of squaring the cards in this shuffle, and it should be used occasionally for that purpose only.

Again, a card may have been returned to the pack and you may have controlled it to the bottom by one of the other methods. Glimpse the card in the manner described above and, after one or two more packets have been shuffled into the left hand, drop those held by the right on top. Offer the pack for shuffling, saying, "Perhaps it would be better if you shuffled." You know the name of the card and are perfectly willing to let him shuffle as long as he likes.

THE STEP

Assume that a card has been drawn and noted.

1. Spring the cards into the left hand, rather slowly, asking the spectator to replace his card. When his hand advances with the card, stop the spring, retaining a part of the pack in the right hand. Say, "Do you want to replace your card here?" and rap the inner end of the cards in the left hand with the knuckles of the right, squaring them. If he replaces the card, well and good; if not, spring a few more cards until he is satisfied, and square these as before. Do not look at your hands while squaring.

2. Drop the cards remaining in the right hand upon those in the left, so that about a half inch of the packet extends beyond the outer end of the lower packet.

3. Place the right hand over the pack to square it, with the thumb resting against the inner end of the lower packet. Press downwards lightly on the outer end of the upper packet before pushing it flush with the lower packet. This forms a break between the two packets at the inner end, which you pick up with the left little finger at the right side near the inner corner.

4. Remove the right hand, and the pack appears to be in good condition, although the little finger retains the break.

5. Control the card to the top by means of the overhand shuffle or the pass.

NATURAL JOG

Suppose a card has been drawn.

1. Hold the pack in your left hand, as for dealing, but with the index finger curled up around the outer end.

2. Cut off the upper half with the right hand by the ends, and have the spectator replace his card on the top of the left-hand packet.

3. Hold this packet slanting downwards a little. Toss the right-hand packet upon it, so that its outer end strikes against

the middle of the left-hand packet at a slight angle (Fig. 103). The upper half will slide down to the left index finger, which will automatically jog its bottom card at the inner end (Fig. 104).

4. Press the left thumb on top of the pack, and place the right hand over it, with the fingers at the outer end and the thumb at the inner end. Place the tip of the thumb against the inner edge of the jogged card; press it inwards and upwards flush into the pack, forming a break under the card and holding the break by the left little finger at the right side near the inner corner.

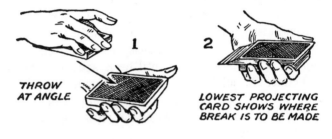

NATURAL JOG
Fig. 103   Fig. 104

5. The card at the top of the packet under the break is the spectator's card. Bring it to the top by means of the overhand shuffle or the pass.

Do not look at your hands at any time but converse naturally as you perform the control.

TWELVE-DOWN RIFFLE

This is one of the best card controls.

1. Spread the cards from your left into your right hand as if to have one drawn. Secretly count the first twelve cards, insert your left little finger tip under them to hold a break, and square the deck. Give the impression that you have changed your mind.

2. Place your right hand over the pack, with the fingers and the thumb at the ends, and slowly riffle the cards upwards from bottom to top. Ask a spectator on your left to insert his index finger anywhere in the pack as you riffle and remove the card under it. Contrive to have him take one near the middle.

3. When he has removed a card and all are looking at it, slant

the outer end of the pack downwards and lift off the twelve cards above the break between the right fingers and thumb. Hold the pack and the cards with their backs squarely to the spectators, preventing them from noting how many cards you hold in either hand.

4. Say, "Kindly replace your card where you took it from." Extend the left hand a little and have the card replaced at the top of the packet. Drop the cards held in the right hand on top of all, and square the pack meticulously.

The spectators believe the card is lost, for they think it is returned to the haphazard position from which it was taken. You know it is the thirteenth card from the top and are ready to use it for whatever trick you have in mind.

TRICKS WITH THE HINDU SHUFFLE

ALL CHANGE HERE

In this effective feat the Hindu shuffle is used to show that apparently every card in the deck is the same. It is an artifice that is useful in several other good tricks.

1. Have the deck shuffled by a spectator. Instruct him to remove one card and then pass the deck to a second person. Let this person also remove one card and then return the deck to you.

2. Have the selected cards returned to the deck, and control them to the top by means of the Hindu shuffle so that the top card is the second spectator's card.

3. Hold the deck in your left hand and with the right fingers and thumb at the ends remove the top half, at the same time making the backslip and thus placing the second card on top of the lower half in the left hand. Place this packet aside for the moment.

4. Ask the first man to name a number, say between five and fifteen. Suppose he calls ten. Have him name his card, say the five of hearts. Place the packet you hold in your left hand and count off ten cards, pushing them off one by one with your left thumb, and taking them one on top of the other in the right hand. On reaching the tenth card, turn your right hand with the back upwards, and slap the counted cards face upwards onto the

cards still in your left hand. "There it is!" you exclaim. "The tenth card, the five of hearts!" Immediately remove these face-upwards cards and spread them, showing the five of hearts with nine cards above it. Close the spread, place the packet underneath the cards in your left hand, and place all face downwards on the table.

5. Pick up the other packet, and in the course of an overhand shuffle place one card above the second spectator's card at the top. Address him, saying, "Will you kindly name another number between five and fifteen?" As you say this push the two top cards off the pack to the right a little, and in squaring the pack again secure a left-little-finger break under these cards.

Let us say that the spectator names the number eight. Remove the top card and turn it face upwards, counting "One" and placing it squarely on the pack. Square the deck at the ends, grasping the two top cards at the ends between the right thumb and middle finger, moving them inwards so that they protrude over the inner end for about an inch. Immediately draw out the card which is under these two—the third card—and turn it over inwards, bringing it face upwards, and lay it on the first two, counting "Two."

Remove the next card—the fourth card—and turn it face upwards and lay it on the first three, counting "Three." Continue counting cards in this manner until you have turned one less than the number named—in our example, seven. Under these, and hidden by them, is the chosen card, which is face downwards.

"I want you to be satisfied that my count is accurate," you say. Push the protruding cards squarely on the pack and slowly deal the cards which are face upwards at the top, counting them. "Seven cards," you point out. Tap the chosen card, which is now the top face-down card. "This is the eighth card, the card at your number. Will you name your card, please?"

"The jack of clubs," let us assume he says. Slowly turn the card face upwards, showing his card.

6. Drop this card, face upwards, on the seven cards which lie face upwards on the table. Pick them all up and place them at the bottom of the deck, thus placing the jack of clubs at the bottom.

7. "Now, really," you continue, "I do not as a rule explain how these feats are done. But this one is so delightfully simple that I will show it to you, and you will be able to have some fun with it yourselves." Place the packet you hold to one side and pick up the first packet, holding it in position for the Hindu shuffle. "The fact is that all these cards are fives of hearts, hence it made no difference to me what number you called. Look!" Begin a Hindu shuffle by pulling off a small packet into your left hand, then lift your right hand, bringing its packet to a vertical position with the bottom card facing the audience squarely. Lower the right hand, continue the shuffle by pulling off a few more small packets from the top, and again lift the right-hand packet, showing the five of hearts. Repeat the same motions until only the five of hearts remains in the right hand. Drop it on top of the packet, square the cards, and palm it in your right hand.

8. Pick up the second packet by drawing it back towards yourself, and in the action add the palmed card to the top. The second person's card is on the bottom of this packet, and you show apparently that all these cards are jacks of clubs by using the moves detailed in step No. 7, with this difference: In the first movement, draw off the top card only—the five of hearts—into the left hand, so that when the action is completed it will be the bottom card of the packet. When you have apparently shown that all the cards are jacks of clubs, drop the jack on top of the packet as in step No. 7. Square the packet and palm the jack in your right hand, placing the rest of the cards on the table.

9. Pick up the first packet with your right hand, adding the palmed jack of clubs. Force it on the first spectator by means of the lift shuffle force. "These cards are all fives of hearts," you say. "Take one and put it face down on the table."

10. Put the packet down, take the second packet, shuffle the five of hearts to the top, and force it on the second spectator by the backslip force. He places it face downwards on the table before him.

11. The trick is done; it only remains to bring out the climax as strongly as possible. On turning their cards face upwards, each spectator finds he has the other man's card. Then with a flourish

you spread each packet face upwards, ribbonwise, and all the cards are seen to be different, making up a regular deck.

Ewephindit

Suitable for close-up and impromptu work, this fast revelation of a chosen card has a spectator locating his own card without knowing how he did it.

1. Have a card drawn, noted, and returned to the pack, bringing it to the top by means of the Hindu shuffle.

2. Overhand shuffle, taking the card to the bottom.

3. Spread the cards, remove one at random, and hand it face upwards to the spectator, saying, "that's not your card, is it? It's not? Good, then we'll use it for the trick."

4. Spread the cards in a fan between your hands, in readiness for the sliding key move, drawing the chosen card under the fan with the right fingers. "Kindly push that card into the pack, face upwards, anywhere you like."

5. When the card has been inserted in the spread, place the chosen card above it as you would place a sliding key card above a chosen card.

6. Square the pack, saying, "There is only one chance in fifty-one that you placed the marker card next your chosen card." Run through the cards until you come to the face-up card. Turn the card above it, showing the chosen card. "And that's exactly what you did!"

XVI

THE CLASSIC FORCE

Forcing a card is the act of making a spectator remove from the pack a card which you wish him to take, although he believes that he has a free choice.

Of all the methods evolved for accomplishing this, the classic force is the oldest and still the best. In this method you spread the deck and invite someone to draw a card. You place the card you want him to take under his fingers at the moment they touch the pack. He removes this card, confident that he has had an uninfluenced choice.

The mechanics of this force are as follows:

1. Let us say that you wish to force the ace of hearts, and this is at the top of the pack. Give the cards an overhand shuffle taking the card to the bottom and back to the top.

2. Next take the force card to the middle of the pack in the following way: Give the pack another overhand shuffle by undercutting the lower half, injogging the first card, and shuffling off. Turn the left hand so that the pack is horizontal, with the backs of the cards uppermost. Place the right hand over the pack, with fingers at the outer end and the thumb at the inner end. Place the tip of the thumb under the inner edge of the injogged card, pressing it upwards and inwards, so that when it is pushed flush with the pack there will be a small break under it and above the card to be forced. Hold this break with the right thumb, then shift the left hand so that it holds the pack, with the little finger holding the break above the card to be forced.

Unlike the usual method of holding a break, the tip of the left little finger in this case rests against the face of the card above the break.

3. Push cards off the top of the pack with the left thumb, taking them with the right hand, and request someone to take a card.* Press the left little finger firmly against the side of the lower packet, preventing these cards from spreading to the right.

4. Time the spreading of the cards so that, at the moment the spectator's hand reaches the pack, all the cards above the break have been pushed into the right hand and you are beginning to push the cards *under* it; the first of these cards, you will remember, is the card to be forced.

At the very moment that you begin to push off this lower portion, the spectator's hand arrives at the deck to make a choice.

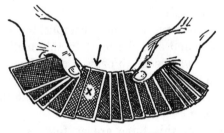

FORCING A CARD
Fig. 105

Advance both hands two or three inches toward his hand and literally place the force card under his fingers. That must be done with finesse, and this is where experience enters into the picture. After you have done a good deal of forcing, you will find that there is a knack in spreading the cards so that the force card is under the spectator's fingers at precisely the right moment.

If, when you first begin to force cards, you find that you have exposed the force card too soon, here is what you do: Spread a few more cards with the left thumb and stop. Hold the pack as in Fig. 105. A little more of the force card is exposed than of any other card. Now, as the spectator's hand approaches, turn *both* hands and the cards a little to the right or left a matter of less

---

* Robert-Houdin, in *Secrets of Conjuring and Magic*, has this to say: "It is well to say *take*, and not *choose*, though the latter word is frequently used. The word *choose* implies a liberty of action which it is better not to suggest too strongly."

than an inch, to make the force card the most convenient to his hand. In ninety-nine cases out of a hundred he will take the card.

We have mentioned that the tip of the left little finger presses up into the break against the face of the lowermost card of the upper packet. This is a great help in forcing, for when the left thumb pushes this card to the right you can feel it glide over the finger tip and thus you know that the next card is the force card. With experience you can force a card without looking at the pack, relying solely on your left little finger's sense of touch to tell you when you have come to the force card.

The force is certainly simple, but to do it with dead certainty calls for experience and for the timing which comes only with experience. There are also psychological factors which must be kept in mind.

(a) You should shuffle the cards before the force so that you cannot seem to know the position of any card. If the spectator believes this to be the case, he will remove any card without suspicion, since it does not seem to matter which card he takes.

(b) You must not, by your manner or by anything you say, lead anyone to believe that you have a reason for forcing a card. Your manner must be easy and relaxed. If you are tense, this will be noticed, and although the spectator may not know what you have in mind he will be difficult to control.

You may think: Very well. But, while I am gaining experience, what shall I do if the force fails?

Let us say that the force *has* failed and that a card has been drawn two or three beyond the force card. Have the card returned at the place from which it was taken and count the number of cards intervening between it and the force card. The force card, the name of which you know, thus becomes a key card, and to locate the chosen card you need only count the number of cards above or below it that you noted previously.

If the card has been removed from a point too far distant from the force card to enable you to count the intervening cards, you do this:

Have the card withdrawn from the pack and, as its name is

being noted, remove all the cards to the right of the force card with the right hand. This is easy, because the tip of the left little finger still presses up against the face of the card just above it. Hold these a few inches away from those spread in the left hand and have the selected card replaced on the left-hand portion. Dropping the cards held by the right hand on top of all completes the action. To find the chosen card, look for the card just above your force card, which acts as a key card.

You may still think: But what if the force fails and I cannot use the force card as a key card? In such a predicament, you then do another trick which does not require that a card be forced. You have not stated what you would do with the drawn card, and no one will know that you have changed your plans. This is very important for you, because the knowledge that failure is not going to prove a disaster will prevent tenseness, which spoils more forces than any other single factor.

A final word on the matter of experience. To get experience, make it a practice to attempt to force a card in every trick you perform, whether it calls for a force or not—if, of course, the nature of the trick permits this. In that way you will get invaluable experience and learn the timing of the force, and if you fail in the first few attempts it is a matter of no consequence. You should never, however, force the same card repeatedly simply to show how clever you are, for this is tantamount to revealing a method which you should keep secret.

ONE-HAND FORCE

Few modern cardmen use this force, although in some respects it is more convincing than the classic force.

1. Shuffle the cards, and in so doing take the card to be forced to the middle of the pack, holding a break above it with the left little finger by using the method given for the classic force.

2. Shift the cards above the break a little more than a quarter of an inch to the right, the right hand making this adjustment, so that there is a step between the two packets. The topmost card of the packet below the step is the card to be forced.

3. Take the pack in the left hand and with the right hand

spread the cards in a fan, contriving to expose a little more of the surface of the force card than of any other.

4. Extend the fan and request someone to take a card. Because the force card is more accessible than the others, it is almost invariably taken. Further to assure this, the slightest movement of the left hand to the right or left will place the force card directly under the spectator's fingers as they reach the pack.

As with the classic pass, the preliminary shuffle makes the force easier, since the spectator believes the cards to have been well mixed; hence the particular card he removes seems to be of no great importance. Care, however, must be taken not to expose too much of the force card, or the device will be obvious. If it is exposed a quarter inch more than the others, this will be sufficient.

The one-hand force is useful for forcing a number of cards one after the other without closing the fan.

Bottom Force

Place the card to be forced at the bottom of the pack and make an overhand shuffle, retaining it there. Follow this shuffle with a false cut (second method, page 134, or fourth method, page 135).

1. Grasp the deck at the ends with the right fingers and thumb, and place it on the left palm, holding it as for dealing.

LEFT HAND

FORCE CARD

THE BOTTOM FORCE
Fig. 106

2. Move all the cards, except the bottom force card, forward two inches with the right hand.

3. Pat the outer end with the right fingers, beveling it inwards from bottom to top until the bottom protruding card is covered (Fig. 106).

4. Request someone to remove as many cards from the bottom of the pack as he desires, and point out that the sloping end makes it possible for him to remove as many as he likes.

5. He will remove a number of cards from the bottom, but he cannot remove the bottom force card which is beyond his grasp. The cards above those he removes drop onto the left palm and on the bottom force card. Immediately square these cards by rapping on the inner end with the right knuckles. Invite the spectator to look at the bottom card "to which you cut in the fairest possible manner" and have him show it to everyone as you turn your head.

6. Have him shuffle his packet, then hand him the remaining cards and have him shuffle the whole deck. Knowing the card, you can find it and dispose of it as required for the purpose of the trick in hand.

SLIDE-OUT FORCE

The card to be forced is at the bottom of the pack.

1. Shuffle the pack, running the bottom card to the top and back to the bottom.

THE KNIFE FORCE
(KNIFE CUT BELOW FORCE)
Fig. 107

2. Make the key undercut, dropping the lower half of the pack on top, but inserting the tip of the left little finger between the two packets to hold a break. The force card is now the card just above the little finger tip.

3. Hand a spectator a table knife and ask him to thrust it into the pack as you riffle the cards. Place the right hand over the pack and riffle upwards from the bottom, contriving to have the blade thrust into the outer end below the break.

4. Tip the outer end of the pack upwards a little, and grasp all the cards above the break at the ends, between the right thumb and middle finger, shifting these cards outwards an inch beyond the outer end of the pack.

5. Grasp the knife blade and the cards you have shifted over the outer end between the right thumb and middle finger, and draw them outwards and away from the pack (Fig. 107).

6. Show the card under the blade—the force card—and ask all to note and remember it.

A reversed playing card, or a borrowed business card, can be used in place of the knife.

Two-Card Force

The two cards to be forced are at the top and bottom of the deck.

1. Run through the cards and hand someone the joker.

2. Make the pass at a point a little above the middle of the deck, but after the packets are transposed press the tip of the left little finger between the packets, holding a break. One force card is the bottom card of the upper packet; the other is the top card of the lower packet.

3. Place the right hand over the pack, with thumb at the inner end and the fingers at the outer. Riffle the cards upwards, and ask the spectator to insert the joker, face upwards, wherever he likes.

4. Time the riffle so that he thrusts the joker into the pack among the cards *above* the little finger break. Grasp all the cards above the break at the sides, near the inner end, between the right thumb and middle finger, and draw these inwards and away from the deck. Hold the protruding joker at the outer end with the left thumb and index finger, to prevent it from being drawn away with the upper packet (Fig. 108).

The illusion is that the pack is separated at the point at

which the joker is inserted. Actually the cards under the joker slide away with those above it. This is concealed by the joker itself.

5. Show the card at the face of the packet in the right hand, and the one at the top of those remaining in the left hand. These are the force cards.

This two-card force may be used as a 'discovery' of two chosen cards which have been controlled to the top and bottom of the pack, a spectator being invited to thrust the joker into the pack, after which you show that one of the chosen cards is above the joker, the other is below it.

Fig. 108

RIFFLE-BREAK FORCE

One or more cards can be forced by this method. These are at the top of the pack.

1. Shuffle the card to be forced to the center of the deck, and hold the pack in the left hand, with the thumb along one side, the middle and ring fingers at the other, and the little finger holding a break above the card to be forced. Bend the forefinger under the outer end of the pack.

Hold the pack with its outer end sloping downwards, and be careful that no one on your right can see the little-finger break. To avoid this, turn the left hand inwards toward the body.

2. Riffle the left outer corners downwards with the thumb, explaining that when you repeat the riffle you would like someone to call "stop" whenever he pleases.

3. Riffle downwards again rather slowly, but do not riffle below the break. If the command to stop does not come soon enough, simply begin the riffle again. Try to have the command come when you have riffled to a point just above the break.

When it does come, stop the riffle at this point and press down with the thumb tip upon the cards under it, forming a wide break at this corner.

4. Place the right hand over the pack, with the thumb at the inner end and the fingers at the outer end, which they cover completely. Grasp and slide away to the right *all the cards above the little-finger break at the inner end*. Do not lift these cards away; slide them flatly. Simultaneously press down with the left thumb on the corners of the packet remaining in the left hand, so that its condition appears unchanged.

5. Extend the left hand and have the top card removed, thus forcing the card.

SLIDING-KEY FORCE

This very deceptive and easy method of forcing a card makes use of the sleight described as the *sliding-key card* (see page 80).

1. Have the card to be forced on the bottom of the pack; shuffle overhand, keeping it in that position.

2. Spread the cards between your hands, at the same time sliding the force card underneath to the center, and invite a spectator to *touch* the back of any card he pleases.

3. Place the tip of your left thumb upon the card to the left of the one touched by the spectator and draw away to the right, with your right hand, the card touched by the spectator and all the cards above it, together with the force card, which automatically becomes the bottom card of the right-hand packet.

4. Square the cards in your right hand by tapping their sides against the cards in the left hand.

5. Turn your head and lift the right-hand packet to a vertical position, asking the spectator to note and remember the card he has chosen freely.

At this point it is not advisable at once to hand the deck to the spectator to be shuffled. It is better to square the pack and execute a short overhand shuffle yourself, and then hand the cards out to be shuffled.

DOUBLE-LIFT FORCE

Place the card to be forced at the top of the pack.

1. Give the deck an overhand shuffle, retaining the force card at the top; then take the pack in the left hand, face downwards, as for dealing. Ask someone to name a number between five and fifteen, emphasizing that he has a free choice and may change his mind as often as he likes. As you make this statement, prepare for a double lift by inserting the tip of your left little finger under the two top cards.

2. Suppose you are given the number nine. Say, "Number nine? Very well." Grasp the two cards above the little finger break at the ends between the right index finger and thumb and carry them away as one card, counting "One." Push a second card off the pack with the left thumb and drop it *upon* the two held by the right hand, counting "Two." Continue to deal the cards until you have counted to a number one less than the number given. In the illustration we have used you would count to eight.

3. "The next card is the card at your number and you will have to admit that, since you yourself named the number, I could not know it in advance. I want you—" Break off abruptly, as though struck by a thought. Replace the cards you hold in your right hand on top of the deck, and extend it to the spectator. "I don't even want to touch your card," you explain. "You take the cards, turn your back, count down to the ninth card, look at it, remember it, and then shuffle it back into the pack. Surely nothing could be more fair than that."

It would be much fairer, of course, if by your subterfuge you had not placed the original top card in the ninth position from the top.

CUT FORCE

This method of forcing is bold.

1. Place the card to be forced at the bottom of the deck, and retain it there while shuffling.

2. Square the pack, place it on the table, and request someone to cut it, placing the cut to the right.

3. Next invite him to pick up the lower packet and place it at right angles upon the cut (Fig. 109).

4. Pause for a moment, conversing or performing any action which is a part of your trick, then have someone lift the upper crosswise packet and look at the card at its face, as you say, "Please note and remember the card at which you cut." This will be the original bottom card. So few people understand the nature of the cut that your statement will not be questioned.

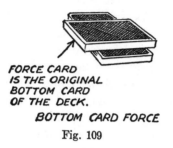

FORCE CARD
IS THE ORIGINAL
BOTTOM CARD
OF THE DECK.

BOTTOM CARD FORCE

Fig. 109

You should never repeat a force of this type for the same audience. Knowing what you will do, the spectators will analyze the action and may fathom the method.

TRICKS WITH THE FORCE

JUSTICE CARD TRICK

Card tricks that are performed while the magician is blindfolded make a particularly profound impression upon laymen. For this reason it is a good plan to include one such trick in a routine of card tricks.

1. Ask someone in the gathering to assist you, and when you have a volunteer place him on the left side of your table while you stand behind it. Have him shuffle the deck, and when you take it back glimpse the bottom card. Let us say it is the four of spades. Force this card upon your assistant, preferably using the classic force or the one-hand force, and have him show the card to all present.

Invite him to replace the card in the deck, make a short shuffle, then hand him the deck and ask him to shuffle it himself.

2. As he does this, take a white linen handkerchief from your pocket and fold it diagonally into a blindfold about two inches wide. Ask another spectator to tie the blindfold over your eyes. You will find, when you have been blindfolded in this manner, that you can see down the side of your nose and by tilting your head back a little—but not too much—and glancing downwards you can see a certain area of the table top. You are supposed to be sightless, however, and therefore now you close your eyes, which will make your actions convincingly realistic.

3. Keeping your eyes tightly closed, take the deck and cut it into two packets, one of which you keep in your hand. Open your eyes and, glancing downwards and holding the cards within your area of vision, deal them face upwards on the table. Count the cards as you deal and when you see the force card—the four of spades—remember the number at which it lies from the top of the packet. Complete the deal without any hesitation, and ask the spectator if he has seen his card.

If the card is not in this packet, take the other one and repeat the deal with it, noting the position of the force card—how far it is from the top.

4. Hand the packet containing the force card to the assistant, and close your eyes tightly throughout the remainder of the trick; your consequent fumbling will be convincing. Request the assistant to hand you the cards one by one, face downwards, and to think intently of his card. Let us suppose that you know that the force card is the eighteenth card in his packet. Take the cards one by one, appearing to concentrate on each card and leading the audience to believe that you will announce when you have been given the proper card. Instead, you wait until you are given the card before the one you know is his; in the present illustration, you will take the seventeenth card and hesitate before discarding it.

5. Abruptly you exclaim, "Just a moment! Hold that next card face downwards." Lift off the blindfold with your left hand. "What was the card of which you have been thinking?" Gesture toward him with your right hand.

"The four of spades."

"Right! Show that card to everybody!"

He does, and everyone sees that you have stopped him on his card.

FOURS OF A KIND

The plot of this trick is similar to that of the feat described as *the sevens* (see page 123). It has, however, a delayed climax of the turn-the-tables type.

Prior to performance remove the fours of clubs, hearts. spades, and diamonds. Arrange the deck so that one of these is at the top and the second is directly below it; after the second there is an indifferent card with a third four-spot below it. Place the remaining four-spot second from the bottom.

1. Shuffle the cards by means of the riffle shuffle, without disturbing the two cards at the bottom or the four cards at the top.

2. Force the four-spot at the top by means of the backslip force, and have it placed on the table before the drawer, without permitting its face to be seen.

3. Prepare for a double lift, saying, "There is a sympathy among cards which has often been commented upon. I believe that I can show you what I mean." Turn the two top cards as one, showing the indifferent card, which let us say is a nine, and replace the two face downwards on the deck. Remove the top card, a four-spot, and place it face downwards before you, saying, "This card tells me the value of the card you drew. It is a nine."

4. Hold the pack in the left hand face downwards as for the glide, tip it up so that the face card, which we shall say is a diamond, can be seen, and say, "This card indicates the suit. A diamond. We know your card must be the nine of diamonds." Turn the pack face downwards as you say this, glide back the bottom card, remove the card above it (a four-spot), and place it face downwards before you on the table.

Remove the card that is now above the glided card at the bottom and, using it as a pointer, indicate the two cards before you. "Remember," you say, "A nine here and a diamond here. The nine of diamonds." Replace the pointer card at the bottom, thus effectually concealing the glided card.

5. At this point the indifferent card is at the top of the pack, with a four-spot directly under it. Make the pass, transposing the upper half to the bottom, and hold a left-little-finger break between the two packets. Spread the cards from hand to hand and *force the fourth four-spot upon yourself*—a feat that should give you very little trouble! It is only necessary to remove the card below the one above which the little finger maintains control.

Place this card face downwards beside the other three, explaining, "The purpose of this card will be clear in a moment. As you have seen, the cards say that the one you drew a moment ago is the nine of diamonds. Please turn your card face upwards and show everyone that this is the case."

6. The spectator turns his card and shows it. Let us say it is the four of the heart suit. Appear a little discomfited; then exclaim, "My original trick hasn't worked, so I shall do another trick instead. Your card is the four of hearts. Very well. *Cards, change!*" Tap each of the three cards before you, turn them over, and show that each is a four-spot.

Pulse Trick

You will be surprised at the number of pseudo-scientific explanations which will be offered to explain this trick, in which you name a selected card by reading a lady's pulse, and she in turn reads your pulse and names a card you have selected.

1. Force a card on a lady and, after she has noted its value, have her place it to one side face downwards.

2. Say, "It is an interesting fact that the principle of the so-called lie-detector has been used by magicians for over a century. For instance, it is entirely possible for me to name the card you have chosen by reading your pulse."

3. Hold her wrist so that you can feel the pulse. Say, "The lie detector measures physical reaction to stimuli, as we all know. When a significant question is asked, no matter how well the subject may discipline his emotions, his body reacts abnormally. To show you how magicians have used this principle in the past, I shall call out *ace, two, three,* and so on, and, no matter how well you dissemble, I shall know the value of your

card when I name it. I will ascertain the suit in the same way."

4. Count, "One, two, three, four," and so on up to "king." Immediately say, "When I counted five, your pulse jumped. Your card was a five." Of course you name the value of the forced card.

5. Repeat this with the four suits, naming the proper one, and have the card turned to prove that you are correct.

Usually there will be some discussion of this phenomenon, and after a moment you offer to prove that what you say is so.

1. Take the pack and shuffle it, withdraw a card, and note its value. Place it face downwards to one side without letting anyone see it.

2. Have the lady feel your pulse and instruct her to call the values and suits as you did. Press the tip of your middle finger firmly against the tip of your thumb, and when the value of your card is named slide your thumb inward on your finger tip for a fraction of an inch. The muscles of the wrist tighten and this is felt by the lady taking your pulse. When, at the end, you ask her to name the value of your card, she names the proper one.

3. Repeat this with the suit, have it named, turn your card, and show that she has named it correctly.

Since you have mentioned "jumping pulses," the lady in many cases is prepared to swear that your pulse jumped!

XVII

TOP AND BOTTOM CHANGES

Top Change

THERE is no other sleight in all conjuring with cards which will give you so much pleasure as this. More than any other sleight, it lends itself to improvisation, the delightful ad-libbing with a pack of cards which causes so much laughter and more nearly approaches a battle of wits with your audiences than any other conjuring maneuver. To exchange one card for another boldly and under the very noses of those who watch, without being detected, is a sweet triumph! It is also good entertainment; indeed, Robert-Houdin, the father of modern magic, observed

RIGHT HAND

CARD HELD AT CORNER BY MIDDLE FINGER AND THUMB. INDEX FINGER IS FREE.

Fig. 110

almost a century ago, "I know of nothing more surprising than the effect of a card neatly 'changed'." The words are as true as though written yesterday.

Let us say that you are going to exchange secretly a card held in the right hand for the one at the top of the pack, which is held in the left hand, as for dealing, but with the index finger resting at the outer end.

216

1. Hold the card in the right hand, at its inner right corner, between the outermost phalanges of the middle finger and the thumb. Place the index finger lightly alongside the middle finger, but do not hold the card with it. The other fingers are free (Fig. 110).

2. Move the right hand to the left hand and slide its card under the left thumb flush onto the pack. The left index finger at the outer end prevents the card from overlapping. Do not draw it onto the pack with the left thumb.

3. Simultaneously with the preceding action, and as the right hand approaches, push the top card of the pack over its side to the right for about an inch, then lift the thumb a little so that the right hand can slide its card under it. *Do not push off the top card before the right hand begins its swing to the left.*

Although we have described the actions in steps Nos. 2 and 3 as separate processes, we have done this only for clarity. Actually the left thumb pushes the top card to the right as the right hand approaches and slides its card under the thumb and onto the pack.

4. Grasp the inner right corner of the card pushed off the pack between the right index finger and thumb (Fig. 111). Hold

LEFT THUMB HAS ALREADY PUSHED FORWARD THE CARD TO BE TAKEN.

RIGHT HAND WHILE LEAVING THE CARD ON TOP, TAKES CARD IMMEDIATELY BENEATH IT WITH THUMB AND INDEX.

Fig. 111

the right hand motionless with the card, and move the left hand and the pack away to the left. *The right hand must not move away to the right.*

The hands should be held well away from the body, and the action should be easy and natural and should be explained by a subsequent action. For instance, you show the card held by the right hand and lower it so that it is about a foot away from the left hand and the pack, but on the same level. Glance to the left, at a table or a chair; look back at your audience, saying, "I will put the card on the chair."

Turn your body to the left toward the chair and as you do this move the right hand toward the left a little faster than the left hand moves. The two hands meet at the middle of the turn and exchange the cards without the least hesitation. Move the left hand with the pack backwards and away, perhaps grasping the rail of the chair, as you face left and drop the card the right hand now holds on the chair seat.

Again, you may hold the hands a foot apart and speak to someone on your right, turning a little toward him. "I shall ask this gentleman on my left to blow upon the card," you say, at the same time turning toward your left, executing the change as the hands meet. Hold the right hand motionless, and move the left hand with the pack outwards to the left, gesturing to the person to whom you refer.

Still again, when you are doing close-up card magic, you may show a card in your right hand, then lower it so that it is horizontal. Say to someone, "Will you hold your hand palm upwards?" and, when he raises his right hand, move the right hand to it as though to place the card on his palm. Apparently change your mind, saying, "We'd better use your other hand," and at this moment glance up to meet his gaze. Bring the right hand to the left, exchange the cards, and move the left hand away a little. A moment later, when you place the changed card on the spectator's palm, he is unaware that it is not the card you showed a moment before.

The entire process of the top change is a smooth and natural blending of actions, and we need not tell you that to look at your hands would be fatal. You must look at the audience or at the object on which you will place the card.

The Changing Card

Here is a feat so simple that you will not realize how much laughter it can evoke until you use it. Because the best way to learn a sleight is to do it, we urge you to perform this fine trick as often as you can.

1. Go to someone on your left and have him choose a card, *show it to everyone* (this is important if all are to enjoy the trick), and replace it in the pack. Control the card to the top by means of the Hindu shuffle.

2. Turn and walk to someone on your right. Spread the cards in a wide fan, saying, "Sir, I shall ask you to point to a card, and I promise you that whatever card you point to will be the card chosen by the gentleman across the room. Kindly make a careful choice."

3. When a card has been indicated, do not let the spectator draw it from the fan of cards, but remove it yourself, making sure that its face cannot be seen.

4. Return to the center of the platform, holding the card in your right hand well away from the body, its back to the audience. Turn to the first spectator, saying, "Ladies and gentlemen, here is the card!"

Turn the card to show its face and glance from right to left, bowing a little as if to acknowledge applause but at the same time turning the card into a horizontal position on a level with the pack in the left hand.

5. Next turn to the spectator on your left; as you do so, bring the right hand to the left so that it overtakes the left hand, and make the top change. Immediately the change is made, hold the right hand motionless, with its card slanting downwards so that its face cannot be seen. Move the left hand, with the pack, on to the left in a gesture toward the first spectator. "This is your card, sir?"

6. Someone (and usually several persons) will tell you that it is not. Turn to the right again, moving the right hand and the card away from the body with its back to the audience. Look at the card, then glance back at the spectator on your left. Now, for the first time, ask him the name of his card. He says, "The seven of diamonds" or whatever his card was. "Well, this is the seven of diamonds, isn't it?" you say, turning the card face outwards as you mention the name of the card.

Hold the card in this manner for about five seconds, and *do not move until the laughter has subsided.*

When you have performed this trick as we have described it you will understand the psychology of the top change better. You must not snatch the card in making the change—you do not need to make it with great speed. We have tried to emphasize that naturalness is the keynote of good conjuring, and this is especially true of the top change.

At first it may seem to you that everyone must see the exchange of cards, but a century of experience on the part of card conjurers is that, smoothly and easily performed, the exchange goes wholly unnoticed.

TOP-CHANGE BYPLAY

This is another quick card trick especially suitable for an impromptu or close-up performance.

1. Have a card drawn and shown to all. When it has been replaced in the deck, control it to the top by means of the Hindu shuffle.

2. "Ah, I've made a mistake!" you apologize. "Let's start over again. Take another card." Force the same card on the same spectator, using the classic force. When he and those around him glance at it, they will laugh and may make some remark that it is the same card. If this happens, you must act as though it is a genuine surprise to you. You must never be smug and pleased with yourself when you make a force.

3. Reach out and take the card in your right hand. Turn to address someone on your left. "My mother told me there'd be nights like this!" you say wryly. As you make the turn, top change the forced card for the indifferent card at the top of the pack. "Here, let's get rid of that card!"

4. Toss the card face downwards on the first spectator's lap, if he is seated, or drop it on a convenient table or chair if you are all standing. Immediately pass the forced card to the middle of the pack and force it again on the same spectator.

5. When, for the third time, the spectator draws a card which he now believes rests on his own lap, the resultant laughter will be most gratifying to you.

6. Do not touch the card you discarded in step No. 4. Usually some curious soul will reach for it and turn it over, and this will cause more laughter.

BOTTOM CHANGE

In the bottom change the card held in the right hand is placed at the bottom of the pack, the top card being taken in its place. It is generally agreed that this change is not so smooth as the preceding method, but there are certain tricks in which it must be used if the trick is to be performed at all. You must not gather from this fact that the bottom change is difficult or de-

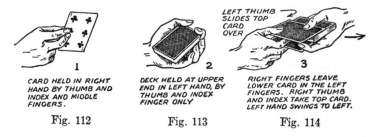

CARD HELD IN RIGHT HAND BY THUMB AND INDEX AND MIDDLE FINGERS.

DECK HELD AT UPPER END IN LEFT HAND, BY THUMB AND INDEX FINGER ONLY

LEFT THUMB SLIDES TOP CARD OVER

RIGHT FINGERS LEAVE LOWER CARD IN THE LEFT FINGERS. RIGHT THUMB AND INDEX TAKE TOP CARD. LEFT HAND SWINGS TO LEFT.

Fig. 112   Fig. 113   Fig. 114

tectable. Actually it is easier than the top change and, when neatly performed, it is imperceptible. We simply point out that, all things being equal, the top change is the preferable method.

The principle of the bottom change is the same as that of the top change—that is, one card is changed for another under cover of a larger movement of the hands and the withdrawal of the left hand from the right after the change has been made.

1. Hold a card face downwards in your right hand, between the thumb and index and middle fingers, and about a foot from the left hand. Unlike the top change, in which the card is held at the lower corner, here you grasp it at the middle of the right side (Fig. 112).

2. Hold the pack face downwards in the left hand between the thumb and index finger at the extreme outer end. Place the pack well into the crotch of the thumb. Keep the other three fingers free of the pack, so that by extending them an opening will be made between them and the index finger; into this opening the right hand card may slide and be gripped as in a forceps.

Rest the thumb on the top card, in readiness to push it off the pack to the right (Fig. 113).

3. Make a turn to the left and move the right hand toward the left, simultaneously moving the index finger from below the card onto its back, so that it is gripped between the two fingers and the thumb is free.

4. The right hand overtakes the left at the middle of the body and slides its card between the left index and the other three fingers, which drop slightly to permit this. Close the right thumb and index finger on the top card, which is pushed off the pack to the right by the left thumb (Fig. 114). Move the left hand away with the pack, the right hand following on more slowly with the former top card.

The changed card is now gripped squarely under the pack between the left index and the other three fingers. Close the latter on the pack and move the index finger outwards, allowing the card to be pressed up against the bottom of the pack by the fingers.

5. Continue the swing to the left, moving the left hand away from the right. At the end of this turn, the two hands are some distance apart as at the beginning. Now turn the left hand so that its back is to the audience and the bottom card cannot be seen.

6. Drop the card held by the right hand on a table or chair, or extend it to someone to blow upon if the trick calls for this handling, or use the hand in a gesture to emphasize what you are saying, being careful that the face of the card cannot be seen until you are ready to reveal the change.

The entire action should be an exact simulation of a natural turn to the left for any of the purposes mentioned in the preceding paragraph. A speedy movement of the hands is to be avoided, since it will warn the audience that something has been done, although they may not know what.

The bottom change is excellent for use with a single card in each hand or with a packet in each hand.

TOP AND BOTTOM CHANGES

It should be noted that, in giving instructions for the changes, we have told you that the change should be made while turning to the left. You should practice the changes in this manner until you have the knack. When you can perform them smoothly and elusively, you should learn to make changes while moving the pack to the right. When performed in this manner, the left hand moves to the right to indicate an object or person, and as it passes the right hand the exchange is made, with the right hand remaining absolutely motionless.

The exchange must be made without an instant's pause, and it is covered by a turning of the body to the right as the left hand makes its gesture and the exchange.

In the case of both the top and bottom changes, it is advisable to practice them by going through the same action you will use in the trick you plan to perform.

The following points are important:

(a) You must not snatch the card from the left hand.

(b) You must not pause noticeably at the moment when the hands meet and the cards are exchanged.

(c) When the exchange has been completed, the hands should be about the same distance apart as at the beginning.

(d) After the exchange, hold the right hand card tilted downwards so that its face cannot be seen.

(e) Divest the sleight of importance in your own mind. Remember that the larger movement of the turn conceals the smaller movement of the hands and that to the audience the hands never meet.

One final word of caution. Do not watch yourself in a mirror as you practice. You cannot perform the action naturally if you divide your attention between what you do and how it looks. Moreover, mirror watching has a tendency to cause the eyes to widen; this is not attractive and can become a fixed habit.

XVIII

ARRANGEMENTS

I N THE present chapter we shall give you a number of tricks requiring an arrangement of the cards which will bring about a result you desire. These arrangements must be made without the knowledge of the audience, and this may be accomplished in one of these ways:

1. You may prepare the arrangement before you perform, place the cards in their case, and offer the trick as your first feat.

2. You may place the arrangement in your pocket before performance. The absence of six or seven cards, or even a dozen, will rarely be noticed. When you need the arrangement, palm the cards and secretly add them to the pack.

3. You may arrange the cards openly between tricks. You will already have seen how this is done in the feat described as the obliging aces (see page 125). The general rule is that when you are making an arrangement openly you must do it boldly. The moment your manner becomes furtive you will create suspicion.

Between impromptu tricks there are always a few moments of laughter and comment, and you can make your arrangement at this time if you do it as you talk, dividing your attention between the cards and those about you. You must remember that, although you know you are making an arrangement and may at first be self-conscious, those about you do not know what you are doing. You can let them think you are searching for the joker as you shift cards about, or you need offer no explanation at all.

Some of our most adept card experts make arrangements with

the utmost *sang-froid*. Their manner is so disarming that, though they are seen arranging the cards, their audiences never connect this with the trick that follows.

4. You may arrange the cards during the course of the trick which precedes the one requiring the arrangement. Let us say that you are performing a key location trick and have found the correct card and are prepared to reveal it. Instead of doing so immediately, you pretend perplexity and run through the cards, occasionally removing one and returning it, then moving a few cards here and there, as if in search of the card.

Actually you are arranging the cards in readiness for use. Most short arrangements can be made in a matter of seconds. With the cards properly arranged, you bring the trick in hand to its proper conclusion and are ready to perform the feat requiring the arrangement.

After the arrangement has been made and before the trick is introduced, always shuffle the cards thoroughly by the overhand method, controlling the arrangement in the manner that has been fully described.

TRICKS WITH ARRANGEMENTS

THE SELECTIVE TOUCH

"Jimmy Valentine" made popular the notion that one's finger tips could be made so sensitive that they would acquire abnormal qualities, and this idea was seized upon to dress the presentation of a number of conjuring tricks.

In this trick a shuffled pack is placed in your pocket, and the suit and value of a chosen card are matched by removing cards from the pack, presumably because of the sensitivity of the finger tips.

Preparation. Secretly place the ace of clubs, two of hearts, four of spades, and eight of diamonds with the backs outermost in your upper right vest pocket. The eight of diamonds is nearest your body.

Procedure. The steps are as follows:

1. Have someone shuffle the deck, remove any card, note it, and place it face upwards on the table.

2. Open your coat and have him place the remainder of the pack in your inner coat pocket. See that he places it back outermost.

3. Discourse on the sensitivity of your finger tips. "We all know that it is possible to read raised figures with the finger tips, but it is not so generally known that it is possible to read printing in the same manner," you say. "I frankly admit that I am unable to read fine print, such as that found in a magazine or newspaper; but I can read the large indexes of the cards, both the numerals and the pips."

4. "I'll try it with your card." Turn toward your left, open your coat a little with your right hand, and slide your left hand into the inner coat pocket, moving the fingers so that the movement shows through the cloth. Remove your hand from the pocket and remove one of the cards from your vest pocket, the suit of which matches that of the spectator's card. Knowing the sequence of the cards makes this an easy matter. Bring it out as if from your inner coat pocket, saying, "Here is a card of the same suit!"

5. Again reach under the coat. "Now to see if I can match the value of your card." Remove your hand and rub it briskly on your right coat sleeve, then plunge it under the coat again. Fumble about in the inner coat pocket, finally removing the card or cards necessary to match the value of the card—for example, for an ace bring forth the ace; for a three, the ace and two; for a four, the ace and three, and so on. Any number can be matched with the four cards—the jack, queen, and king being considered as eleven, twelve, and thirteen.

If the suit card you have already removed is needed to match the value, remove the other card or cards and place these upon the suit card, arriving at the proper value in this manner. For example, let us say that the spectator has the seven of spades. Bring forth the four of spades and show it, a spade, as the suit card. Now remove the ace and two, placing them beside the four, pointing out that the three values total seven.

A little experiment will show you that any card can be matched by using the four cards. The trick is simple but when given a good presentation it is, like other simple things, very entertaining.

A FUTURE IN CARDS

This feat is made possible by a simple arrangement. A person thinks of a card and you instantly produce it, thus proving by conjurers' logic that you have read his mind.

1. Take a shuffled pack and spread the top cards as if to have one chosen. Secretly count the cards and, when you have spread fifteen, cut these off the pack, saying that instead of having one selected you will do a much more difficult trick.

2. Place the remainder of the pack to one side and remove any club, any heart, any spade, and any two diamonds from the fifteen—keeping them in this order, which can be remembered easily if you think of the consonants in the word *CHaSeD*. Hold the five cards in your right hand, retaining the other ten cards in your left hand.

3. "I promised you the trick would be a difficult one," you say. "I do not want you to touch a card or remove it from the pack. Instead, please think—just think—of one of these cards." Spread the five cards and remember the name of the second diamond, which will be the fifth card in the fan. Let us say it is the ace.

4. Drop the five cards on the pack, and place the ten in your left hand on top of all. "I shall prove to you that I can read your mind." Shuffle the cards without disturbing the position of the first fifteen cards, then take five cards from the top and push them into the center. Remove five from the bottom and push these also into the center. Finally remove five more cards from the top and thrust these into the center of the pack. As a result, the five cards from which the choice was made are now at the top of the pack.

5. Place the pack in your right coat pocket. "Kindly name your card, and I will offer my proof," you say, thrusting your hand into your pocket. When the card is named, instantly secure the proper card and withdraw it from your pocket, saying, "I was sure that was your card. Here it is!"

In finding the proper card you are guided by the *CHaSeD*

formula. If a card named is a club, you withdraw the top card; if a heart, the second card; if a spade, the third; if a diamond, the fourth. But if the diamond named is the one the name of which you memorized (in this illustration, the ace) you remove the fifth card.

JACKS WILD

Professing to demonstrate a gambler's sleight, you repeatedly deal three jacks to a spectator. Offering to deal him the four jacks, you deal him the four aces instead.

Secretly take the four aces and alternate them with four indifferent cards, placing the aces first, third, fifth, and seventh. Place this set-up on four indifferent cards, and place all face upwards at the bottom of the pack.

Now arrange the jacks so that they are in the following order from the top of the deck down: jack of spades, jack of diamonds, jack of clubs, any card, jack of hearts, and so on.

1. Bring the conversation around to gamblers' sleights, explaining that although you are not an authority on matters of this kind nevertheless you have been shown the sleight known as the second deal and that you will demonstrate it.

2. Take the pack, saying, "See if you can catch me when I deal the second card." Deal the top card to a spectator, the next to yourself, the third to the spectator, the fourth to yourself, the fifth to the spectator. Slide your next card, the sixth, under the two before you, pick up all three, and replace them on the deck.

"Did you see the second deal?" you inquire. "I gave you three jacks." Turn his cards face up on the table, showing two black jacks on top of a red jack. Slide the top black jack under the other two, pick up all three, and place them face downwards on the pack.

3. "I'll do it again." Repeat the deal, and he will again have two black jacks and a red jack. Since the red jack is below the two blacks each time, it is not noticed that it is the other red jack. Again slide the top black jack under the other two, and replace them face down on the pack.

4. "Listen and you'll hear the second card as it slides from

under the top card," you suggest. "It makes a hissing sound." Repeat the deal once more. Show that the spectator has the three jacks, pick them up, and drop them face downwards on the pack.

5. "They tell me it takes twenty years to develop a good second deal," you comment. Drop both hands to your sides and grasp your chair, hitching it forward as if to make yourself more comfortable. Under cover of this natural action, turn the pack over with your left thumb. Bring it up into view, the reversed cards uppermost.

6. "I'll deal a regular poker hand this time," you continue, "and I'll try to give you all four jacks." Deal the cards in the ordinary manner. When he turns his cards, he finds the four aces!

"Some day," you say, "I'm going to find out how the gamblers do that!"

While everyone's attention is centered on the four aces, drop your hands under the table top and turn over the two remaining reversed cards so that the pack is in its regular condition.

Think Stop

An arrangement of the cards of one suit is used in this intriguing effect.

Beforehand arrange the thirteen cards of the club suit in numerical order by placing the ace on the table, face downwards, and on it placing the two, then the three, and so on up to the king. The king will therefore be the top card of the packet, and the ace will be the face card. Place this packet on the bottom of the deck.

1. False shuffle the deck, using the overhand false shuffle, keeping the arranged cards on the bottom. Spreading the upper three-fourths of the deck, invite a spectator to select a card.

2. Square the deck and place it on the table. Have the spectator show his card to the onlookers, and announce that you will have the card replaced in such a way that all must be convinced that it is lost in the deck.

3. Invite the spectator to place his card on top of the pack

and then cut and square the deck himself. This done, have him cut a second time and complete the cut.

4. Take the deck and place it on your left palm, extend your left fingers, and invite the spectator to cut again and place the cut on your fingers. Complete the cut yourself, lift the deck, and replace it on the left palm. By holding your hand rather high you can secretly glimpse the bottom card as you replace it on the palm of your left hand. If the bottom card is a club, square the deck and place it on the spectator's left hand. If the bottom card is not a club, simply repeat the cutting until a club appears on the bottom.

5. Stress the fact that the repeated cuts make it impossible for anyone to have any conception of the position in which the chosen card lies in the deck. Let us suppose that after several cuts you glimpse the seven of clubs at the bottom of the deck. Square the deck and place it on the spectator's outstretched left hand. Announce that by long practice you are able to estimate exactly how many cards have been cut each time and that therefore you are able to tell exactly where the chosen card lies from the top of the pack. "It is now," you assert confidently, "exactly twenty-one cards from the top."

6. "However," you continue, "there's no magic about that. Simply a matter of keen observation. Anyone can do it with practice. I propose to do something really magical. I will count backwards from twenty-one, mentally, and you, sir, will call 'Stop' at any time you please. The chosen card will rise in the deck as I count, and you will then find the card at the number I have arrived at. I am counting now, so say 'Stop' whenever you please." When the spectator calls, assert that you had reached the number seven, always naming the value of the club at the bottom of the pack as your number. The jack, queen, and king are valued at eleven, twelve, and thirteen, respectively.

7. Have the spectator deal six cards onto your hand, and then name his card. The seventh card is turned face up, and it is the chosen card!

Note that if you count the cards dealt onto your hand, reversing their order under pretense of verifying the number dealt, they will be back in their original sequence. By placing them on the bottom of the deck you can repeat the trick or use the set-up for the following feat:

DEAL AWAY

There is nothing more surprising to the layman than to be allowed to find his own selected card under conditions over which he seems to have complete control. That is what seems to happen in this self-working feat.

1. Having shown the trick we have just described, and having replaced the dealt packet at the bottom after reversing its order—so that the arrangement of clubs at the bottom runs from ace to king, the ace being the face card—say, "Perhaps you are unwilling to believe that there is such a thing as mental control. I can assure you that there is and that one person can dominate the thoughts of another. For instance, I am now thinking of one of the cards, and I am projecting my thought to you. I want you to make your mind a complete blank and then name the first card that comes to mind. That card will be the card I am projecting to you. Are you ready? All right—*quickly!* Name a card!"

"The seven of hearts."

"*Right!*" you exclaim. No matter what card he names, you tell him he has named the correct card. "Why, it's marvelous!" Look quizzically at him, and everyone will be amused at your swindle.

2. After a moment, say, "Ah, you don't believe I projected my card to you. Very well, I'll offer you proof that there is such a thing as mental control. Here, please take a card." Spread the pack and have one removed from the upper three-fourths. Square the pack and place it on the table; have the card shown to all and then placed on the top of the pack, after which you invite the spectator to make one complete cut, thus burying his card at the middle, with the arrangement of clubs directly above it.

3. Pick up the pack and make an overhand false shuffle, which will not disturb the order of the cards. "I give you my word of honor that I do not know the position of your card in the pack

at this moment," you say. This is true. "But I do not need to, because I am not going to find your card. You're going to find it yourself." Hand him the pack. "Please deal cards face downwards on the table, ten or twelve or fifteen, as many as you like. When you feel an impulse to stop the deal, stop."

4. The spectator deals a number of cards and stops the deal. "Kindly turn over the last card you dealt," you say. Let us assume that it is a four of diamonds. "You stopped on a four-spot. Very well, deal four cards." He deals four cards, and you have him turn the last card face upwards as before. It is, say, the eight of clubs. You then know that, if he deals eight cards and turns the last card dealt, it will be his chosen card. In other words, soon or late he will turn a card of the club suit face upwards, and whatever its value, if he deals down that many cards more, the last card dealt will be his card.

5. You therefore announce, "You are being guided as inevitably as if by destiny itself. You have turned an eight-spot. Deal eight cards." He does so. "Now name your card." He does so. "Look at the last card you dealt." He turns it face upwards and it is his chosen card!

Pick up all the cards and idly give them a riffle shuffle, thus removing any possible clues to the feat. As in the preceding trick, jacks, queens, and kings are valued at eleven, twelve, and thirteen respectively.

THE EDUCATED CARDS

In this excellent trick a spectator finds his own card and has not the faintest idea as to how he found it.

First you must secretly place an arrangement at the top of the pack. Run through the pack and place any nine, seven, five, three, and ace at the bottom in sequence, the ace being the face card. Turn the deck face downwards and grasp it at its ends between the left thumb and fingers, the hand being arched over the pack.

With the right thumb at the top and the fingers at the bottom of the pack, draw off the top and bottom cards and drop them on the table. Repeat this six times. You will have a pile of twelve cards which run, from the top down, x, x, x, 9, x, 7, x, 5, x, 3, x, A.

Push this packet to one side without disturbing the sequence of the cards, and draw off six more sets of two cards in the same way as before. Glance up, saying, "Ever see this before? It's the faro shuffle, the only shuffle the faro dealers use." Drop the pack upon this pile you have just dealt, then carelessly scoop up the first pile and place it on the deck. Thus you have placed your arrangement of twelve cards at the top.

1. Shuffle the deck, retaining the first fifteen cards at the top, then place the pack in your left hand and spread it as if to have a card removed, secretly counting the first twelve cards. Square the deck as if you had changed your mind, and secure a little-finger break under the twelfth card in preparation for the twelve-down riffle control.

Riffle the cards upwards with the right hand, saying, "Take any card you like. I'll riffle slowly so that you have a free choice. Please show your card to everyone." Split the pack at the twelfth card, have the drawn card replaced, and drop the twelve cards upon it, thus placing the chosen card thirteenth from the top. This is the twelve-down riffle control (see page 196).

2. Undercut the lower half, injog the first card, and shuffle off. Undercut at the injog, forming a break, and shuffle off to the break. Throw the cards under the break on top, thus returning the arrangement and chosen card to the top. As you do this, say, "Let me show you how simple it is to find your card, even after a genuine shuffle. In fact, to show you how simple it is, I'll let you find the card yourself."

3. Take the pack face downwards in your left hand and begin to deal cards slowly face upwards on the table. "Tell me when to stop the deal." The first three cards you deal are indifferent and every other card thereafter is one of your arrangement. When the command to stop the deal comes, glance at the card face upwards on the table. If it is one of the cards of your arrangement—a nine, seven, five, three, or ace—point to it, saying, "You stopped me on a five—" (or whatever it is) "—so I'll deal five cards." Deal the five cards, pushing the last card dealt to one side. "This is the card at your number," you point out. "What was the name of your card?" He tells you and when you turn the card you placed to one side, it is the spectator's card.

If, however, he stops the deal on an indifferent card, you remove the *next* card from the top of the pack, saying, "You stopped the deal on this card." Whatever its value, deal that many more cards and the last one will be the chosen card.

The trick has an effect out of all proportion to the simple means involved.

REDS AND BLACKS

This is a trick the secret of which is well known to everyone. That it is a good trick is attested to by the fact that it is used by many cardmen of the first rank, who present it with such polish that it deceives even those who know the method.

Before presenting the trick, place all the red cards at the top of the pack, the black cards at the bottom. Turn the first of the black cards face upwards in the deck.

1. False shuffle the cards, using the overhand false shuffle. Spread the cards and notice that one card is "accidentally" reversed. Run all the cards above the reversed card into the right hand, turn the reversed card face downwards, and reassemble the pack, inserting the tip of your little finger between the two packets as you do so.

2. Riffle the outer end of the pack with the right hand; apparently cut the pack haphazard but actually cut at the little-finger break. Place all the red cards at your right, the black cards at your left.

3. Turn your back and instruct someone to cut either packet, remove one card, and replace the cut. Have him look at and remember the card, then thrust it in the center of the *other* packet, finally shuffling this packet.

4. Next have him cut the first packet, place the shuffled packet on the lower portion of the cut, and replace the upper portion on all.

5. Turn around, take the deck, and hold it with its face toward yourself so that no one else can see the cards. Pretend to search for the chosen card, but actually cut the pack to bring all the reds and blacks together for a repetition of the trick if this seems desirable.

6. Finally remove the spectator's card. It will be the only

black card among the reds, or vice versa. Have the card named
and show that you hold it in your hand.

Repeat the trick if this seems warranted. If not, shuffle the
deck, thus destroying all clues to the ways and means.

XIX

ROUTINES

Routining Card Tricks

WHEN the neophyte has mastered several tricks, he is faced with the necessity of *routining* them, that is to say, arranging them in the best possible order so that the fullest effect can be drawn from each feat and so that they will follow one another smoothly without any hesitation or delay. This programming of tricks is most important. If one relies solely on knowing a number of separate tricks, all too often one's mind goes blank after a trick or two before an audience. This is true even with advanced cardmen. A floundering attempt is then made to recall some simple feat, and instead of arriving at a triumphant climax one has to close ignominiously.

To avoid such disaster, the only plan is to arrange one's tricks in a certain sequence, so that, having started with one trick, the rest follow automatically with no effort of memory whatever. This routining will be found to be an interesting study. Roughly the plan should be to start with a good trick, one that arouses interest at the very beginning, continue with tricks the effects of which are on an ascending scale of interest, and finish with the strongest effect of the series.

In using the word "mastered" in the first sentence of this chapter, we mean that the student has his tricks literally at his finger tips and that he can do them at a moment's notice, anywhere and with any pack that may be handed to him. This is the only way in which to get complete satisfaction from performing and to give complete satisfaction to your audiences. Make up your mind at once that it is better to know a few tricks thoroughly than it is to half know several dozens.

Let us suppose that the conditions are that you are called

upon to entertain a small group and that a pack of cards has been handed to you. Begin with:

Topsy-Turvy Cards

Introduce the trick with some remark about testing the cards to see if they have been well trained. Finding that the cards are satisfactory, continue with:

Now You See It

This is a "mistake" trick, in which it appears that you cannot complete your trick successfully and yet at the last moment you turn the tables and finish triumphantly. It is a good trick, because it gives you a psychological advantage over your audience. At first those present think you are a hopeless dub with cards, and they feel a little sorry for you. When you seem to be in the deepest trouble and they feel most sympathetic, you startle them by showing that you have had command of the situation from the start. The climax is amazing and causes laughter and bewilderment. The trick can be performed in about two minutes, and this is important, for the first tricks should be quick and good.

The trick is a good one for another reason. While performing it, you prepare for the next in your routine, in this manner: While searching for the spectator's card in step No. 9, move the cards around and, in doing this, place any nine-spot at the ninth position from the top, with the four aces immediately following it. In this manner, while doing one trick, you prepare for the next, which is:

The Obliging Aces

This is a trick which seems to call for great skill. In performing it, you convince those present that you have genuine ability. When finished, thrust the four aces into the pack and hand it for shuffling. Next, you perform:

Do as I Do

Your audience is now watching attentively for sleight-of-hand, hence you make a change of pace and instead perform a self-working feat which requires no skill but has a tremendous effect. You follow this with:

Card in the Pocket

Here you change the *type* of trick, performing a pseudo-mind-reading feat, which you follow with:

Three Cards Across

This concludes the routine with a fine trick which to the audience is the most surprising feat of all those you have performed.

A routine of card tricks which may serve one person admirably may not be nearly so effective in the hands of another, for the personality of a performer has much to do with the entertainment value which is got from the routine.

As you perform the tricks given you in this book, you will find that you enjoy performing some of them more than others, and usually you will get a stronger audience reaction from these tricks. You should remember the ones from which you get the most effect and use these in building your routines. You should also try to remember any amusing byplay or incidents which happen, so that you can keep these in your presentation. You will find that the more you perform a trick the better your presentation will be, for a good presentation grows, like Topsy, as you incorporate these extemporaneous bits of business in your routine.

The building of a routine is one of the most fascinating aspects of doing magic with cards. The clever performer always considers his tricks from the viewpoint of the audience and strives to make them more and more entertaining. Your talk, or *patter*, is an integral part of the routine and should be given as much thought as the mechanics of the trick. In some of the tricks in this book we have sketchily indicated a suitable patter, but if possible you should contrive your own talk, which will then be in keeping with your personality. You will find that as you perform your tricks you will make amusing or showmanly remarks extemporaneously, and you should remember these, if you can, as carefully as you remember the bits of byplay we have mentioned.

In constructing your patter, which will follow the plot line of your trick, be careful not to be verbose. The student often feels that he must talk interminably, and this becomes boresome. You will know quickly enough if what you are saying is effective. If it is not, rewrite your patter. If you are talking too much and your audience looks unhappy, cut your patter mercilessly. If you have attempted to be humorous and no one laughs, throw out the pseudo-humorous lines and find others that are really amusing or witty. It is only by self-criticism that you will perfect and smooth your talk.

The plot line of a trick is usually indicated by the trick itself. In devising your presentation, you should apply the laws of interest. If you say, "Let me show you a card trick," you have not necessarily succeeded in arousing interest. But if you say, "You have, no doubt, heard of the lie detector, the complicated machine which science has devised to determine if a person is lying or telling the truth. Well, this pack of cards is my lie detector, and I'd like to show you how it operates." If you make some such introductory statement, you have piqued the curiosity of everyone present. Even so simple a statement as "This is a trick which Herrmann the Great performed for over thirty years" will arouse interest, for everyone has heard of Herrmann, and the spectator's reaction is, "If this trick was so good that Herrmann used it for thirty years, it must be worth watching." Your patter thereafter will follow the plot line which you have suggested in your opening statement.

It may be wise to tell you at this time that you cannot gauge the effect of a trick accurately when you perform for your family or intimate friends. They know you too well. They will either tell you that you are wonderful or that you are not very good, and neither may be the exact truth. To determine the value of a trick and its presentation, perform it for strangers.

One final word concerning routining: Construct your routines so that they can be performed in from ten to fifteen minutes. You will build a number of them, using different types of tricks— those performed at the table, those for use when standing and surrounded by people, and so on—and by limiting them to fifteen minutes at the most you will be sure that you do not monopolize a gathering. If when you have finished a routine your audience clamors for more, you have only to perform one of the other routines.

This routine is designed for use on occasions when an intimate group is being entertained at the table.

Beforehand have the four aces on the top of the pack, the pack in its case, and the case in your pocket. For your first trick perform:

The Poker Player's Picnic

Take out the pack and shuffle it thoroughly by the overhand method, retaining the aces on the top, and finally cut the cards by means of the palm cut. Place the pack before a spectator and proceed with the trick.

At the end of this feat you have four piles of cards with an ace face upwards on top of each. Turn the aces face downwards. For the next trick you require the aces to be on the top of the pack. Place them there secretly as follows:

1. Pick up packet A and place it in your left hand in the position for an overhand shuffle. Pick up packet B and with it begin an overhand shuffle by running one card (the ace) onto packet A. Jog the next card and shuffle off freely. Undercut to the jogged card and throw on top. You have two aces together on top of the cards you hold.

2. Pick up packet C. Repeat the same shuffle to bring the three aces together, but this time finish the shuffle by using the break, shuffle off and throw; bringing the three aces to the top of the cards you hold.

3. Take the last packet, D, and control its ace in the same way. Finally execute the lift shuffle with the whole deck, then cut the pack, using the palm cut.

Having thus assembled the four aces secretly at the top of the deck, proceed to the next trick:

A Poker Puzzle

At its finish, gather up the cards of the hand just exposed and also the fifth hand which was dealt to yourself. Three poker hands of five cards each remain on the table. Use these to introduce the following trick:

The Good Luck Card

The student should have no difficulty in presenting these three tricks effectively. The collection of the four aces from the top of the four packets should be done in a casual manner, without looking at the cards while shuffling them and telling about the trick you are about to do.

A ROLLICKING ROUTINE

This is a fast-moving routine in which the cards jump about, change, and generally perform in a rollicking manner.

Hand the pack to someone and have him shuffle it.

Rapid Transit

"Let's see how the cards are behaving tonight," you say as you take the pack. "I'll place the top card, the ace of hearts, on the table. The next card is—let's see, it's the ten of clubs. I'll place the ten of clubs over here. Watch it closely. I'll replace the ace of hearts on the pack while you watch that ten of clubs. Now we'll see if the pack is in a good mood tonight, for if it is I shall have the ten of clubs at the top of the pack and you will have the ace of hearts on the table. Yes, the pack is full of tricks tonight. I feel emboldened to try a most difficult feat—"

The Piano Trick

Perform this trick as given in the chapter on the palm. At its conclusion, continue with:

Leapfrog

"The cards are certainly in high spirits tonight. Let's see what else they have to offer. Here, will you take a card, and you too, sir?" Have two spectators each remove a card and, when they have been replaced, control them to the top by means of the overhand lift shuffle. Casually run the top card to the bottom as if about to shuffle again overhand, change your mind and make a riffle shuffle, retaining the bottom card (the second selected card) and the top card (the first selected card) in position.

Key undercut one-third of the deck and work this trick.

"My cards are athletic, aren't they?"

A Vested Interest

Gather the scattered cards and place them under the packet in your left hand, thus retaining the first selected card on the top of the pack. Shuffle, retaining the first card in position, and for the finale work this trick.

The opening trick is an intriguing one, and the two discoveries smartly worked are most effective.

CARD-DISCOVERY ROUTINE

Hand the deck for shuffling and, when it has been returned to you, ribbon spread the cards on the table, turn them over, and gather them with a sweep. "So far, so good!" you comment. Spring the cards from hand to hand. "Better and better!" Perform the Charlier cut. "A perfect pack. I think it will give surprising results."

A Tipsy Trick

Present this amusing feat as described in the chapter on reverses.

The Double Speller

"I doubt if anything like that could happen tonight in the present company," you continue. "Still, one never knows how the cards will act." Spread the cards with a flourish, saying, "Will you take a card, sir? And you? And you too, sir? The more the merrier." After the cards have been shown to everyone, begin a lift shuffle and, having shuffled about one-third of the pack, throw the lifted packet onto the cards in your left hand and have the third spectator's card placed on top. Continue the shuffle by jogging the first card and shuffling off.

Form a break at the jog and repeat exactly the same procedure with the second person's card, and finally do the same with the third person's card. You have all three cards on the top of the pack in the order of their selection.

Shuffle once more, placing one card above the three chosen cards on the top of the pack.

Perform this trick as described in the chapter on the pass. When the first spectator finds his card reversed in the pack, the other two chosen cards will be second and third under the reversed card at the top of the packet remaining in his hands. Take this packet from him, drop it on the dealt cards and square the deck. Bury the reversed card and the one under it in the center.

Pinkie Does It

Shuffle again, using the lift shuffle, then execute a riffle shuffle and finally the palm cut, retaining the two cards in position at the top. Perform the rising card trick exactly as explained in the chapter on tricks with the overhand shuffle, and at the conclusion allow the second spectator to withdraw his card himself.

A Smash Finish

You are now left with the third spectator's card at the top of the pack. Overhand shuffle, taking it to the bottom and back to the top. Palm the card in your right hand and hand the deck to be shuffled by someone on your left, and thereby sighting the card.

When the spectator has shuffled to his satisfaction, instruct him to hold the deck in his left hand by one end. No matter how he holds it, remove the pack with your right hand and place it in your left, secretly adding the palmed card.

Take hold of his left hand and turn it palm upwards, then place the pack face upwards on it, so that he can grip the cards between his thumb near the inner end of the deck, on the face, and his fingers on the back of the deck extending about half its length. Instruct him to take a firm hold of the cards.

Turn to the person who selected the third card. Ask him to hold out his right hand, and say, "In taking your card the tips of your fingers came in contact momentarily with its index at one end or the other. A minute impression of that index was thus left on your fingers. No, it is not visible and can only be detected by a highly sensitive sense of touch. This is much more difficult than reading the face of a card, but I shall try. Allow me."

Feel the tips of his fingers with your left hand, since "that is the more sensitive, being nearer the heart." Announce the color, then the value, and finally the suit of his card, which you previously glimpsed.

Turn to the spectator who is holding the pack. "Now, sir, please hold the pack tightly." See that he has not changed the grip, his thumb near the inner end and his fingers protruding under the pack, and suddenly strike the pack with a sharp downward blow. All the cards except the lowermost will be knocked out of his hand and scattered on the floor. Have him hold up this card and show it to everyone. It is the card just named, the card that was selected by the third spectator.

We have mentioned elsewhere that it is always advisable to have several persons note a selected card in order to guard against the possibility that the drawer may forget its name, misread it, or misname it in an attempt to disconcert you. There is the possibility, too, that you may have erred in some manner and lost control of one of the cards.

In such a case you must never concede defeat. Let us say that you have lost control of a chosen card and now must extricate yourself from your predicament. Do it in this manner:

1. Hold the pack in your left hand as for the color change. Turn to the spectator, saying, "Kindly name your card." Place your hand over the pack and simulate the action of the color change. When the card is named, say, "I'll do something very surprising for you!"

2. Pass by this spectator's card and go on to the next drawn card. While discovering it, fan through the pack, find the lost card, place it at the top of the pack, and then go back and make your discovery of the card.

RAZZLE-DAZZLE ROUTINE

This short routine contains many surprises and can be performed under almost any conditions; for this reason it is excellent for impromptu use. As with all routines, you should practice it until you can go through it without watching your hands or having to stop to remember what to do next. The action should be automatic, smooth, and graceful.

The Sevens

Since this is the opening trick of the routine, arrange the four sevens as required for the trick before your performance. When you have finished the feat, hand the pack to someone for shuffling.

Righting a Wrong

After performing this trick, again have someone shuffle the cards. Take the pack, glance at it, and say, "Did you know that shuffling the cards generates electricity? Look what you've done." Place the deck face downwards in your left hand and do the *pop-up card* trick. Quickly place the card on the top of the pack and hold it down with your forefinger. "You shocked that card. It's still trying to get away from me." Remove your right hand and hold it in position for the *self-cutting pack*. "Why, the whole pack's in a ferment," you exclaim, shooting the lower half into your right hand. "I don't think I'll be able to control the cards. However, I'll try. I'll use the two red aces."

The Acrobatic Aces

Spread the cards face upwards and remove the red aces, and with them perform this trick, concluding by saying, "As you can see, the cards have a whim of iron."

Top-Change Byplay

Shuffle the cards, using the waterfall shuffle, and when the cards are squared, cut the pack using the method described as a pretty cut. Place the deck face upwards in your left hand, and change the face card by means of the color change, muttering, "The cards are absolutely uncontrollable tonight. No one knows what will happen next."

Fan the deck, have a card removed and noted by all, and proceed into the top-change byplay.

When you have extracted all the fun to be had from the trick, glance at someone and say, "I'll read your mind. Think of a card." Spread the cards with their faces toward yourself, find the eight of clubs, and cut it to the top of the pack. Hesitate, shake your head, and say, "Concentrate, please." Fan the pack, find the nine of clubs, remove it, and hold it with its back to the audience, saying, "Remember, all you did was think of this card. Kindly name it." He names it and once in fifty-two times it should be the card you hold. On the other fifty-one occasions, glance at the card, say "Oh" in an expressionless tone, and place it at the top of the pack.

Immediately and blandly say, "Well, I'll do another trick for you. This time *I'll* think of a card and you name it. Ready? Good. Name the first card that comes to mind, and that will be my card. . . . All right, what's the card I'm thinking of?" No matter what card he names, say, "That's correct!" All this the audience believes to be amusing nonsense, but actually you have set up the eight and nine of clubs at the top of the pack in preparation for:

The Ambitious Card

Perform the trick as given, finally finding the card under your coat. "You see how the cards are tonight? Can't do a thing with them!" you say, pocketing the deck.

PART THREE

XX

PLATFORM TRICKS

Conus Ace Trick

THE number of four-ace tricks is now almost legion, but one of the first and still the best is the one devised by the French conjurer Conus a century ago. With slight modification the trick is as effective today as it ever was. The plot, as in all great tricks, is simple: The four aces are transformed in a spectator's hands into four other cards, and they are finally found in one of his pockets.

Preparation. You will need a deck of cards and four duplicate aces. On the top of the deck place the four duplicate aces, with the ace of clubs uppermost. On top of all place the ace of clubs from the deck, so that at the top you have two aces of clubs followed by the three duplicate aces. The other three aces of the deck are scattered through it. Remove any four indifferent cards from the pack, then put it in its case and put the case on your table.

Procedure. The steps are as follows:

1. Invite a spectator to come forward to assist you. Seat the volunteer at a small table at your left. Pick up the card case and, saying that you will use a deck of cards, remove the cards and lay the case on the table. Spread the cards with their faces outwards, showing them but keeping the aces at the top bunched together. Close the spread and insert your left little finger under the five top cards. Square the deck and hold the break under the five top cards by pressing the little finger firmly against the side of the deck. You can then hold the deck quite openly, yet you are ready to palm the five cards whenever you please.

2. Address the spectator: "You, sir, are to act as a committee

of one on behalf of this large and intellectual audience, so I want you to be absolutely satisfied about everything that takes place. You agree to that?"

"Yes."

"First, we haven't made any arrangement about this trick, have we?"

"No."

"As a matter of fact, you have never seen me before in your life, have you?"

"No." (Sometimes when the assistant is an acquaintance and people know it, you get some fun out of his accommodating answer.)

"Fine, you will be satisfied about everything that takes place?"

"Yes."

"You won't say yes if you mean no?"

"No."

"You mean no?"

"Yes."

"Good! Now that we thoroughly understand each other, will you take the deck, remove the aces, and see that there are only four all together?" In the meantime you have quietly palmed the five top cards and taken the pack in your right hand.

3. Place the deck on the table before him and, as he begins to run through it, turn to the audience. "You cannot be too careful. Some people, especially when playing poker, use a lot of aces." Turn to your assistant, who has found and removed three aces and is searching for the ace of clubs. "One, two, three aces," you say. "What have you done with the fourth?" Seize his right lapel with your right hand, pulling his coat open. Hold it for a moment as you say to the audience, "Did you see what he did?" Then take the lapel with your left hand and thrust your right hand into his inner breast pocket. Bring out the first ace of clubs and leave the other four aces in the pocket. Show it, and under cover of the laughter this causes whisper to him, "Button up your coat just to make them laugh." He does this, and the action always causes amusement. It also safeguards you against any premature discovery of the duplicate aces, safely ensconced in the buttoned coat.

4. "You mustn't do that. *I'm* the one to do the trick, *you* are the committee." Take the deck, open it bookwise, and have the spectator insert the four aces. Close the pack on them, and in putting it on the table make a pretence of manipulating the cards. "Now, sir, the aces are in the middle of the deck?" Having seen you make a suspicious move, he will express doubt about that. "You are quite right," you say. "I want you to be perfectly satisfied. Watch." Take the deck, turn it face upwards, run through it to the four aces and show them in the middle. "Right?" Close the spread, inserting your left little finger tip above two of the aces. Make the pass in turning the deck face downwards, and lay the cards on the table.

5. "Now, sir, those four aces placed in the middle by yourself will travel to any position you may like to name. For instance, would you like them all at the top or all at the bottom, or one on the top and three on the bottom, or one on the bottom and three on the top, or . . . say, two at the top and two at the bottom?" Rattle off the first choices very rapidly, the last after a momentary pause, then say, "Wait; for greater safety, place your hand on the deck."

Nearly always the spectator chooses the last suggestion. "Two above and two below," he says. Tap the deck with your right forefinger, say "Pass!" and then have him remove the cards himself. A round of applause is sure to follow.

If another position is chosen, you have at least one ace already there. Take the pack and let the spectator remove that one; then, as he shows it, make the pass to bring the others to the position required.

6. Show the four aces and place them on the top of the deck. "You did that very well. With a few years' practice I'm sure you will make a good magician. Now, suppose I place the aces on the table, so—" (deal them face downwards) "—and you place your hand on them." Grasp his hand and place it on the four cards. "Do you think I could take them away from you and send you four other cards? You'd like to see me try? By the way, are you quite sure that you have the four aces?"

The spectator, not having seen the aces since they were placed on the deck, expresses his doubts. "That's right. I'm glad you are a little skeptical, for I want you to be quite certain. See—" (take the four cards and show them) "—they are the four aces." Replace them on the top of the pack.

7. *Look at your hands,* make a rapid movement as if making the pass, then deal the four top cards on the table, and again place his hand on them. "This time you have them?" The spectator responds that he is not at all sure about that. "There is such a thing as being too skeptical," you say. "Turn the cards over yourself." As he does so slip the tip of your left little finger under the top card. He turns the cards over and shows the aces.

8. Take them again. Casually place them on the deck, then remove them, taking the top card with them. "There has been no change so far," you say, holding the packet of five cards up so that he and the audience can see the face of the indifferent card. Drop the packet on the deck, and then deal off the four aces. Grasp his hand and place it on them. "This time you have the aces." The spectator vigorously protests that he has not. Appeal to the onlookers, "You are all satisfied that the aces are on the table?" There will be cries of "No! No!"

Pretending to be at a loss as to how there can be any doubt about the matter, turn to the spectator, "I can't do the trick until you are perfectly satisfied. Please turn the aces over and show them to everybody." In the meantime you have had ample opportunity to palm five cards from the top of the deck in your right hand. Retain the deck in that hand.

The aces are shown amidst laughter and much to the surprise of all. Maintain your attitude of being a little bewildered by the attitude of the audience. Take the aces one by one in your left hand, and hold them face downwards. Lay the pack down and suggest that the spectator look it over. Take the aces with your right hand, adding the five palmed cards to them. Hold the packet face outwards by the ends between the right thumb and fingers and say, "Now, to make quite sure there can be no mistake, I'll give the aces a good bend, so." Squeeze the ends, making the face of the packet concave. "There can be no doubt about the aces now."

9. Take the deck in your left hand, and drop the packet from your right hand on top. "Can you tell me where the aces are

now?" you ask. Seeing the bent cards, the spectator answers confidently, "On the top." "Satisfied at last. Watch very closely." Deal the four top cards very delicately one by one and place them in a pile before him. As you remove the fourth card press the left thumb on the pack, taking the bend out of the other cards. Turn the top indifferent card face upwards, saying, "You see, they're all gone." In replacing it slide it under the top ace, which you push off the pack a little to facilitate this. "Place your hand on the aces and your other hand on top of that. Don't move your hands or the audience will think you are doing the trick and not me.

10. "Here's the impossible thing I shall try to do. I shall change those four aces you are holding so tightly and send you four other cards. Here is one card." Make the double lift and turn-over, showing the indifferent card seen just before. Turn them down as one card, and thumb off the top card—an ace—face downwards on the table.

Begin an overhand shuffle by pulling out all except the top and bottom cards, thus keeping the changed card out of sight, drop the pack on the two cards, undercut half the deck, injog the first card, and shuffle off. Undercut to the injog, bringing the three aces back to the top. Take off two cards as one and, holding them toward the spectator, ask him to breathe on the card. As he does so, slide the two cards rapidly apart, saying, "I didn't ask you to *blow*. You've made two!" Drop them on the first ace without showing their faces.

11. Spread the cards and ask the spectator to remove one. "Show it to everyone," and, as he does so, palm the top card in your right hand and take the deck in that hand. "What card did you take? The ten of diamonds," you say, taking it face down-wards in your left hand. Lay the pack down and take the card in your right hand, adding the palmed ace to it. Hold the card (s) up by the ends showing it (them), and place it (them) in your left hand, face outwards, the thumb on the face and the fingers on the back (Fig. 115).

"I shall change this card into one of your aces. Would you like me to do it visibly or invisibly? Visibly? Very well, I pass my hand over the cards, so—" (pass your empty right hand across the card) "—and nothing happens. I pass it over again—" (this time push the rear card with the left fingers into the right hand and palm it) "—and again nothing happens." Change the grip

TWO CARDS HELD AS
ONE. AS RIGHT HAND
PASSES OVER FACE THE
LEFT FINGERS SLIDE
BACK CARD INTO THE
RIGHT PALM.

Fig. 115

of the card in your left hand so that it is held between the thumb on one side and the middle finger on the other, with the fore-finger resting on the middle of the top end (Fig. 116). "This is the critical time. Watch!" Pass the right hand over the card and deposit the palmed card on it without pausing a moment. The tips of the fingers and thumb make a frame into which it fits snugly.

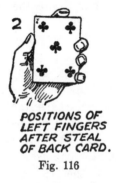

POSITIONS OF
LEFT FINGERS
AFTER STEAL
OF BACK CARD.

Fig. 116

"One ace!" you exclaim. Pick up the other three one by one, placing them in the left hand fanwise and saying, "Two! Three! All four! . . . Will you look at your four cards and see what I have sent you? Show them to everybody."

The spectator turns his four cards and shows four indifferent cards. Take this opportunity to slip the indifferent card from the back of the four aces in your right hand onto the deck, which you have picked up with your left hand. Pause while you display the four aces, and acknowledge the applause as if the trick has ended.

12. Casually place the aces on the top of the pack and immediately palm them in your right hand, taking the pack in that hand. Then say to the spectator, "You did that very nicely. I'd like you to try another trick before I put the deck away." Pick up the card case with your left hand, put the pack down with your right hand, and take the case in that hand. "Place your hand on the deck. Right. Now I shall make the aces pass up your sleeve into one of your pockets. *Pass!* Did you feel them go? No? Well, run through the deck. . . . No aces? Then kindly search your pockets." As he does this, take the pack, adding the palmed aces to it, and place it in the case.

The spectator finally unbuttons his coat and much to his surprise finds the four aces in his breast pocket. The duplicate aces were placed in his pocket so long before that no one remembers that you even so much as touched him.

Not only is the trick a most effective one but it affords ample opportunities for inoffensive fun which the assisting spectator will enjoy as much as the audience.

LADIES' LOOKING GLASS

This fanciful title was given to the feat by its inventor, Comte, a famous French magician who flourished in the early years of the nineteenth century. The trick is one of the great card tricks, and we have retained the title but somewhat modified the procedure.

Four spectators each remove a pair of cards from the deck, which are then replaced and the deck shuffled. Three of the pairs appear in rapid succession at the top and bottom of the deck, and the magician tosses the cards into the air and catches the last pair at the tips of his fingers.

Requirements. A deck of cards and eight duplicate cards. Since these cards must be memorized, it is well to take eight cards of some known arrangement, for example, the first eight cards of the Nikola system. These are:

Six of diamonds
Five of clubs
King of clubs
Jack of hearts
Five of spades
Nine of diamonds
Nine of spades
Queen of hearts

Place these eight cards on the top of the deck in that order. Take any indifferent card from the deck, place it on top of the duplicate set of eight cards—which are in the same order—and place the packet of nine cards in your right trousers pocket, with the backs outermost.

Procedure. Present the trick as follows:

1. "Many years ago," you begin, "when I was a boy, I saw a famous magician do a feat with cards which was so extraordinary that I have puzzled over it ever since and have never been able to find a solution to it. I shall show you what he did, and perhaps some of you may be able to suggest an answer to the problem.

2. "First, he had a number of cards taken." Take the deck, shuffle overhand, using the lift shuffle and retaining the arranged cards at the top. "Since it makes no difference what cards are taken, will you, sir," addressing someone on your right, "just call "Stop" whenever you please as I shuffle the cards." Begin the lift shuffle, and at the word "Stop" drop the controlled packet onto the cards in your left hand. Hold this hand out to the spectator and have him take the card stopped at. "Do you think you can remember two cards? Very well, take the next as well." Address another person on his right and have him take the next two cards.

3. Place the cards in your right hand underneath those in your left, begin another lift shuffle, and ask a third person to the right of the second to call "Stop" in the same way. Have him take the two top cards of the left-hand packet, and have a fourth person take the next pair. This is the easiest, quickest, and most con-

vincing way of forcing a number of cards. "Please remember your cards. Show them to those near you so that there can be no mistake."

4. "This done, the old master handed the deck to the first person, asking him to replace his cards, shuffle the deck, and hand it on to the next person, who did the same thing. In this way all the cards were replaced and each person shuffled the deck. Will you do that?" Hand the deck to the first person.

While the cards are being thus shuffled into the deck, casually place both hands in your trousers pockets, palm the nine cards in your right hand, and relax.

5. When the fourth person, who will be well on your left, has replaced his cards and shuffled the deck, go to him, hold out your left hand palm upwards, and with your right hand pull up your left sleeve a little, keeping the hand on your left forearm. "Will you place the deck on my left hand? Thank you. You have shuffled freely, now I want you to make a free cut." When he has lifted off a portion of the deck, take the remainder in your right hand, adding the palmed cards, then take the cut from him with your left hand and place it below, thus completing the cut. Place the pack face downwards on your left hand and hold it there in full view.

6. "A number of freely selected cards have been replaced in the deck, each of you has shuffled it, and finally the deck has been cut freely. It would be entirely possible for one of the

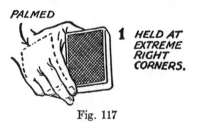

PALMED

1 HELD AT EXTREME RIGHT CORNERS.

Fig. 117

selected cards to find its way to the top or bottom." Lift the deck with the right hand, with the thumb at one end and the fingers at the other, and show the bottom card. If by chance it is a card someone has selected, simply remove it and thrust it into the middle of the deck. Lift the top card, show it, and ask, "Did anyone draw this card?" Since this is the indifferent card you have added to the deck, nobody will claim it. Slip the left little finger tip under the top card of the deck and replace the card on top. Square the deck, palm the two cards in your right hand, and take the deck in that hand by the extreme right corners between the thumb and the *forefinger only* (Fig. 117), bending the other fingers well into the palm.

7. "Now here is the mystery. The old master simply placed the deck on his left hand, so." As you do so, reach out with the left fingers and draw the two palmed cards to the bottom of the deck, thus bringing the first pair of cards to the top and the bottom. The action takes a moment and is covered by the right hand. "Then by simply shaking the cards, so—" (move the left hand up and down slightly) "—he made the first pair of cards appear, one on the top and the other on the bottom. An absolute impossibility, but just for the fun of it I'll try. Will you, sir—" (addressing the first spectator) "—kindly name your two cards? The six of diamonds and the five of clubs. I have tried this hundreds of times and never succeeded." Shake the pack, raise the inner end of the top card, and shake your head. "It never comes right with me. Just once more." Shake the deck again, lift the inner end, and exclaim, "A miracle!" Lift the pack by the ends with your right hand and hold it with the face card, the six of diamonds, facing the audience.

Pause a moment, then replace the pack on your left hand, shake it, and lift off the top card, the five of clubs. "Incredible! I can hardly believe it, but there it is!"

Slip the left little finger tip under the top card as before, replace the five of clubs on top, and palm the two top cards. Take the pack in your right hand by the extreme top right corners and look at the bottom card. "Yes, they are both there." Replace the pack on your left hand and pull the two palmed cards to the bottom as before, thus bringing the second pair to the top and bottom of the deck.

8. Address the second spectator, "What were your cards? The king of clubs and the jack of hearts. We can hardly expect to succeed again, but this seems to be my good night." Shake the deck and lift it to show the bottom card, the king of clubs. "There

it is! Now for the jack of hearts." Another little shake and you lift off the top card, showing the jack of hearts.

Replace this card on top and repeat exactly the same moves to bring the next pair, the five of spades and the nine of diamonds, to the bottom and the top.

9. Proceed in the same manner to show these two cards, keeping up the same attitude of bewilderment at your success. After showing the third pair, bring the last pair to the bottom and top as before, and lay the deck on the table as if the feat were finished, shaking your head and saying, "I simply cannot understand it." The fourth spectator will remind you that there is still another pair of cards to be discovered.

10. Apologize, saying that you have been so astounded at your success with the other pairs that you forgot all about his cards. "The spell is broken, I'm afraid," you continue. "You see I have put the deck out of my hands, and it would be impossible to find your cards in the same way. I'll have to try another method for discovering them. . . . Ah, yes. Just let me touch my fingers to yours" (rub the tips of your right fingers on the tips of his).

Pick up the deck in your right hand, pressing it well into the fork of the thumb. Grip it firmly, with the thumb on the top card and the fingers on the bottom card. "I'll toss the whole pack into the air and I'll try to catch your two cards!"

RIGHT HAND.

2

Fig. 118

Strike an attitude, your right side toward the spectators. Make a few preliminary up-and-down movements with your right arm, then with a sharp upward jerk let all the cards except the top and bottom ones fly upward a foot or so. Instantly close your thumb and fingers on the two cards retained in your right hand

and with the same hand strike the pack in the air, scattering the rest of the cards in all directions. Slide the two cards apart, insert the forefinger between them, and grip the lower one between it and the thumb. Move the middle finger onto the face of the upper card and grip it against the ring finger, then separate the cards as far as possible (Fig. 118).

Hold the pose for a few moments, keeping the backs of the two cards outwards. "Please name your cards," you say to the spectator. "The nine of spades and the queen of hearts," he replies. Slowly turn the two cards face outwards, take one in each hand, and display them.

The discoveries of the cards, and especially that of the last two, must be done dramatically. When well acted, this feat will be remembered and talked about long after other card tricks are forgotten.

EVERYWHERE AND NOWHERE

Nothing is quite so amazing to the general public as witnessing the mysterious transformation of one card to another; perhaps that is because it so nearly approximates the popular concept of "magic." Here we have a fine feat of this type. The magician, attempting to find a chosen card, shows three indifferent cards. Each of these, a moment later, is shown to be the chosen card; still a moment later, everything is as it should be, with the chosen card flanked by two indifferent cards.

You will require two duplicate aces of spades, with backs matching those of the pack you use. Place these, together with the ace belonging in the pack, at the top of the deck. Have three clear-glass tumblers on your table, neatly spaced.

1. "Ladies and gentlemen," you say, "a card trick which proves that, although seeing may be believing, you should not always believe what you see." Advance to someone on your left, shuffling the cards by the overhand method to place the aces at the middle in position for forcing. "Will you help me, sir? Take any card." Force one of the aces, preferably by the one-hand force or the classic force.

Have the card shown to all and replaced at the point from which it was taken, then square the cards neatly and give them one riffle shuffle, doing this slowly so that all may note its fairness. When performing for a small group it is most convincing to permit the spectator himself to make this shuffle. Take the pack, saying, "A very minor card trick, a simple little feat. I shall find your card in the easiest possible manner, by looking for it."

2. Openly run through the cards. A single riffle shuffle will not separate the three aces by more than two or three cards. Openly rearrange the cards so that two indifferent cards separate the three aces, then cut the pack, placing the first ace at the top, the second ace third from the top, and the third ace fifth from the top.

An amusing bit of business to use as you do this is the following: Let us say that you are performing for a small group in a home and have arranged with someone to provide soft waltz music at appropriate intervals. You now turn to this person, saying, "A little waltz, professor—looking-for-a-card music, if you please," and the instant the music starts you say, "Thank you, professor, that's little enough!" and the music stops.

3. Turn to the person who selected the card, saying, "I think I have found your card. Do not tell me its name—let me show you." Double-lift the two top cards and turn them face upwards on the pack, as one card, showing an indifferent card. "There is your card!" This is denied and you glance worriedly at it. "It does not matter," you say, brightening. "I will find it another way." Turn the two cards face downwards as one, remove the top card, the ace of spades, and place it on your table leaning against one of the tumblers. The face of the card, naturally, is away from the audience.

4. "I will find it by cutting," you announce. Hold the deck between the first phalanx of the left thumb on one side and the first phalanges of the middle and ring fingers on the other, with the forefinger's first phalanx bent on the outer end.

With the right thumb and middle finger seize the upper half of the deck at the inner corners and press the tip of the right forefinger on the top card. Push this card slightly forwards with the right forefinger and swiftly draw the upper half away to the right, the top card being retained by the pressure of the left forefinger. In the action, separate the hands, moving them in opposite directions for about six inches. Drop the cards held by the right hand on top of the other packet.

You have made what seems to be a genuine cut, in the course of which you have got rid of the indifferent card at the top of the pack, at the same time placing an ace at the top with an indifferent card under it.

5. Prepare for a double lift. Turn the two cards at the top face upwards on the pack, as one, saying, "This time I am confident that I have found your card. It *is* your card, is it not?" Again this is denied, and for a moment you appear to be reviewing what you have done, glancing unhappily at the pack. Again you brighten, shrugging off your misfortune as you say, "It is of little consequence. I will try again." Turn the two cards face downwards as one, remove the top card, an ace, and place it against a second glass with its face away from the audience.

6. Cut the pack again as given in step No. 4, bringing the third ace to the top. Prepare for another double lift, and turn the two cards face upwards on the pack, this time not quite so confidently, saying, "Would this be the card? No? Just as I thought, something has gone wrong. . . . My mother told me there would be nights like this." Turn the two cards face downwards as one, remove the top card, the third ace, and place it with the others on your table as before.

7. "Apparently I have made a miserable failure," you comment. "But you will remember that I told you that you should not always believe what you see. I will tell you a little secret. Sometimes I cheat. . . . Tell me, sir—if you were to choose one of the three cards, which would you take—the one on the right, the one in the middle, or the one on the left? Whichever you choose, I promise that it will be your card."

Pick up whichever card is selected and hold it before you in readiness for display. "Will you name your card? The ace of spades?" Slowly turn the ace face outwards, saying, "You see, it is your card after all!"

8. You will be applauded at this point, for the audience thinks the trick is ended. Turn to your left to replace the card on the table, but as you do so make the top change, exchanging the ace

for an indifferent card. It is the latter card which you replace on the table, with its back to the audience.

9. As you say the following, cut the cards as in step No. 4, thus burying the ace somewhere in the middle of the pack: "But, you may say, what would I have done if you had chosen one of the other two cards? Suppose you had chosen this card—" (pick up one of the other two) "—I then would utter the potent spell 'arbadacarba,' which is abracadabra spelled backwards, and—" (slowly turn the card face outwards) "—you see, it too is your ace of spades."

10. "I know what you are thinking. What about the third card?" Turn to your left toward your table and make the top change, placing an indifferent card on the table. Pick up the third card and hold it face outwards, showing still another ace of spades. "It too is your card!"

11. "Now you are thinking, 'Ah, they are all aces of spades!' That is not so." Pick up the other two cards and place them on either side of the ace, showing them to everyone. "One ace of spades only! *That* you must believe, for seeing is believing!"

In the hands of a good actor—and we say "actor" advisedly, for all good magicians are good actors—this feat is one of the most delightful imaginable.

EGYPTIAN POCKET

This feat is one of the few that are suitable for the stage or platform only. It was one of Alexander Herrmann's favorites, and he it was who gave it the name by which it has been known ever since. Successful presentation of the trick calls for considerable address rather than technical skill.

The effect is that a spectator takes a pack of cards and has four cards freely selected by four other spectators. He collects the cards, and they are replaced in the deck, which is then shuffled and placed in his breast pocket. He himself then draws three of the four chosen cards from the deck, but he fails to find the fourth. Examination of the deck shows that the card is missing, but on blowing on his pocket he finds the card there. He blew too hard, however, for the magician pulls an avalanche of cards from various parts of his clothing.

The only preparation required is to have a duplicate deck in your left coat pocket. The deck to be used should be a new one, with the seal unbroken. If it is encased in a cellophane wrapper, this should be removed beforehand. Have the deck on your table.

1. "At the present time," you begin, "many people are concerned with the workings of what is termed the subconscious mind. We have our psychoanalysts and psychiatrists busily probing into its workings and coming up with curious results. I would like to make an experiment which I am sure will interest you. Will you, sir," addressing a gentleman who looks good-natured and appears to be enjoying the show, "be kind enough to help me? Thank you. Please take this pack of cards—" (toss the pack to him) "—break the seal, take out the cards, and certify to their condition? Kindly stand up as you do, so that all can see."

2. The spectator opens the case, removes the cards, and tosses the case back to you. Instruct him to shuffle the cards and then spread them neatly, face downwards, with both hands. "Now, sir, I want you to smile amiably and ask this lady—" (indicating a lady in the front row and well to your right) "—to choose a card." As he does this, address the lady (A): "Please look at the card and remember it. Hold it in your right hand only for the moment, and don't let my assistant know what card it is."

3. Indicate another lady (B) a few seats away from the first and toward your left. Instruct your volunteer assistant to repeat his performance of smiling and having that lady take a card, asking her to use the same precautions, hold the card in her right hand, and conceal its face from your assistant.

Have these same maneuvers repeated twice more with two other ladies (C and D), always working toward your left. Some amusement may be had by telling your man each time to smile, and when he reaches the fourth lady you remark, "Hard work, isn't it? I think you can manage one more smile."

4. Four cards having been selected, you continue, "You will have to use both hands now, so I'll relieve you of the deck." Take the cards from him. "This is what I want you to do, and it is most important. Hold out your left hand, flat and palm upwards, and request the lady—" (he is still standing in front of D)

"—to place her card face downwards on that hand. . . . That's right. Now with your right hand grasp the lady's right hand, with which she held her card, and hold it for a few moments. Let the impression sink in. Fine! I think you have been impressed enough."

Indicate the next lady (C) and have the same maneuvers repeated, laying emphasis on the impressions he is receiving from the lady's hand. Have the same act done with ladies B and A, but, when he has grasped A's hand, turn away to put the card case on the table and leave him holding the lady's hand. Turn again and pretend to be surprised that he is still "holding hands." "Well," you say, "I think you must have received a very good impression this time."

5. "Kindly bring me the four selected cards." He does this, and you seat him at your table so that he is on your left, with the little table between you. Shuffle off about half the deck by the overhand method, hold the packet in your left hand toward him, and have the four cards placed on it. Immediately resume the shuffle, jogging the first card and shuffling off on top of it. Form a break at the injog, shuffle to the break, and throw on top. Finally execute the lift shuffle control, leaving the four chosen cards on the top. While shuffling talk briskly to the assistant, asking him if he likes magic, if he has enjoyed his work so far, and so on. Look at him and not at your hands.

6. "For our experiment we really should have the objects, that is the cards, placed in a dark room, so let's improvise one. Will you empty your inner breast pocket for a few moments?" As he moves his hand to do this, palm the four top cards in your right hand and take the pack in that hand. "One moment," you continue, "will you shuffle the cards first?" Hand the deck to him and, when he has shuffled, take it back, replacing the palmed cards on top by the method we have already given you. Then have him empty his breast pocket. Generally some amusement may be caused by naming the miscellaneous articles brought forth. Give him the deck and have him place it in his pocket.

You require to have the cards with their faces toward his body, therefore watch carefully. "The cards must be completely isolated. You are sure that you left nothing else in your pocket?"

So saying you plunge your hand into the pocket. If the deck has been placed wrongly (it should be on end and backs outwards), turn it into the correct position and push off the top card, A's card, turning it so that it lies on its side at the bottom of the pocket. "That's right," you go on, "nothing in the pocket but the cards."

7. "We are going to see how well your subconscious mind responds to the impressions you received from the ladies. Suppose we begin with this lady's card," and you indicate the second lady (B). "Kindly name the card you chose." "The six of spades," let us suppose the lady replies. "You, sir, now have to find the lady's card, the six of spades. Oh, you won't have any trouble. Your subconscious will do it for you. Please hold your left hand over your head. By the way, you had better stand up. Thank you. Take hold of your lapel with your right hand, hold your coat open, and when I say "Three" dive your left hand into your pocket and bring out the six of spades. You must work as fast as you can, or the impression left on your hand and the card will fade. Are you ready? One, two, three!"

He thrusts his hand into the pocket and naturally, taking the first card his hand comes in contact with, brings out the six of spades. Take the card from him and display it to the audience.

8. "That was excellent. Your subconscious is working very well tonight. Let's see if it will lead you to this lady's card," and you indicate C. Follow exactly the same procedure with her card and with D's, each card being named and found by the assistant in the same way. Encourage him to work with you by making little asides complimenting him. Watch him when he plunges his hand into the pocket, and if he does not withdraw it at once with a card this means he is taking one from the center of the pack. Stop him, saying, "No, no, sir! You are letting the impression escape. Let's start again. You must be quick, or the card will get away from you."

9. With the last card, the one drawn by the first lady (A), naturally he fails and brings out a wrong card. Let him try twice more and then remark, "Really, I'm surprised. I thought that would have been the strongest impression you received. You held the lady's hand quite a while. We must try another method,

the simplest possible." Take the deck out of his pocket, leaving there A's card, the one you turned on its side. "Run through the deck, take out the card which the lady has named, and we'll try another experiment with it."

10. He searches, but the card is not there. Take the pack from him. "Do you know how to make a ten of hearts?" (or whatever the card was). "No? Very simple. Just blow on your pocket." He does so and of course finds the card there. Seize the moment of surprise at this discovery to put your left hand in your left coat pocket and add the second deck to the one you hold. Cover the extra thickness with your right hand and palm off about twenty cards.

11. "Unfortunately you blew a little too hard. You made quite a lot of cards." With your right hand, still holding the palmed cards, seize his right lapel, pulling his coat open, and then grasp the lapel with your left hand. Dive your right hand into the pocket and bring out six or eight cards, fanning them, and leave the rest behind. "Perhaps you had better take them out yourself." As he does so, palm another large packet of cards, thrust your hand under his vest, and bring out one card, leaving the others. Pull out four or five more singly, then lift the edge of his vest so that the rest of the cards will drop out in a stream. Don't let them fall in a bunch; regulate the flow by the pressure of your hand holding the edge of the vest. As the last cards fall, palm the cards remaining in your left hand. Place your right hand just above his nose, and squeeze the cards as in the spring flourish, so that a stream of cards appear to issue from his nose. As you do this, say to him *sotto voce*, "I hope you don't mind this little fun. You've helped me splendidly."

All that remains to be done is to shake hands with your assistant, thank him, and usher him off stage.

Such is the trick with which Herrmann always created a sensation. As we have said, the technical work is of the simplest character and allows the performer to give his whole attention to the presentation. With good acting the feat cannot fail.

CARDS TO THE POCKET

This trick is a favorite with cardmen, who have found that it has a fascination for audiences. A number of cards vanish from the left hand and one by one find their way into an empty pocket. The trick is unusual in that it is equally suitable for large or small audiences.

It has been said that a performer's worth can be determined by his presentation of this feat, for it calls for a skilled technique, an interesting presentation, and the ability to make credible a feat which logic rejects as impossible. Perhaps more than any other card trick, it is a feat which must be lived with and performed over a period of years before it will yield all its riches.

1. Make a brief introductory statement along these lines: "I should like at this time to present one of the great feats of card magic." Hold the pack in the left hand at arms' length, gesture toward it with the right hand, and make the Charlier cut, which audiences mistakenly believe to be a most difficult manipulation.

Fan the pack gracefully, with the card faces to the audience, saying, "A pack of fifty-two cards. I shall ask one of you to take the deck in his own hands and give me any ten cards taken from the top, the bottom, or the middle, as he chooses. I want you to be satisfied that I could not know beforehand which ten cards would be given me."

If you are performing on a platform, you should walk into the audience as you say this, thus shortening the interval spent away from the stage.

2. Approach a gentleman, hand him the pack, and extend your left hand. "Ten cards, please." If he removes some from the bottom or the middle, you say, "A card from the bottom, *one*. A card from the middle, *two*. One from the top, *three*," and so on to ten. You do that because one of the most important factors in making this trick incomprehensible is to convince your audience that you do not know which cards you will use in performing it. Never under any circumstances remove the cards from the pack yourself, for presently you will make these cards leave your left hand and appear in your right trouser pocket. You must not give the audience reason to think afterwards, "Ah,

but he had duplicates of the cards in a secret pocket in his trousers. That's how he did it!"

3. Leave the remainder of the pack with the spectator, saying earnestly, "If you will take the rest of the pack, sir, place it under your pillow when you retire tonight, and make a wish, I promise you that when you awaken tomorrow morning . . . the cards will still be there." Transfer the ten cards from your left to your right hand and hold them aloft, well over your head, as you return to the platform.

4. "Ten cards!" you continue. "I shall count the cards for you, and may I suggest that each of you remember one or two of them." You must not explain *why* you want this done, for that would violate a most important rule: You must never tell an audience beforehand what you propose to do. Given this knowledge, it might conceivably fathom your methods. Forewarned is forearmed.

5. Hold the packet of ten cards face downwards in your left hand as for dealing, holding both hands well away from your body but not so high as to obscure your face. Push the top card off the packet with the left thumb and take it in the right hand, with the fingers at the face and the thumb at the back of the cards, grasping it at the middle of the right side. Count "One!" as you do this and move the hands apart.

Bring the hands together and push off a second card with the left thumb. Slide this in *front* of the card in the right hand, counting "Two!" Continue in this way until you have counted the fifth card. When you push the sixth card into your right hand, and all cards thereafter, allow the cards to project a half inch to the left of the first five cards. You must not watch your hands as you make this count. Instead, meet the gaze of several persons in the audience in a friendly manner. "Ten cards, no more and no less," you summarize.

6. Bring the hands down to your waist, with the right hand holding the cards in a horizontal plane. Bring both hands together casually and place the cards in the left hand, pressing the left little finger tip up against the lowermost card of the first five. This is why you stepped the ten cards into two packets of five. Square the packet with your right hand, taking and holding

a break under the first five cards with the left little finger. Turn the left hand so that the break cannot be seen.

As you do this you say, "May I call attention to my right trousers pocket." Without ostentation, show that your right hand is empty in a natural movement, then thrust it into the pocket and withdraw the lining. "Absolutely empty, a truly unfortunate circumstance which I shall be happy to give away absolutely free of charge." Replace the lining and withdraw your right hand. Square the packet of cards in your left hand once or twice, then remove the right hand.

7. Make an amusing remark and, as the audience reacts to it, palm the top five cards in your right hand. Grasp the remaining five cards in the same hand, at the ends near the right corners, between the index finger and thumb. Move the empty left hand away to the left, and hold the right hand absolutely motionless for the moment.

"My trick is this, ladies and gentlemen. I shall place the ten cards in my left hand and cause them to pass up my sleeve, across the vest from my left to my right shoulder, and down into the pocket which I have just shown you was empty." *Now* unhurriedly place the five exposed cards in the left hand, face downwards, and move the right hand with the five palmed cards up the sleeve to the crook of the elbow, tugging at it as if to raise it a little. Any hurried action in the trick will destroy the illusion you are seeking to create, and you must not hurry the action in the mistaken belief that the sooner you get rid of the palmed cards the better off you will be. The contrary is quite the case. "If you watch closely, you will not only see the cards make their mysterious journey, but hear them go as well."

8. Ruffle the cards in the left hand, at the same instant moving the hand up and down about an inch to conceal the smaller movement of the finger. Tug a little at the left sleeve with the right hand. Hold this position as you say, "Did you hear the card go?" Move the right hand smoothly and unhurriedly down to the right trouser pocket, thrust it in and release the five cards it holds. Simultaneously grasp the outermost card between the tips of the right index and middle fingers, and draw this card slowly from the pocket, back outwards. Drop your thumb

under it and lever it face outwards, calling its name. "The first card, the five of clubs! Some of you will remember the card." After a moment, drop it to one side.

9. Square the packet in the left hand, then move your right hand back to the left sleeve, tugging at it. It is not unlikely that many of those watching will believe that you have removed a card from those in the left hand, for now they know what your trick is and they are alert to learn how it is done.

"The second card follows in the path blazed by the first." Again ruffle the packet. Move the right hand to the pocket, but before thrusting it into the pocket turn it *naturally* so that its palm may be seen to be empty. You must not give any sign that you know that some of the spectators are surprised to see that it does not contain a card. Your purpose in misleading your audience into thinking that you *might* have palmed a card is this: All laymen have heard of palming cards and in this particular trick their first reaction is, "Ah, he palmed it into his pocket." You first convince these persons that they have hit on the correct solution and then you demonstrate, by showing the hand empty, that they are mistaken.

You have thus gained an important psychological advantage, for now they will not jump to conclusions without positive proof. (It is a curious fact that, although audiences are willing to believe that a performer may palm *one* card, they are blind to the fact that it is just as easy to palm five.)

Thrust your hand into your pocket, remove the uppermost card between the right index and middle fingers as before, and show it in the same manner as before. "The second card!" Display it and drop it to one side.

10. Move the right hand directly back to the left sleeve. "The third card!" you exclaim. "Before you can wink an eye, it moves like lightning, up, across, and down into my pocket." Ruffle the packet as you say this, then remove a card from your pocket as before, display it, and discard it.

11. "Three cards have passed from my left hand into my pocket," you recapitulate. "Three from ten—seven. I have seven cards remaining in my left hand."

Count the five cards you hold in such a manner as to convince everyone that they are actually seven, by using the following false count:

(a) Hold the packet of five in the left hand, as for dealing, but in a vertical position and with the little finger resting against the inner end.

(b) Push off the top card and take it, face outwards, in the right hand between the fingers at its face and the thumb at its back, at about the middle of the right side. Count "One."

(c) Push off the next card and take it in front of the one held in the right hand, counting "Two."

(d) Push off and take the next card in front of those held in the right hand, counting "Three." At the same instant drop the left thumb upon the rearmost card of those in the right hand, and secretly draw it back on top of the two remaining in the left hand. The left little finger, at the end, keeps this card in alignment with the others. The movement of the rearmost card of those in the right hand back onto the left-hand packet is completely concealed by the cards in front.

(e) Take another card in front of those in the right hand, counting "Four."

(f) Push off still another card, counting "Five," and as you take it in the right hand, draw back the rearmost card with the left thumb as you did before, adding it to the card in the left hand.

(g) Place the two remaining cards in the right hand, counting "Six. Seven!"

This false count is extremely deceptive, but in the following manner you should guard against the unlikely possibility that someone may notice that two cards are shown twice: Face a little to your left as you count the first two cards. Face directly ahead when you count the next three. Face to the right as you count the last two.

12. Place the five cards, which the audience thinks are seven, in your left hand and prepare to pass another card. "The fourth card!" you say. "Watch it go!" Ruffle the packet and thrust your right hand in your pocket. Palm one of the cards already

there, and remove the right hand. "I often have trouble with the fourth card," you explain. "For some reason it has ideas of its own. It isn't in my pocket. I should say that right now it is digging into my elbow." Bring your right hand behind your left elbow and press the palmed card against it with the fingers. Move the hand down, retaining the card pressed firmly against the elbow, then grasp it between the right index and middle fingers at its lower end, and with a little tug bring it into view. "Couldn't negotiate the curve," you explain unhappily.

13. "Six cards remain." False count the five cards as six, drawing back the rearmost of those in the right hand in making the count of three. If you are performing under circumstances in which you can move to a spectator without loss of time, hand him the packet of cards. "One, two, three, four, five, six cards," you say as you hand him the packet, retaining a grip on one corner. "How many cards do you hold, sir?" Ask him this abruptly and almost invariably he will reply, "Six." All those except the few close to the spectator think that he has actually counted the cards, and this makes the passage of the next card all the more baffling. In the rare case when the spectator replies "I don't know" or starts to count the cards, you override him by saying strongly, "Six cards. *Watch!*"

Ruffle the corner of the cards, saying, "Did you feel it go? One of the cards slipped away from you. Kindly count the cards." Extend your left palm and have him deal them onto it, counting the cards aloud as he does so, "One, two, three, four, five!"

Turn so that your right side is toward him, saying, "Please remove the card which only a moment ago you yourself held in your hands." Perhaps a little awkwardly, he will dip into your pocket with two fingers and remove the card. Take it from him and hold it high in the air, exclaiming, "And here is the fifth card!" This is a climax, so make the most of it.

Turn immediately and return to your place, still holding the card aloft. In most cases you will be applauded at this point if you have performed the trick well. When the applause has subsided, drop the last card to one side.

14. "Five cards remain. I'll count them for you again." Count the five, but this time, when you place the fourth card in front

of those already in the right hand, jog its lower end a half inch below the other cards. Replace the five cards in your left hand and, in squaring them, press down on the jogged card with your right thumb and take a left-little-finger break above it, in readiness to palm off the three cards above it.

15. "May I call your attention to the fact that my trouser pocket remains empty at all times between the passage of the cards." In a natural movement let the right hand be seen empty, withdraw the lining of the pocket, and replace it.

Bring the two hands together, square the cards once or twice, and utter some amusing pleasantry. When the audience reacts, palm the three top cards. Hold the remaining two cards as before, between the right thumb and index finger, and move the left hand away, holding the right motionless.

16. "I shall now attempt a feat rarely seen," you announce. "The passage of *two* cards at one and the same time—a feat so difficult that I hesitate to contemplate it, and therefore shall not contemplate it." *Now* place the two exposed cards in the left hand, and carry your right with the palmed cards up to the sleeve. Ruffle the two cards, thrust your right hand into your pocket, drop one of the cards, and remove the other two, holding them aloft. "Here they are!"

17. "Three cards remain," you point out. If convenient, advance to someone and extend the packet you hold. "Will you kindly breathe upon the cards?" The instant he does so, spread the two cards, saying, "Two cards only! One has shot into my pocket." Turn your right side to him, saying, "Kindly remove the card." Take it from him when he removes it from your pocket, and hold it high so that all can see it. However, if it is inconvenient to approach a spectator, blow upon the cards yourself, spread them, showing only two, and remove the card from your pocket as usual.

18. "Two cards!" Hold one in each hand, face outwards. Place them squarely together and take them face inwards in the left hand. Touch the cards with the right hand and make a throwing motion toward your right pocket. "Another card in the pocket!" Grasp the two cards at the ends between the right fingers and thumb, then grasp them firmly at the middle of the left side

between the left thumb at the back and fingers at the face. Snap the two cards sharply with the right middle finger, exclaiming, "One card only!"

19. You are going to palm the rearmost of the two cards, and this must be done well. Take the two, as one, at the ends between the right thumb and fingers, and hold "it" up so that all can see it. Place the two cards, face downward, in the left hand and, at the moment the left fingers take it, palm the top card by means of the first method of palming. Do not look at your hands as you do this. Immediately and smoothly move the right hand with the palmed card to your pocket, then dip into the pocket and remove the palmed card, showing it. "Here's the card!"

20. "One card remains, and it is the hardest of them all!" Hold the card in your right hand, showing it. Hold your left hand with its back towards the audience, the fingers pointing downwards. Thrust the card between the thumb and the palm of the left hand and pat it well into the hand with the tips of the right fingers. Rub the back of the left hand with the right fingertips, then turn the left hand showing the card. "The last card often refuses to make its journey," you explain ruefully. "I'll try again."

Again show the card with the right hand and thrust it into the left hand as before. This time, however, when the right fingertips have patted the card into the left hand and only an inch of the card extends from the hand, press outward against the end of the card with the right fingertips. This levers the card against the side of the left forefinger causing it to spring back into the right palm, the left thumb moving back a little to permit this. Palm the card in the right hand and rub the back of the left hand with the fingertips as you did before.

Move the left hand, still back outwards, away from the right hand, fixing your gaze upon it. Blow upon the hand, then slowly turn it and show that the card has vanished. Move your right hand with the palmed card rather slowly to the right trouser pocket, thrust it in and a moment later withdraw it with the card clipped between the first and second fingers, saying, *"And here it is!"*

Because we think so highly of this feat, we have described it in the fullest possible detail. Although it is a trick that demands the utmost of a performer, it is worth learning to do well. A trick so charming to watch is a rarity, and the time spent in mastering it is time well spent. Once you have made it yours, you will never drop it from your repertoire.

ENLARGING AND DIMINISHING CARDS

This feat in which a pack of unprepared cards is made apparently to grow larger, then to diminish in size, and finally to disappear was devised by the great magician, Robert-Houdin, and was used by him to follow the trick of the *cards passing up the sleeve*. It is perhaps the prettiest effect of pure skill that is possible with cards. Unfortunately, because of the modern tendency for substituting mechanical appliances for skill wherever possible, the feat is seldom seen. Decks of various sizes are now used, the substitution of one for another giving the illusion of the cards being diminished in size. Anyone who has mastered Robert-Houdin's method will look down on these as mere makeshifts.

For the purpose of the trick the performer must be able to spread the cards in his left hand with one swift motion of his right hand, by pressing the thumb against the left side of the deck and then sliding it to the right, releasing the cards progressively. The action is practically the same as that of opening a fan.

The cards should be of a flexible type and in perfect condition, and unless the performer has very large hands a packet of about thirty cards only should be used. Any ace except the ace of spades placed at the face of the packet helps to disguise the subterfuge that is used.

The trick can be introduced as a plausible explanation of how the cards are passed up the sleeve, or indeed of any trick in which cards have apparently been passed from one place to another.

1. Show the deck in your left hand, face outwards, about half its length protruding above the left forefinger, as you begin by saying, "These are specially prepared cards. I confess it. They

have rubber in their composition so that by pulling or squeezing them they can be made any size required. You see that they are just the usual size at present." Fan the cards swiftly and display them (Fig. 119). Then close the fan smartly, bringing the pack back to its original position.

2. Seize the upper end of the deck with the right hand, and with assumed effort pull it upwards, making the cards protrude half an inch more above the left forefinger. Spread the cards again and display the enlarged fan, saying, "You see the cards are somewhat larger." Close the fan as before.

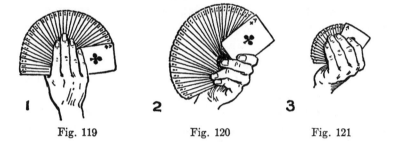

Fig. 119   Fig. 120   Fig. 121

3. Again with pretended effort pull on the upper end of the deck until its lower end is almost flush with the upper side of the left forefinger. Spread the cards and at the same time push outwards with the left thumb on the inner ends, making them project from the tips of the left fingers to almost their full length (Fig. 120). They will appear to have almost doubled in size.

4. "If I want them to be smaller I have simply to tap them, so." Close the fan, squaring the pack, and with the right hand pat the upper end smartly, pushing the cards down in the left hand to their original position. Fan them again as you say, "You see they are back to their original size" (Fig. 119).

5. Close the fan once more. The cards should now project about two inches above the left forefinger. "With considerable pressure I can make them smaller still." Bring your right hand over the top of the pack and press downwards, pushing the cards down until they protrude an inch only. Spread them again swiftly as you remove the right hand.

6. Repeat the same action of squeezing the cards, and push them downwards so that only the extreme ends show. Spread them as in Fig. 121 so that they appear to be tiny cards. The indexes will help this illusion.

7. Close the fan and again bring the right hand over to squeeze the pack, but this time press on the outer end, move the left thumb aside momentarily, and lever the pack up into the right hand, palming it. Press the left thumb tightly against the tips of the left index and middle fingers, as if holding the compressed cards with considerable effort, and move the right hand away, its forefinger pointing to the left hand.

8. Raise the left hand, keeping your whole attention fixed upon it, and with your right hand tug lightly at your left sleeve near the elbow. "When the cards are this size I can snap them up my sleeve with the greatest of ease." Snap your left middle finger against the tip of the thumb, and open the fingers widely. The cards have vanished.

Pause a moment, then thrust your right hand under your coat toward the arm pit, and produce the palmed cards in as large a fan as possible, saying, "The moment the pressure is released the cards spring back to their original size."

Three Cards Across

This trick is one of the finest in all card magic. When neatly presented it never fails to entertain and mystify an audience. It was a favorite with the great English magician, David Devant, and with countless card conjurers since.

The plot is simple. A spectator counts off a number of cards and puts them in his pocket or holds them in his hands. A second spectator chooses a card, the value of which is used to indicate how many cards shall be caused to fly invisibly to the cards held by the first assistant. The magician takes the pack, snaps it sharply, and when the spectator again counts his cards he finds that the required number of cards have been added to those he holds!

This is one of the oldest plots in magic and, like all the old tricks which have survived the passage of time, it is a truly great classic.

Preparation. Beforehand place two of the three-spots on the top of the pack, the other two at the bottom.

Procedure. The steps are as follows:

1. If you are performing for an intimate group, seat yourself at a table and request one of those present to sit opposite you. If you have a larger audience, use a small table and stand your assistant on your left, with the table between you. In selecting a spectator to assist you, choose if you can a person who has shown that he enjoys your tricks, for he will be less likely to attempt to embarrass you and will follow your instructions implicitly.

Place the pack before your assistant and instruct him to cut it into three packets fairly equal in size. When he has done this, request him to select any one of the three and take it in his hands. Note which he takes, and in picking up the other two assemble them so that you will have two three-spots either on the top or on the bottom.

If you have two three-spots at the top of the pack, well and good. If not, shuffle one of those at the bottom to the top. Approach another spectator and force the three-spot on him, preferably using the classic force. Have him place the forced card in his pocket without looking at it.

2. Return to the table and address your assistant somewhat as follows: "I shall ask you, sir, to count your cards, but I want you to do so in a manner which will prove to all that you have counted them correctly. Kindly hold them about eighteen inches above the table and drop them one by one, thus." Illustrate by dropping three cards singly from those you hold. "We shall all be able then to count with you and you will be sure that none of the cards cling together."

The reasons given for counting the cards in this manner are logical, and you have a private purpose too. Thus counted, the cards will spread and not be dealt in a neat pile—an essential point as you will see in a moment.

Pick up the three cards you have dropped, replace them on the top of the cards you hold, and keep them separate by inserting the tip of your left little finger under them.

3. Count with the spectator as he drops the cards, and at the

same time palm the three cards at the top of the pack in your right hand. There is no risk of detection, for all eyes will be watching the spectator deal the cards. When the count is completed, let us say sixteen cards, glance at the spectator and say, "You counted sixteen cards. That is correct?" Whatever the number may be, he will agree.

Reach forward with your right hand and with a careless off-hand gesture push the cards toward him, releasing the three palmed cards on them. Your hand must rest on the cards for only a moment, and you must not look at them. The entire action should seem to be a gesture *toward* the cards to indicate what you want done. This is the crux of the trick, and when it is done properly no one later remembers that your hand was anywhere near the cards. It would seem that everyone should see what you do, but you must remember that you have not said what you are going to do and for this reason the spectators do not grasp the significance of your gesture.

At the moment you push the cards toward your assistant, catch his eye and say, "Kindly pick up the cards and place them in your pocket." If he is seated, have him hold them tightly between his hands.

4. Address the audience, saying, "My trick is this, ladies and gentlemen. My friend here has taken a given number of cards determined by himself. He counted them in such a manner that we are all assured that the count was correct." Turn to the assistant and say, "How many cards do you hold?" "Sixteen," he replies. Again address the audience, "I call your attention particularly to the fact that never once have I touched the cards."

This is not true—you did touch the cards and secretly added three more to them—but, if you have done this naturally and easily, no one will question the statement. The gesture will have passed unnoticed. Indeed, the authors many times have heard spectators afterwards affirm that not once had the performer touched the cards.

5. Turn to the second spectator, upon whom you forced the three-spot. "Will you, sir, now for the first time show the card you chose? The three of diamonds. Very well, I shall use the

value of that card for my trick. I shall cause three cards to pass from the cards I hold in my hand to the packet of sixteen cards which are being held tightly by my friend at the table. Are you ready, sir? Ah, you needn't look so worried. The impact of the cards will be negligible, hardly more than a slight tickling sensation."

Hold the cards in your left hand, as for dealing, with the thumb pressing firmly on the back of the packet, and as you count "One!" bend the outer ends of the cards upwards with the right middle finger and riffle them sharply.

Repeat the riffle, counting "Two!"—and once again, counting "Three!" This time, palm the top card, reach over and pretend to pull the card out of his sleeve, as you say, "Sorry, that one went only halfway. I'll try again." Replace the card on top of your packet, being careful that no one sees its face, riffle again, and call, "Go!"

6. Address the assistant, "A moment ago you had sixteen cards. You now hold nineteen. Please count them in the same way that you did before, so that we may all see the result of this truly inexplicable feat."

Count aloud with the spectator, and when he reaches "sixteen" raise your hand and your voice emphasizing the last three numbers with crescendo effect.

This is the feat in its best form. The student cannot appreciate how fine a trick it is until he has himself witnessed the utter amazement it induces in an audience.

EVERYBODY'S CARD, I

Card tricks may come and card tricks may go, but the really great card classics go on forever. This feat has been performed by countless magicians for almost a century and no doubt will be charming audiences a hundred years hence. Robert-Houdin, who included it in his programs under the title *the metamorphoses*, writes of it, "I may once more remark that this trick, skillfully executed, is one of the most surprising that can well be performed." The authors can only urge their readers to master this delightful bit of hanky-panky.

The plot is simple. Four cards are drawn by as many persons. One of them is shown to each in turn, and it changes successively, the one card becoming everybody's card.

1. Advance with the pack in hand and make a short introductory statement. "Ladies and gentlemen, I should like to show you one of the great card tricks." As you say this, fan the cards and hold them with their faces toward the audience. Square the pack smartly in the left hand, with the card faces toward the audience, and say, "A pack of playing cards."

Glance at the face card, appear to notice something unusual, and brush the card with the right finger tips. "The four of spades." Cover the pack for a moment with the right hand, make the color change and show that the face card has changed to another card. Gesture with the right hand toward the pack, but do not say anything and, during the laughter which the color change provokes, do not move. Shrug a little, helplessly. "An unusual pack of cards!"

2. Approach someone well on your right, holding the pack as for the Charlier cut, and ask the spectator to cut the cards. At the moment his hand is about to close on the pack, make the Charlier cut, saying, "Thank you." This will usually amuse an audience if you are careful not to give the impression that you are a wiseacre.

3. Spread the cards widely between your hands, and invite the spectator, whom we shall call A, to take a card. Let it be amply clear that he has a free choice, but do not mention this fact, because you should never lead an audience to believe that there is such a thing as a forced choice. "Remember your card, please." Extend your right hand for the card, saying, "I will place your card on the table for a few moments." Turn to your left, making the top change, and drop an indifferent card on the table.

4. Approach a second spectator, whom we shall call B and who is seated somewhat to the right of the center of the audience. Shuffle A's card to the middle of the pack in preparation for a force as you do this. Square the cards, holding a break over A's card, and say to B: "You, too. Will you take a card?" Break off, glance back at A, saying, "No, no! Stay for a while and

enjoy the show!" Revert to B and force A's card upon him. Take it from him, and in turning to your table again make the top change, placing an indifferent card upon the first card.

5. Prepare in the same manner to force A's card upon a third person, C, who is seated to the left of center. A moment before you make the force, glance back toward spectator A worriedly, apparently note that he is still in his seat, smile broadly at him as if you have a little joke between you, and invite C to take a card. This incidental "business" helps to make the spectator's choice of a card seem unimportant, since you are more interested in spectator A than in what you are doing. It also helps to enliven the slow part of the trick, which is the time spent in having cards selected.

6. Take C's card, turn back to your table, and actually drop this card upon the other two. Care must be taken that only those close to A, B, and C see the cards they take. It is for this reason that you choose spectators in widely separated parts of the audience. You must also handle the card so that its face is not seen after the top change.

7. Now move on to spectator D, who is at the extreme left. Extend your left hand with the cards in position for the Charlier cut, saying, "Will you cut the cards?" Glance back at spectator A, laughing, and say, "Remember?" Before D can move to cut the cards (it is unlikely that he will fall into the trap you set for A), you say, "I'll shuffle them myself." Spring the cards from the right into the left hand, saying, "A Chinese shuffle I learned in Canton . . . Ohio."

8. Place the pack face downwards on the extreme finger tips of the left hand. Hold the hand well away from the body. "And a cut!" Remove the upper half with the right hand and place it beside the lower portion. Pick up the lower portion, leapfrog it over the upper half, and place it to the left of the latter portion. Finally, pick up the upper half and place it on top of the other. Clearly the pack has not been cut at all, and your swindle will cause some amusement. You must make this cut neatly in about three seconds, so that it will not slow your presentation.

9. "The cards have been shuffled and cut," you say blandly to

spectator D. "Kindly take one of the fifty-two cards." Riffle the pack close to your ear, as though counting the cards, and say in a surprised tone, "Hmm. Only forty-nine!" Then note the three on the table. "Oh yes, three on the table, forty-nine here."

Spread the cards before D. Abruptly glance at him in mild indignation. "Sir, do you think I cheat?" Pause and say, as if the thought had just struck you, "Why, I *do*! Here, take the cards in your own hands and remove one."

10. As he removes a card, walk to your table, and pick up the three cards there—two of which are indifferent cards and the third the cards taken by A, B, and C. Move to A, show him the three cards, and say, "You see your card?" He affirms that you hold it. Next move to B, showing him the three cards. "You also see your card?" Finally show the three cards to C, asking him the same question. You will have received three affirmative answers, and the audience, seeing that you hold three cards, assumes that each of these is a card drawn by one of the spectators!

11. Now you return to the last spectator, D, saying, "You have found a card to your liking? Good. May I have the pack?" Take it in your left hand, drop the three cards you hold in your right hand on top of it; the top card of the pack will then be the one taken by A, B, and C. Take D's card with your right hand.

Glance toward A, at the other side of the audience, bow formally, and say in a satiric tone, "I hope you're having a good time." Again smile as though you had some pleasant and private understanding with him. Move toward him and make the top change, taking his card in your right hand but holding it horizontally so that its face cannot be seen by anyone.

Stand before him, with the card extended. "Will you breathe on the card?" At the moment he blows, make the ruffle with a single card. Glance toward spectator D, saying, "Your card has metamorphosed into this gentleman's card." Tip up the card so that A, and only a few others near him, can see it. "It *is* your card, sir?" A will admit that it is. Immediately move away from him, effectually silencing him and thus preventing any possible remark which might reveal the name of his card.

12. Hold the card well away from your body, with its outer end sloping downwards so that its face cannot be seen. Let it be clear to all that the card is not exchanged for another. Approach B, extend the card, have him blow on it, and again ruffle the card. Tip it up so that he can see it, and say, "And now it is your card, too."

13. When he has agreed, move on to C, again holding the card so that its face cannot be seen. Request C to blow on the card, and when he does so say, "Oh, come now, sir! What a feeble attempt! Surely you can do better?" The spectator, entering into the spirit of the occasion, rewards you with a full-blown zephyr, and you ruffle the card, at the same time tilting it so that he can see its face. "Unbelievable as it may seem, the card is also your card!"

14. Glance back at A, saying, "Aren't you glad you stayed?" At the same time move on to spectator D. "And now, last but not least, let us see if we can transform the card into your card. Kindly blow upon it." When he has done so, tilt it up so that he can see it, and say, "You see—it's your card, too."

Turn to your left a little, and top change the card you hold for that at the top of the pack, which is D's card. D will deny that the card you showed him is his card; but if he does not you say, "It *is* your card, isn't it?" in which case he will state that it is not. "Of course," you exclaim. "The ruffle was missing. Kindly blow again." Ruffle the card as he blows upon it, then tip it upwards so that he can see it. Finally hold it up so that all can note that it is the same card they saw at the start. "You see, ladies and gentlemen," you exclaim, "this card is everybody's card!"

Although there are two forces and four top changes in the trick, these sleights are made when there is no reason for the audience to anticipate trickery; for this reason they are easy to perform without detection. The trick is entirely delightful and will charm any audience when done easily and naturally. We have outlined a possible presentation in an attempt to convey the informality which is so important in making the feat entertaining. The tone set here may not be suitable to everyone, but the plot adopts itself to any style of presentation which the student may wish to evolve for himself.

Note particularly the use of the glance toward a spectator away from you in order to offer misdirection during the execution of a sleight or in preparation for it. This device is extremely useful, for it capitalizes upon the universal human urge to see that which another looks at.

When performing this trick for small groups, it is advisable to follow it immediately with another trick; this will prevent the four spectators from mentioning the names of their cards, which would reveal the *modus operandi* of the trick.

EVERYBODY'S CARD, II

This version of the preceding trick is more suitable for performance before a drawing-room audience or some other small group, where seating conditions would make the four-card presentation impracticable. We shall give only the barest outline of the procedure:

1. Spectator A takes a card, which you control to the top of the pack.

2. Force the same card on B.

3. Let C remove any other card. Control this to the top, above A-B's card, by means of the Hindu shuffle.

4. Shuffle the cards, retaining C's card at the top, with A-B's card under it.

5. Approach C, riffle the pack, and request him to stop the riffle. This done, backslip C's card to the top of the lower packet in removing the upper half. Remove C's card, and reassemble the pack with A-B's card on the top.

6. Show C his card and ask him if you have found the proper card. He acknowledges that you have.

7. Move toward A, top changing the card you hold for the one on the top of the pack. Have A blow on this card. Ruffle it, and show that it is his card.

8. Move to B, have him blow on the card. Ruffle it and tip it up so that he can see that it is also his card.

9. Move to C, have him blow on the card. Show it to him and he denies that it is his card.

10. Top change the card you hold for the one at the top of the pack. Have C blow on this card. Ruffle it at the same time, then show that it is his card.

INDEX

A CATALOG OF SELECTED
DOVER BOOKS
IN ALL FIELDS OF INTEREST

A CATALOG OF SELECTED DOVER
BOOKS IN ALL FIELDS OF INTEREST

CONCERNING THE SPIRITUAL IN ART, Wassily Kandinsky. Pioneering work by father of abstract art. Thoughts on color theory, nature of art. Analysis of earlier masters. 12 illustrations. 80pp. of text. 5⅜ x 8½. 0-486-23411-8

CELTIC ART: The Methods of Construction, George Bain. Simple geometric techniques for making Celtic interlacements, spirals, Kells-type initials, animals, humans, etc. Over 500 illustrations. 160pp. 9 x 12. (Available in U.S. only.) 0-486-22923-8

AN ATLAS OF ANATOMY FOR ARTISTS, Fritz Schider. Most thorough reference work on art anatomy in the world. Hundreds of illustrations, including selections from works by Vesalius, Leonardo, Goya, Ingres, Michelangelo, others. 593 illustrations. 192pp. 7⅛ x 10¼. 0-486-20241-0

CELTIC HAND STROKE-BY-STROKE (Irish Half-Uncial from "The Book of Kells"): An Arthur Baker Calligraphy Manual, Arthur Baker. Complete guide to creating each letter of the alphabet in distinctive Celtic manner. Covers hand position, strokes, pens, inks, paper, more. Illustrated. 48pp. 8¼ x 11. 0-486-24336-2

EASY ORIGAMI, John Montroll. Charming collection of 32 projects (hat, cup, pelican, piano, swan, many more) specially designed for the novice origami hobbyist. Clearly illustrated easy-to-follow instructions insure that even beginning papercrafters will achieve successful results. 48pp. 8¼ x 11. 0-486-27298-2

BLOOMINGDALE'S ILLUSTRATED 1886 CATALOG: Fashions, Dry Goods and Housewares, Bloomingdale Brothers. Famed merchants' extremely rare catalog depicting about 1,700 products: clothing, housewares, firearms, dry goods, jewelry, more. Invaluable for dating, identifying vintage items. Also, copyright-free graphics for artists, designers. Co-published with Henry Ford Museum & Greenfield Village. 160pp. 8¼ x 11. 0-486-25780-0

THE ART OF WORLDLY WISDOM, Baltasar Gracian. "Think with the few and speak with the many," "Friends are a second existence," and "Be able to forget" are among this 1637 volume's 300 pithy maxims. A perfect source of mental and spiritual refreshment, it can be opened at random and appreciated either in brief or at length. 128pp. 5⅜ x 8½. 0-486-44034-6

JOHNSON'S DICTIONARY: A Modern Selection, Samuel Johnson (E. L. McAdam and George Milne, eds.). This modern version reduces the original 1755 edition's 2,300 pages of definitions and literary examples to a more manageable length, retaining the verbal pleasure and historical curiosity of the original. 480pp. 5³⁄₁₆ x 8¼. 0-486-44089-3

ADVENTURES OF HUCKLEBERRY FINN, Mark Twain, Illustrated by E. W. Kemble. A work of eternal richness and complexity, a source of ongoing critical debate, and a literary landmark, Twain's 1885 masterpiece about a barefoot boy's journey of self-discovery has enthralled readers around the world. This handsome clothbound reproduction of the first edition features all 174 of the original black-and-white illustrations. 368pp. 5⅜ x 8½. 0-486-44322-1

STICKLEY CRAFTSMAN FURNITURE CATALOGS, Gustav Stickley and L. & J. G. Stickley. Beautiful, functional furniture in two authentic catalogs from 1910. 594 illustrations, including 277 photos, show settles, rockers, armchairs, reclining chairs, bookcases, desks, tables. 183pp. 6½ x 9¼. 0-486-23838-5

AMERICAN LOCOMOTIVES IN HISTORIC PHOTOGRAPHS: 1858 to 1949, Ron Ziel (ed.). A rare collection of 126 meticulously detailed official photographs, called "builder portraits," of American locomotives that majestically chronicle the rise of steam locomotive power in America. Introduction. Detailed captions. xi+ 129pp. 9 x 12. 0-486-27393-8

AMERICA'S LIGHTHOUSES: An Illustrated History, Francis Ross Holland, Jr. Delightfully written, profusely illustrated fact-filled survey of over 200 American lighthouses since 1716. History, anecdotes, technological advances, more. 240pp. 8 x 10¾. 0-486-25576-X

TOWARDS A NEW ARCHITECTURE, Le Corbusier. Pioneering manifesto by founder of "International School." Technical and aesthetic theories, views of industry, economics, relation of form to function, "mass-production split" and much more. Profusely illustrated. 320pp. 6⅛ x 9¼. (Available in U.S. only.) 0-486-25023-7

HOW THE OTHER HALF LIVES, Jacob Riis. Famous journalistic record, exposing poverty and degradation of New York slums around 1900, by major social reformer. 100 striking and influential photographs. 233pp. 10 x 7⅞. 0-486-22012-5

FRUIT KEY AND TWIG KEY TO TREES AND SHRUBS, William M. Harlow. One of the handiest and most widely used identification aids. Fruit key covers 120 deciduous and evergreen species; twig key 160 deciduous species. Easily used. Over 300 photographs. 126pp. 5⅜ x 8½. 0-486-20511-8

COMMON BIRD SONGS, Dr. Donald J. Borror. Songs of 60 most common U.S. birds: robins, sparrows, cardinals, bluejays, finches, more—arranged in order of increasing complexity. Up to 9 variations of songs of each species.

Cassette and manual 0-486-99911-4

ORCHIDS AS HOUSE PLANTS, Rebecca Tyson Northen. Grow cattleyas and many other kinds of orchids—in a window, in a case, or under artificial light. 63 illustrations. 148pp. 5⅜ x 8½. 0-486-23261-1

MONSTER MAZES, Dave Phillips. Masterful mazes at four levels of difficulty. Avoid deadly perils and evil creatures to find magical treasures. Solutions for all 32 exciting illustrated puzzles. 48pp. 8¼ x 11. 0-486-26005-4

MOZART'S DON GIOVANNI (DOVER OPERA LIBRETTO SERIES), Wolfgang Amadeus Mozart. Introduced and translated by Ellen H. Bleiler. Standard Italian libretto, with complete English translation. Convenient and thoroughly portable—an ideal companion for reading along with a recording or the performance itself. Introduction. List of characters. Plot summary. 121pp. 5¼ x 8½. 0-486-24944-1

FRANK LLOYD WRIGHT'S DANA HOUSE, Donald Hoffmann. Pictorial essay of residential masterpiece with over 160 interior and exterior photos, plans, elevations, sketches and studies. 128pp. 9¼ x 10¾. 0-486-29120-0

ANIMALS: 1,419 Copyright-Free Illustrations of Mammals, Birds, Fish, Insects, etc., Jim Harter (ed.). Clear wood engravings present, in extremely lifelike poses, over 1,000 species of animals. One of the most extensive pictorial sourcebooks of its kind. Captions. Index. 284pp. 9 x 12. 0-486-23766-4

1001 QUESTIONS ANSWERED ABOUT THE SEASHORE, N. J. Berrill and Jacquelyn Berrill. Queries answered about dolphins, sea snails, sponges, starfish, fishes, shore birds, many others. Covers appearance, breeding, growth, feeding, much more. 305pp. 5¼ x 8¼. 0-486-23366-9

ATTRACTING BIRDS TO YOUR YARD, William J. Weber. Easy-to-follow guide offers advice on how to attract the greatest diversity of birds: birdhouses, feeders, water and waterers, much more. 96pp. 5³⁄₁₆ x 8¼. 0-486-28927-3

MEDICINAL AND OTHER USES OF NORTH AMERICAN PLANTS: A Historical Survey with Special Reference to the Eastern Indian Tribes, Charlotte Erichsen-Brown. Chronological historical citations document 500 years of usage of plants, trees, shrubs native to eastern Canada, northeastern U.S. Also complete identifying information. 343 illustrations. 544pp. 6½ x 9¼. 0-486-25951-X

STORYBOOK MAZES, Dave Phillips. 23 stories and mazes on two-page spreads: Wizard of Oz, Treasure Island, Robin Hood, etc. Solutions. 64pp. 8¼ x 11. 0-486-23628-5

AMERICAN NEGRO SONGS: 230 Folk Songs and Spirituals, Religious and Secular, John W. Work. This authoritative study traces the African influences of songs sung and played by black Americans at work, in church, and as entertainment. The author discusses the lyric significance of such songs as "Swing Low, Sweet Chariot," "John Henry," and others and offers the words and music for 230 songs. Bibliography. Index of Song Titles. 272pp. 6½ x 9¼. 0-486-40271-1

MOVIE-STAR PORTRAITS OF THE FORTIES, John Kobal (ed.). 163 glamor, studio photos of 106 stars of the 1940s: Rita Hayworth, Ava Gardner, Marlon Brando, Clark Gable, many more. 176pp. 8⅜ x 11¼. 0-486-23546-7

YEKL and THE IMPORTED BRIDEGROOM AND OTHER STORIES OF YIDDISH NEW YORK, Abraham Cahan. Film Hester Street based on *Yekl* (1896). Novel, other stories among first about Jewish immigrants on N.Y.'s East Side. 240pp. 5⅜ x 8½. 0-486-22427-9

SELECTED POEMS, Walt Whitman. Generous sampling from *Leaves of Grass*. Twenty-four poems include "I Hear America Singing," "Song of the Open Road," "I Sing the Body Electric," "When Lilacs Last in the Dooryard Bloom'd," "O Captain! My Captain!"—all reprinted from an authoritative edition. Lists of titles and first lines. 128pp. 5³⁄₁₆ x 8¼. 0-486-26878-0

SONGS OF EXPERIENCE: Facsimile Reproduction with 26 Plates in Full Color, William Blake. 26 full-color plates from a rare 1826 edition. Includes "The Tyger," "London," "Holy Thursday," and other poems. Printed text of poems. 48pp. 5¼ x 7. 0-486-24636-1

THE BEST TALES OF HOFFMANN, E. T. A. Hoffmann. 10 of Hoffmann's most important stories: "Nutcracker and the King of Mice," "The Golden Flowerpot," etc. 458pp. 5⅜ x 8½. 0-486-21793-0

THE BOOK OF TEA, Kakuzo Okakura. Minor classic of the Orient: entertaining, charming explanation, interpretation of traditional Japanese culture in terms of tea ceremony. 94pp. 5⅜ x 8½. 0-486-20070-1

HINTS TO SINGERS, Lillian Nordica. Selecting the right teacher, developing confidence, overcoming stage fright, and many other important skills receive thoughtful discussion in this indispensible guide, written by a world-famous diva of four decades' experience. 96pp. 5⅜ x 8½. 0-486-40094-8

THE COMPLETE NONSENSE OF EDWARD LEAR, Edward Lear. All nonsense limericks, zany alphabets, Owl and Pussycat, songs, nonsense botany, etc., illustrated by Lear. Total of 320pp. 5⅜ x 8½. (Available in U.S. only.) 0-486-20167-8

VICTORIAN PARLOUR POETRY: An Annotated Anthology, Michael R. Turner. 117 gems by Longfellow, Tennyson, Browning, many lesser-known poets. "The Village Blacksmith," "Curfew Must Not Ring Tonight," "Only a Baby Small," dozens more, often difficult to find elsewhere. Index of poets, titles, first lines. xxiii + 325pp. 5⅝ x 8¼. 0-486-27044-0

DUBLINERS, James Joyce. Fifteen stories offer vivid, tightly focused observations of the lives of Dublin's poorer classes. At least one, "The Dead," is considered a masterpiece. Reprinted complete and unabridged from standard edition. 160pp. 5³⁄₁₆ x 8¼. 0-486-26870-5

GREAT WEIRD TALES: 14 Stories by Lovecraft, Blackwood, Machen and Others, S. T. Joshi (ed.). 14 spellbinding tales, including "The Sin Eater," by Fiona McLeod, "The Eye Above the Mantel," by Frank Belknap Long, as well as renowned works by R. H. Barlow, Lord Dunsany, Arthur Machen, W. C. Morrow and eight other masters of the genre. 256pp. 5⅜ x 8½. (Available in U.S. only.) 0-486-40436-6

THE BOOK OF THE SACRED MAGIC OF ABRAMELIN THE MAGE, translated by S. MacGregor Mathers. Medieval manuscript of ceremonial magic. Basic document in Aleister Crowley, Golden Dawn groups. 268pp. 5⅜ x 8½. 0-486-23211-5

THE BATTLES THAT CHANGED HISTORY, Fletcher Pratt. Eminent historian profiles 16 crucial conflicts, ancient to modern, that changed the course of civilization. 352pp. 5⅜ x 8½. 0-486-41129-X

NEW RUSSIAN-ENGLISH AND ENGLISH-RUSSIAN DICTIONARY, M. A. O'Brien. This is a remarkably handy Russian dictionary, containing a surprising amount of information, including over 70,000 entries. 366pp. 4½ x 6⅛. 0-486-20208-9

NEW YORK IN THE FORTIES, Andreas Feininger. 162 brilliant photographs by the well-known photographer, formerly with *Life* magazine. Commuters, shoppers, Times Square at night, much else from city at its peak. Captions by John von Hartz. 181pp. 9¼ x 10¾. 0-486-23585-8

INDIAN SIGN LANGUAGE, William Tomkins. Over 525 signs developed by Sioux and other tribes. Written instructions and diagrams. Also 290 pictographs. 111pp. 6⅛ x 9¼. 0-486-22029-X

ANATOMY: A Complete Guide for Artists, Joseph Sheppard. A master of figure drawing shows artists how to render human anatomy convincingly. Over 460 illustrations. 224pp. 8⅜ x 11¼. 0-486-27279-6

MEDIEVAL CALLIGRAPHY: Its History and Technique, Marc Drogin. Spirited history, comprehensive instruction manual covers 13 styles (ca. 4th century through 15th). Excellent photographs; directions for duplicating medieval techniques with modern tools. 224pp. 8⅜ x 11¼. 0-486-26142-5

DRIED FLOWERS: How to Prepare Them, Sarah Whitlock and Martha Rankin. Complete instructions on how to use silica gel, meal and borax, perlite aggregate, sand and borax, glycerine and water to create attractive permanent flower arrangements. 12 illustrations. 32pp. 5⅜ x 8½.   0-486-21802-3

EASY-TO-MAKE BIRD FEEDERS FOR WOODWORKERS, Scott D. Campbell. Detailed, simple-to-use guide for designing, constructing, caring for and using feeders. Text, illustrations for 12 classic and contemporary designs. 96pp. 5⅜ x 8½.
0-486-25847-5

THE COMPLETE BOOK OF BIRDHOUSE CONSTRUCTION FOR WOOD-WORKERS, Scott D. Campbell. Detailed instructions, illustrations, tables. Also data on bird habitat and instinct patterns. Bibliography. 3 tables. 63 illustrations in 15 figures. 48pp. 5¼ x 8½.   0-486-24407-5

SCOTTISH WONDER TALES FROM MYTH AND LEGEND, Donald A. Mackenzie. 16 lively tales tell of giants rumbling down mountainsides, of a magic wand that turns stone pillars into warriors, of gods and goddesses, evil hags, powerful forces and more. 240pp. 5⅜ x 8½.   0-486-29677-6

THE HISTORY OF UNDERCLOTHES, C. Willett Cunnington and Phyllis Cunnington. Fascinating, well-documented survey covering six centuries of English undergarments, enhanced with over 100 illustrations: 12th-century laced-up bodice, footed long drawers (1795), 19th-century bustles, 19th-century corsets for men, Victorian "bust improvers," much more. 272pp. 5⅜ x 8¼.   0-486-27124-2

ARTS AND CRAFTS FURNITURE: The Complete Brooks Catalog of 1912, Brooks Manufacturing Co. Photos and detailed descriptions of more than 150 now very collectible furniture designs from the Arts and Crafts movement depict davenports, settees, buffets, desks, tables, chairs, bedsteads, dressers and more, all built of solid, quarter-sawed oak. Invaluable for students and enthusiasts of antiques, Americana and the decorative arts. 80pp. 6½ x 9¼.   0-486-27471-3

WILBUR AND ORVILLE: A Biography of the Wright Brothers, Fred Howard. Definitive, crisply written study tells the full story of the brothers' lives and work. A vividly written biography, unparalleled in scope and color, that also captures the spirit of an extraordinary era. 560pp. 6⅛ x 9¼.   0-486-40297-5

THE ARTS OF THE SAILOR: Knotting, Splicing and Ropework, Hervey Garrett Smith. Indispensable shipboard reference covers tools, basic knots and useful hitches; handsewing and canvas work, more. Over 100 illustrations. Delightful reading for sea lovers. 256pp. 5⅜ x 8½.   0-486-26440-8

FRANK LLOYD WRIGHT'S FALLINGWATER: The House and Its History, Second, Revised Edition, Donald Hoffmann. A total revision—both in text and illustrations—of the standard document on Fallingwater, the boldest, most personal architectural statement of Wright's mature years, updated with valuable new material from the recently opened Frank Lloyd Wright Archives. "Fascinating"—The New York Times. 116 illustrations. 128pp. 9¼ x 10¾.   0-486-27430-6

PHOTOGRAPHIC SKETCHBOOK OF THE CIVIL WAR, Alexander Gardner. 100 photos taken on field during the Civil War. Famous shots of Manassas Harper's Ferry, Lincoln, Richmond, slave pens, etc. 244pp. 10⅝ x 8¼.   0-486-22731-6

FIVE ACRES AND INDEPENDENCE, Maurice G. Kains. Great back-to-the-land classic explains basics of self-sufficient farming. The one book to get. 95 illustrations. 397pp. 5⅜ x 8½.   0-486-20974-1

THE MALLEUS MALEFICARUM OF KRAMER AND SPRENGER, translated by Montague Summers. Full text of most important witchhunter's "bible," used by both Catholics and Protestants. 278pp. 6⅝ x 10. 0-486-22802-9

SPANISH STORIES/CUENTOS ESPAÑOLES: A Dual-Language Book, Angel Flores (ed.). Unique format offers 13 great stories in Spanish by Cervantes, Borges, others. Faithful English translations on facing pages. 352pp. 5⅜ x 8½. 0-486-25399-6

GARDEN CITY, LONG ISLAND, IN EARLY PHOTOGRAPHS, 1869–1919, Mildred H. Smith. Handsome treasury of 118 vintage pictures, accompanied by carefully researched captions, document the Garden City Hotel fire (1899), the Vanderbilt Cup Race (1908), the first airmail flight departing from the Nassau Boulevard Aerodrome (1911), and much more. 96pp. 8⅞ x 11¾. 0-486-40669-5

OLD QUEENS, N.Y., IN EARLY PHOTOGRAPHS, Vincent F. Seyfried and William Asadorian. Over 160 rare photographs of Maspeth, Jamaica, Jackson Heights, and other areas. Vintage views of DeWitt Clinton mansion, 1939 World's Fair and more. Captions. 192pp. 8⅞ x 11. 0-486-26358-4

CAPTURED BY THE INDIANS: 15 Firsthand Accounts, 1750-1870, Frederick Drimmer. Astounding true historical accounts of grisly torture, bloody conflicts, relentless pursuits, miraculous escapes and more, by people who lived to tell the tale. 384pp. 5⅜ x 8½. 0-486-24901-8

THE WORLD'S GREAT SPEECHES (Fourth Enlarged Edition), Lewis Copeland, Lawrence W. Lamm, and Stephen J. McKenna. Nearly 300 speeches provide public speakers with a wealth of updated quotes and inspiration–from Pericles' funeral oration and William Jennings Bryan's "Cross of Gold Speech" to Malcolm X's powerful words on the Black Revolution and Earl of Spenser's tribute to his sister, Diana, Princess of Wales. 944pp. 5⅜ x 8⅜. 0-486-40903-1

THE BOOK OF THE SWORD, Sir Richard F. Burton. Great Victorian scholar/adventurer's eloquent, erudite history of the "queen of weapons"–from prehistory to early Roman Empire. Evolution and development of early swords, variations (sabre, broadsword, cutlass, scimitar, etc.), much more. 336pp. 6⅛ x 9¼. 0-486-25434-8

AUTOBIOGRAPHY: The Story of My Experiments with Truth, Mohandas K. Gandhi. Boyhood, legal studies, purification, the growth of the Satyagraha (nonviolent protest) movement. Critical, inspiring work of the man responsible for the freedom of India. 480pp. 5⅜ x 8½. (Available in U.S. only.) 0-486-24593-4

CELTIC MYTHS AND LEGENDS, T. W. Rolleston. Masterful retelling of Irish and Welsh stories and tales. Cuchulain, King Arthur, Deirdre, the Grail, many more. First paperback edition. 58 full-page illustrations. 512pp. 5⅜ x 8½. 0-486-26507-2

THE PRINCIPLES OF PSYCHOLOGY, William James. Famous long course complete, unabridged. Stream of thought, time perception, memory, experimental methods; great work decades ahead of its time. 94 figures. 1,391pp. 5⅜ x 8½. 2-vol. set.
Vol. I: 0-486-20381-6 Vol. II: 0-486-20382-4

THE WORLD AS WILL AND REPRESENTATION, Arthur Schopenhauer. Definitive English translation of Schopenhauer's life work, correcting more than 1,000 errors, omissions in earlier translations. Translated by E. F. J. Payne. Total of 1,269pp. 5⅜ x 8½. 2-vol. set. Vol. 1: 0-486-21761-2 Vol. 2: 0-486-21762-0

MAKING FURNITURE MASTERPIECES: 30 Projects with Measured Drawings, Franklin H. Gottshall. Step-by-step instructions, illustrations for constructing handsome, useful pieces, among them a Sheraton desk, Chippendale chair, Spanish desk, Queen Anne table and a William and Mary dressing mirror. 224pp. 8⅛ x 11¼.
0-486-29338-6

NORTH AMERICAN INDIAN DESIGNS FOR ARTISTS AND CRAFTSPEOPLE, Eva Wilson. Over 360 authentic copyright-free designs adapted from Navajo blankets, Hopi pottery, Sioux buffalo hides, more. Geometrics, symbolic figures, plant and animal motifs, etc. 128pp. 8⅜ x 11. (Not for sale in the United Kingdom.)   0-486-25341-4

THE FOSSIL BOOK: A Record of Prehistoric Life, Patricia V. Rich et al. Profusely illustrated definitive guide covers everything from single-celled organisms and dinosaurs to birds and mammals and the interplay between climate and man. Over 1,500 illustrations. 760pp. 7½ x 10⅛.   0-486-29371-8

VICTORIAN ARCHITECTURAL DETAILS: Designs for Over 700 Stairs, Mantels, Doors, Windows, Cornices, Porches, and Other Decorative Elements, A. J. Bicknell & Company. Everything from dormer windows and piazzas to balconies and gable ornaments. Also includes elevations and floor plans for handsome, private residences and commercial structures. 80pp. 9⅜ x 12¼.   0-486-44015-X

WESTERN ISLAMIC ARCHITECTURE: A Concise Introduction, John D. Hoag. Profusely illustrated critical appraisal compares and contrasts Islamic mosques and palaces—from Spain and Egypt to other areas in the Middle East. 139 illustrations. 128pp. 6 x 9.   0-486-43760-4

CHINESE ARCHITECTURE: A Pictorial History, Liang Ssu-ch'eng. More than 240 rare photographs and drawings depict temples, pagodas, tombs, bridges, and imperial palaces comprising much of China's architectural heritage. 152 halftones, 94 diagrams. 232pp. 10¾ x 9⅞.   0-486-43999-2

THE RENAISSANCE: Studies in Art and Poetry, Walter Pater. One of the most talked-about books of the 19th century, *The Renaissance* combines scholarship and philosophy in an innovative work of cultural criticism that examines the achievements of Botticelli, Leonardo, Michelangelo, and other artists. "The holy writ of beauty."—Oscar Wilde. 160pp. 5⅜ x 8½.   0-486-44025-7

A TREATISE ON PAINTING, Leonardo da Vinci. The great Renaissance artist's practical advice on drawing and painting techniques covers anatomy, perspective, composition, light and shadow, and color. A classic of art instruction, it features 48 drawings by Nicholas Poussin and Leon Battista Alberti. 192pp. 5⅜ x 8½.
0-486-44155-5

THE MIND OF LEONARDO DA VINCI, Edward McCurdy. More than just a biography, this classic study by a distinguished historian draws upon Leonardo's extensive writings to offer numerous demonstrations of the Renaissance master's achievements, not only in sculpture and painting, but also in music, engineering, and even experimental aviation. 384pp. 5⅜ x 8½.   0-486-44142-3

WASHINGTON IRVING'S RIP VAN WINKLE, Illustrated by Arthur Rackham. Lovely prints that established artist as a leading illustrator of the time and forever etched into the popular imagination a classic of Catskill lore. 51 full-color plates. 80pp. 8⅜ x 11.   0-486-44242-X

HENSCHE ON PAINTING, John W. Robichaux. Basic painting philosophy and methodology of a great teacher, as expounded in his famous classes and workshops on Cape Cod. 7 illustrations in color on covers. 80pp. 5⅜ x 8½.   0-486-43728-0

LIGHT AND SHADE: A Classic Approach to Three-Dimensional Drawing, Mrs. Mary P. Merrifield. Handy reference clearly demonstrates principles of light and shade by revealing effects of common daylight, sunshine, and candle or artificial light on geometrical solids. 13 plates. 64pp. 5⅜ x 8½. 0-486-44143-1

ASTROLOGY AND ASTRONOMY: A Pictorial Archive of Signs and Symbols, Ernst and Johanna Lehner. Treasure trove of stories, lore, and myth, accompanied by more than 300 rare illustrations of planets, the Milky Way, signs of the zodiac, comets, meteors, and other astronomical phenomena. 192pp. 8⅜ x 11. 0-486-43981-X

JEWELRY MAKING: Techniques for Metal, Tim McCreight. Easy-to-follow instructions and carefully executed illustrations describe tools and techniques, use of gems and enamels, wire inlay, casting, and other topics. 72 line illustrations and diagrams. 176pp. 8¼ x 10⅞. 0-486-44043-5

MAKING BIRDHOUSES: Easy and Advanced Projects, Gladstone Califf. Easy-to-follow instructions include diagrams for everything from a one-room house for bluebirds to a forty-two-room structure for purple martins. 56 plates; 4 figures. 80pp. 8¾ x 6⅜. 0-486-44183-0

LITTLE BOOK OF LOG CABINS: How to Build and Furnish Them, William S. Wicks. Handy how-to manual, with instructions and illustrations for building cabins in the Adirondack style, fireplaces, stairways, furniture, beamed ceilings, and more. 102 line drawings. 96pp. 8¾ x 6⅜. 0-486-44259-4

THE SEASONS OF AMERICA PAST, Eric Sloane. From "sugaring time" and strawberry picking to Indian summer and fall harvest, a whole year's activities described in charming prose and enhanced with 79 of the author's own illustrations. 160pp. 8¼ x 11. 0-486-44220-9

THE METROPOLIS OF TOMORROW, Hugh Ferriss. Generous, prophetic vision of the metropolis of the future, as perceived in 1929. Powerful illustrations of towering structures, wide avenues, and rooftop parks–all features in many of today's modern cities. 59 illustrations. 144pp. 8¼ x 11. 0-486-43727-2

THE PATH TO ROME, Hilaire Belloc. This 1902 memoir abounds in lively vignettes from a vanished time, recounting a pilgrimage on foot across the Alps and Apennines in order to "see all Europe which the Christian Faith has saved." 77 of the author's original line drawings complement his sparkling prose. 272pp. 5⅜ x 8½. 0-486-44001-X

THE HISTORY OF RASSELAS: Prince of Abissinia, Samuel Johnson. Distinguished English writer attacks eighteenth-century optimism and man's unrealistic estimates of what life has to offer. 112pp. 5⅜ x 8½. 0-486-44094-X

A VOYAGE TO ARCTURUS, David Lindsay. A brilliant flight of pure fancy, where wild creatures crowd the fantastic landscape and demented torturers dominate victims with their bizarre mental powers. 272pp. 5⅜ x 8½. 0-486-44198-9

Paperbound unless otherwise indicated. Available at your book dealer, online at **www.doverpublications.com**, or by writing to Dept. GI, Dover Publications, Inc., 31 East 2nd Street, Mineola, NY 11501. For current price information or for free catalogs (please indicate field of interest), write to Dover Publications or log on to **www.doverpublications.com** and see every Dover book in print. Dover publishes more than 500 books each year on science, elementary and advanced mathematics, biology, music, art, literary history, social sciences, and other areas.